Google Cloud Platform for Architects

Architects

Design and manage powerful cloud solutions

Vitthal Srinivasan
Janani Ravi
Judy Raj

BIRMINGHAM - MUMBAI

Google Cloud Platform for Architects

Commissioning Editor: Vijin Boricha
Acquisition Editor: Rohit Rajkumar
Content Development Editor: Abhishek Jadhav
Technical Editor: Mohd Riyan Khan
Copy Editors: Safis Editing, Dipti Mankame
Project Coordinator: Judie Jose
Proofreader: Safis Editing
Indexer: Priyanka Dhadke
Graphics: Tom Scaria
Production Coordinator: Shantanu Zagade

First published: June 2018

Production reference: 1220618

Published by Packt Publishing Ltd.
Livery Place
35 Livery Street
Birmingham
B3 2PB, UK.

ISBN 978-1-78883-430-8

www.packtpub.com

`mapt.io`

Mapt is an online digital library that gives you full access to over 5,000 books and videos, as well as industry leading tools to help you plan your personal development and advance your career. For more information, please visit our website.

Why subscribe?

- Spend less time learning and more time coding with practical eBooks and Videos from over 4,000 industry professionals

- Improve your learning with Skill Plans built especially for you

- Get a free eBook or video every month

- Mapt is fully searchable

- Copy and paste, print, and bookmark content

PacktPub.com

Did you know that Packt offers eBook versions of every book published, with PDF and ePub files available? You can upgrade to the eBook version at `www.PacktPub.com` and as a print book customer, you are entitled to a discount on the eBook copy. Get in touch with us at `service@packtpub.com` for more details.

At `www.PacktPub.com`, you can also read a collection of free technical articles, sign up for a range of free newsletters, and receive exclusive discounts and offers on Packt books and eBooks.

Contributors

About the authors

Vitthal Srinivasan is a Google Cloud Platform Authorized Trainer and certified Google Cloud Architect and Data Engineer. Vitthal holds master's degrees in math and electrical engineering from Stanford and an MBA from INSEAD. He has worked at Google as well as at other large firms, such as Credit Suisse and Flipkart. He is currently in Loonycorn, a technical video content studio, of which he is a cofounder.

Janani Ravi is a certified Google Cloud Architect and Data Engineer. She has earned her master's degree in electrical engineering from Stanford. She is currently in Loonycorn, a technical video content studio, of which she is a cofounder. Prior to co-founding Loonycorn, she worked at various leading companies, such as Google and Microsoft, for several years as a software engineer.

> *I would like to thank my family, dogs, colleagues at Loonycorn, and friends for making life so much fun!*

Judy Raj is a Google Certified Professional Cloud Architect, and she has great experience with the three leading cloud platforms, namely AWS, Azure, and the GCP. She has also worked with a wide range of technologies in machine learning, data science, IoT, robotics, and mobile and web app development. She is currently a technical content engineer in Loonycorn. She holds a degree in computer science and engineering from Cochin University of Science and Technology. Being a driven engineer fascinated with technology, she is a passionate coder, an AI enthusiast, and a cloud aficionado.

> *I'd like to thank my coauthors and colleagues for all the support and encouragement I've received. I'd also like to thank God and my parents for everything that I am and everything I aspire to be.*

About the reviewer

Tim Berry is a systems architect and software engineer with over 20 years of experience in building enterprise infrastructure and systems on the internet and mobile platforms. He currently leads a team of SREs building customer solutions on Google Cloud Platform for a managed services provider in the UK. Tim is a Google Certified Professional Cloud Architect and Data Engineer, a Red Hat Certified Engineer, and systems administrator. He holds Red Hat Certified Specialist status for configuration management and containerized application development.

I would like to thank my wife, Sophie, for her patience and inspiration; my amazing kids, Josh, Ellie, Tommy, Isaac, and Noah for making me laugh; and my parents for always supporting me. I'd also like to say hi to my dogs, Ruby, Lilo, and Belle, and ask them to get down now please because I'm working.

Nisarg M. Vasavada is a content engineer in Loonycorn. He has pursued his master's in engineering at GTU, and he has been an active member of technical education and research community with his publications. He loves writing and believes that simplifying complexities is the biggest responsibility of an author.

Being a part of this book's writing process was absolutely insightful. I would like to thank and dedicate this book to my family, colleagues, and mentors for always looking after me. Also, lots of love and warmth to my feline and canine siblings!

Packt is searching for authors like you

If you're interested in becoming an author for Packt, please visit authors.packtpub.com and apply today. We have worked with thousands of developers and tech professionals, just like you, to help them share their insight with the global tech community. You can make a general application, apply for a specific hot topic that we are recruiting an author for, or submit your own idea.

Table of Contents

Preface

The Google Cloud Platform is fast emerging as a leading public cloud provider. The GCP, as it is popularly known, is backed by Google's awe-inspiring engineering expertise and infrastructure, and is able to draw upon the goodwill and respect that Google has come to enjoy. The GCP is one of a handful of public cloud providers to offer the full range of cloud computing services, ranging from Infrastructure as a Service (IaaS) to Platform as a Service (PaaS). There is another reason why the GCP is fast gaining popularity; genre-defining technologies such as TensorFlow and Kubernetes originated at Google before being open-sourced, and the GCP is a natural choice of cloud on which to run them. If you are a cloud professional today, time spent on mastering the GCP is likely to be an excellent investment.

Using a public cloud platform was considered risky a decade ago and unconventional even just a few years ago. Today, however, the use of the public cloud is completely mainstream—the norm, rather than the exception. Several leading technology firms, including Google, have built sophisticated cloud platforms, and they are locked in a fierce competition for market share.

The main goal of this book is to enable you to get the best out of the GCP and to use it with confidence and competence. You will learn why cloud architectures take the forms that they do, and this will help you to become a skilled, high-level cloud architect. You will also learn how individual cloud services are configured and used so that you are never intimidated at having to build it yourself. You will also learn the right way and the right situation in which to use the important GCP services.

By the end of this book, you will be able to make the most out of Google Cloud Platform design.

Who this book is for

If you are a Cloud architect who is responsible for designing and managing robust cloud solutions with Google Cloud Platform, then this book is for you. System engineers and Enterprise architects will also find this book useful. A basic understanding of distributed applications would be helpful, although not strictly necessary. Some working experience on other public cloud platforms would help too.

What this book covers

Chapter 1, *The Case for Cloud Computing*, starts with the brief history of cloud computing. Furthermore, the chapter delves into autohealing and autoscaling.

Chapter 2, *Introduction to Google Cloud Platform*, gets you into the nitty-gritty of the Google Cloud Platform, describing the diversity and versatility of the platform in terms of the resources available to us.

Chapter 3, *Compute Choices – VMs and the Google Compute Engine*, explores GCE, which serves as an IaaS provision of GCP. You will learn to create GCE VMs, along with its various aspects such as disk type and machine types.

Chapter 4, *GKE, AppEngine, and Cloud Functions*, discusses the four compute options on the GCP, ranging from IaaS through PaaS.

Chapter 5, *Google Cloud Storage – Fishing in a Bucket*, gets you familiar with GCS and gives an idea of where it would fit within with your overall infrastructure.

Chapter 6, *Relational Databases*, introduces you to RDMS and SQL. We further dive deep into Cloud SQL and Cloud Spanner that are available under GCP.

Chapter 7, *NoSQL Databases*, takes you through Bigtable and Datastore. This chapter explains how Bigtable is used for large datasets, whereas on the other hand, Datastore is meant for far smaller data.

Chapter 8, *BigQuery*, teaches you about the architecture of BigQuery and how it is Google's fully managed petabyte-scale serverless database.

Chapter 9, *Identity and Access Management*, dives into how IAM lets you control access to all of the GCP resources in terms of roles and permissions.

Chapter 10, *Managing Hadoop with Dataproc*, helps you to understand Dataproc as a managed and cost-effective solution for Apache Spark and Hadoop workloads.

Chapter 11, *Load Balancing*, takes you through HTTP, TCP, and network load balancing with reference to its concepts and implementation.

Chapter 12, *Networking in GCP*, teaches you about Virtual Private Cloud Networks of GCP and their infrastructure and how to create and manage our own VPC networks.

Chapter 13, *Logging and Monitoring*, discusses how Stackdriver offers logging and monitoring services of GCP resources for free up to a certain quota and then monitoring both GCP and AWS resources for premium account holders.

Chapter 14, *Infrastructure Automation*, delves into the idea of how provisioning resources can be done programmatically, using templates, commands, and even code.

Chapter 15, *Security on the GCP*, mostly covers things such as how Google has planned for security on the GCP.

Chapter 16, *Pricing Considerations*, helps avoid sticker-shock and sudden unpleasant surprises regarding the pricing of the services that you use.

Chapter 17, *Effective Use of the GCP*, sharpens all of the GCP features and offerings that you learned in the previous chapters to make sure that we conclude our journey on a satisfactory note.

To get the most out of this book

1. First, go breadth-first. Read each chapter rapidly, paying particular attention to the early bits and to the rhymes. They summarize the key points.
2. Don't forget to laugh while reading the rhymes! Seriously, pay attention to each line in the rhymes as they are particularly packed with information.
3. After you finish going through the entire book quickly, come back to the chapters that relate to your specific use cases and go through them in detail.
4. For the drills in the book, understand what step is trying to accomplish, then try it out on your own. In particular, also search for online updates for your most important use cases—the world of cloud computing and the GCP is changing incredibly fast.

Conventions used

There are a number of text conventions used throughout this book.

`CodeInText`: Indicates code words in text, database table names, folder names, filenames, file extensions, pathnames, dummy URLs, user input, and Twitter handles. Here is an example: "A public dataset named `samples.natality` is queried"

A block of code is set as follows:

```
#standardSQL
SELECT
  weight_pounds, state, year, gestation_weeks
FROM
  `bigquery-public-data.samples.natality`
ORDER BY weight_pounds DESC LIMIT 10;
```

When we wish to draw your attention to a particular part of a code block, the relevant lines or items are set in bold:

```
#standardSQL
SELECT
  weight_pounds, state, year, gestation_weeks
FROM
  `bigquery-public-data.samples.natality`
ORDER BY weight_pounds DESC LIMIT 10;
```

Any command-line input or output is written as follows:

```
curl -f -O
http://repo1.maven.org/maven2/com/google/cloud/bigtable/bigtable-beam-impor
t/1.1.2/bigtable-beam-import-1.1.2-shaded.jar
```

Bold: Indicates a new term, an important word, or words that you see onscreen. For example, words in menus or dialog boxes appear in the text like this. Here is an example: "To upload the datafile, click on the **Choose file** button."

 Warnings or important notes appear like this.

 Tips and tricks appear like this.

Get in touch

Feedback from our readers is always welcome.

General feedback: Email `feedback@packtpub.com` and mention the book title in the subject of your message. If you have questions about any aspect of this book, please email us at `questions@packtpub.com`.

Errata: Although we have taken every care to ensure the accuracy of our content, mistakes do happen. If you have found a mistake in this book, we would be grateful if you would report this to us. Please visit `www.packtpub.com/submit-errata`, selecting your book, clicking on the Errata Submission Form link, and entering the details.

Piracy: If you come across any illegal copies of our works in any form on the Internet, we would be grateful if you would provide us with the location address or website name. Please contact us at `copyright@packtpub.com` with a link to the material.

If you are interested in becoming an author: If there is a topic that you have expertise in and you are interested in either writing or contributing to a book, please visit `authors.packtpub.com`.

Reviews

Please leave a review. Once you have read and used this book, why not leave a review on the site that you purchased it from? Potential readers can then see and use your unbiased opinion to make purchase decisions, we at Packt can understand what you think about our products, and our authors can see your feedback on their book. Thank you!

For more information about Packt, please visit `packtpub.com`.

The Case for Cloud Computing 1

Cloud computing is a pretty big deal in the world of technology, and in addition it is also a pretty big deal for those who are not quite in technology. Some developments, for instance, the rise of Java and object-oriented programming, were momentous changes for people who were completely into technology at the time, but it was rare for a non-technical person to have to wake up in the morning, read the newspaper and ask themselves, *Wow, this Java thing is getting pretty big, will this affect my career?* Cloud computing, perhaps like machine learning or **Artificial Intelligence (AI)**, is different; there is a real chance that it, by itself, will affect the lives of people far beyond the world of technology. Let's understand why.

You will learn the following topics in this chapter:

- A brief history of cloud computing
- Autohealing and autoscaling—good technical reasons for moving to the cloud
- Some good financial reasons for moving to the cloud
- Possible implications of cloud computing on your career

Genesis

In the beginning, Jeff Bezos created `Amazon.com` and took the company to a successful **Initial Public Offering (IPO)** by 1997. Everyone knows `Amazon.com`, of course, and it has become a force of nature, dominating the online retail and diversifying into several other fields. However, in the early 2000s, after the Dotcom bubble burst, the company's future was not quite as certain as now. Even so, one of the many things that Amazon was doing right even then was architecting its internal computer systems in a truly robust and scalable way.

Amazon had a lot of users and a lot of traffic, and in order to service that traffic, the company really had to think deeply about how to build scalable, cost-effective compute capacity. Now you could argue rightly that other companies had to think about the same issues too. Google also had a lot of users and a lot of traffic, and it had to think really carefully about how to handle it. Even so, most observers agree that a couple of important differences existed between the two giants. For one, Google's business was (and is) fundamentally a far more profitable one, which means that Google could always afford to overinvest in compute, secure in the knowledge that its money printing press in the ad business would cover the costs. For another, Google's primary technical challenges came in processing and making sense of vast quantities of data (it was basically indexing the entire internet for Google Search). Amazon's primary technical challenges lay around making sure that the inherently spiky traffic of their hundreds of millions of users was serviced just right. The spiky nature of consumer traffic remains a huge consideration for any online retail firm. Just consider Alibaba, which did $25 billion in sales on *Singles Day* (11/11) in 2017.

Somewhere along the line, Amazon realized that it had created something really cool: a set of APIs and services, a platform in fact that external customers would be willing to pay for, and that would help Amazon monetize excess server capacity it had lying about. Let's not underestimate the magnitude of that achievement; plenty of companies have overinvested in servers and have extra capacity lying around, but virtually none of them have built a platform that other external customers are willing and able to use and to pay top dollar for.

So, in 2006, Amazon launched **Elastic Compute Cloud (EC2)**, basically, cloud **Virtual Machine (VM)** instances, and **Simple Storage Service (S3)**, basically, elastic object storage, which to this day are the bedrock of the AWS cloud offerings. Along the way, the other big firms with the money and technical know how to offer such services jumped in as well. Microsoft launched Azure in 2010, and Google had actually gotten into the act even earlier, in 2008, with the launch of **App Engine**.

Notice how Amazon's first product offerings were basically **Infrastructure as a service (IaaS)**, whereas Google's initial offering was a **Platform as a service (PaaS)**. That is a significant fact and with the benefit of hindsight, a significant mistake on Google's part. If you are a large organization, circa 2010, and contemplating moving to the cloud, you are unlikely to bet the house on moving to an untested cloud-specific platform such as App Engine. The path of least resistance for big early adopters is definitely the IaaS route. The first-mover advantage and the smart early focus on IaaS helped Amazon open up a huge lead in the cloud market, one which they still hold on to.

In recent years, however, a host of other cloud providers have crowded into the cloud space, notably Microsoft and, to a lesser extent, Google. That partially has to do with the economics of the cloud business; Amazon first broke out the financials of AWS separately in April 2015 and stunned the world with its size and profitability. Microsoft missed a few important big trends in computing, but after Satya Nadella replaced Steve Ballmer at the helm, he really made the cloud a company-wide priority in a way that mobile, search, and hardware never were. The results are obvious, and if you are a Microsoft shareholder, very gratifying. Microsoft is probably the momentum player in the cloud market right now; many smart observers have realized that Azure is challenging AWS despite the still-significant differences between their market shares.

Why Google Cloud Platform (GCP)?

Okay, you say, all fine and good: if AWS is the market leader, and Azure is the momentum player, then *why exactly are we reading and writing a book about the Google Cloud Platform?* That's an excellent question; in a nutshell, our considered view is that the GCP is a great technology to jump into right now for a few, very rational reasons, as follows:

- **Demand-supply**: There is a ton of demand for AWS and Azure professionals, but there is also a ton of supply. In contrast, there is growing demand for the GCP, but not yet all that much supply of highly skilled GCP professionals. Careers are made by smart bets on technologies like this one.
- **PaaS versus IaaS**: Notice how we called out Amazon for being smart in focusing on IaaS early on. That made a lot of sense when cloud computing was new and untested. Now, however, everyone trusts the cloud; that model works, and people know it. This means that folks are now ready to give up control in return for great features. PaaS is attractive now, and GCP's PaaS offerings are very competitive relative to its competitors.

- **Kubernetes for hybrid, multi-cloud architectures**: You may or may not have heard about this, but Amazon acquired a US-based grocery chain, *Whole Foods*, some time ago. It gave many current and potential AWS consumers pause for thought, *what if Amazon buys up a company in my sector and starts competing with me?* As a result, more organizations are likely to want a hybrid, multi-cloud architecture rather than to tie themselves to any one cloud provider. The term hybrid implies that both on-premise data centers and public cloud resources are used, and multi-cloud refers to the fact that more than one cloud provider is in the game. Now, if the world does go the hybrid, multi-cloud way, one clear winner is likely to be a container orchestration technology named Kubernetes. If that does happen, GCP is likely to be a big beneficiary. Kubernetes was developed at Google before being open-sourced, and the GCP offers great support for Kubernetes.

Autoscaling and autohealing

The technical rationale for moving to the cloud can often be summed up in two words—**autoscaling** and **autohealing**.

- **Autoscaling**: The idea of autoscaling is simple enough although the implementations can get quite involved—apps are deployed on compute, the amount of compute capacity increases or decreases depending on the level of incoming client requests. In a nutshell, all the public cloud providers have services that make autoscaling and autohealing easily available. Autoscaling, in particular, is a huge deal. Imagine a large Hadoop cluster, with say 1,000 nodes. Try scaling that; it probably is a matter of weeks or even months. You'd need to get and configure the machines, reshard the data and jump through a trillion hoops. With a cloud provider, you'd simply use an elastic version of Hadoop such as Dataproc on the GCP or **Elastic MapReduce (EMR)** on AWS and you'd be in business in minutes. This is not some marketing or sales spiel; the speed of scaling up and down on the cloud is just insane.

Here's a little rhyme to help you remember the main point of our conversation here—we'll keep using them throughout the remainder of the book just to mix things up a bit. Oh, and they might sometimes introduce a few new terms or ideas that will be covered at length in the following sections, so don't let any forward references bother you just yet!

Autoscaling in Compute

Once stretched, stays stretched - that's plastic
Stretches and rebounds - that's elastic

These words we learnt in high school physics
Twenty years on, they're back in the mix

Remember buddies, the compute choices are five,
Five different ways to get your app live

GCE VMs are where most people start
Managed Instance Groups, for which the next part

App Engine Standard is the entry-level PaaS
Scales super fast, before seconds can pass

App Engine Flex is better for bespoke runtimes
Scaling a bit slower, like one-minute fun times

Kubernetes has autoscaling of its own
Horizontal Pod Autoscalers, a name that makes you moan

That's just the start, it doesn't end there though
Autoscaling in BigQuery, Datastore and Dataflow

Autoscaling is the single reason for moving to the cloud
AWS, GCP and Azure all say it out loud

- **Autohealing**: The idea of autohealing is just as important as that of autoscaling, but it is less explicitly understood. Let's say that we deploy an app that could be a Java JAR, Python package, or Docker container to a set of compute resources, which again could be cloud VMs, App Engine backends, or pods in a Kubernetes cluster. Those compute resources will have problems from time to time; they will crash, hang, run out of memory, throw exceptions, and misbehave in all kinds of unpredictable ways. If we did nothing about these problems, those compute resources would effectively be out of action, and our total compute capacity would fall and, sooner or later, become insufficient to meet client requests. So, clearly, we need to somehow detect whether our compute resources got sick, and then heal them. In the pre-cloud days, this would have been pretty manual, some poor sap of an engineer would have to nurse a bare metal or VM back to health. Now, with cloud-based abstractions, individual compute units are much more expendable. We can just take them down and replace them with new ones. Because these units of compute capacity are interchangeable (or fungible—a fancier word that means the same thing), autohealing is now possible:

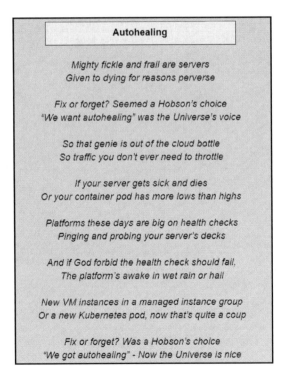

Capital expenditure (CAPEX) versus operating expenses (OPEX)

The financial considerations for moving to the cloud are as important as the technical ones, and it is important for architects and technical cloud folks to understand these so that we don't sound dumb while discussing these at cocktail party conversations with the business guys.

- **CAPEX** refers to a large upfront spend of money used to get an asset (an asset is a resource that will yield benefits over time, not just in the current period)
- **OPEX** refers to smaller, recurring spends of money for current period benefit

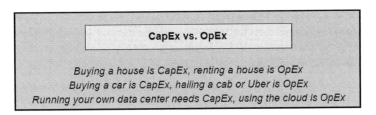

Now, that the last line in the previous image makes clear the big difference between using the cloud versus going on-premise. If you use the cloud, you don't need to make the big upfront payment. That in turn has several associated advantages:

- **No depreciation**: When you buy a house, hopefully, it appreciates, but when you buy a car, it loses a fourth of its value as soon as you drive it out of the dealer's parking lot. Depreciation is called an intangible expense, but try selling a barely used car, and you will find it tangible enough. With the cloud, you don't worry about depreciation, but the cloud provider does.
- **Transparency**: Let's face it folks—big contracts are complicated and have been known to have big payoffs for people concerned. This is a reality of doing business: procurement and sourcing are messy businesses for a reason. Using the cloud is far more transparent and simpler for internal processes and audit

- **Flexibility in capacity planning**: The worlds of business and history are littered with unfulfilled ambitions and unrealistic plans and targets that went nowhere. Your firm might have a target to triple revenues in 3 years: such ambitious plans are common enough. If you, as an architect, sign off on a commensurate tripling in your server capacity and that business growth does not happen, the finance guys will come asking you why overspent if you are still in this firm 3 years down the line. At that point, you will likely not have the luxury of pointing a finger at the CEO who launched the 3X plan. He likely will have moved on adroitly to another shiny plan.

Note, incidentally, that we did not include straight cost as a reason to move to the cloud. The big cloud providers are all rolling in the money, their stock prices are surging on the heady cocktail of high revenue growth and high profitability. The cloud business is a great business to be in if you can get in. It stands to reason that if the suppliers of cloud services are doing so well financially, the consumers of cloud services are paying for it. So, cloud services are not necessarily cheap, they do, however, offer all of these other attractions that make it a real win-win for both sides in the bargain.

Career implications

Our considered opinion is that the move to the cloud is going to affect a lot of folks more than they expect. In particular, employees at a host of IT services companies and system integrators will need to retool fast. Now that's not to say that these companies are clear losers, because the cloud services are pretty complex too and will provide lots of room for several different ecosystems. Some things that used to be hard will now be easy, and some things that used to be easy will now be hard. Workforces will need to be retrained, and the expectations of career trajectories will need to be changed. So, if you are new to the cloud world, here are three topics you might want to spend time really understanding—these are now a lot more important than they used to be:

- Containers, Docker, and Kubernetes
- Load balancers
- IaaS technologies such as Terraform or Google Cloud Deployment Manager

On the other hand, folks who are in the following teams probably need to think long and hard about how to get with today's (and tomorrow's) hot technologies because the cloud is radically simplifying what they currently work on:

- Virtual Machines and IaaS sysadmins
- Physical networking, router, and VPN engineers
- Hadoop administrators

Summary

You learned about the rise of public cloud computing and how GCP, AWS, and Azure came to where they currently are in the market. We also examined some important technical reasons for switching to the cloud. We looked at some good and bad financial implications of moving to the cloud. Finally, we pointed out some technologies that stand to gain from the rise of the cloud and some others that stand to recede in relevance.

Introduction to Google Cloud Platform

2

Now let's get into the nitty-gritty of the Google Cloud Platform. Any cloud platform really is all about resources. It allows you to use resources for a fee. What's cool about Cloud Platforms is the great diversity and versatility in terms of what resources are available to us. This might include hardware such as virtual machine instances, or persistent disks, services such as BigQuery or BigTable or even more complex software such as Cloud ML Engine and the various APIs for machine learning. But in addition to just the hardware and software, there is a lot of little detailed networking, load balancing, logging, monitoring, and so on. The GCP, like other major cloud platforms, provides a great variety of services; take load balancing for instance, GCP load balancing options span to four different layers (that is, data link, network, transport, and application layers) of the OSI networking stack.

You will learn the following topics in this chapter:

- The difference between regions and zones
- The organization of resources in a GCP project
- Accessing cloud resources using Cloud Shell and the web console

Global, regional, and zonal resources

Now, of course, there is no free lunch in life and you have to pay for (almost) all of this, and the payment models are going to differ. For instance, with persistent disks, you pay for the capacity that you allocate, whereas with cloud storage buckets, you pay for the capacity that you actually use. However, the basic idea is that there are resources that will be billed. All billable resources are grouped into entities named **projects**.

Let's now look at how resources are structured. The way the Google Cloud Platform operates, all resources are scoped as being the following:

- Global
- Regional
- Zonal

Now you might think that this geographical location of resources is an implementation detail that you shouldn't have to worry about, but that's only partially true. The scoping actually also determines how you architect your cloud applications and infrastructure.

Regions are geographical regions at the level of a subcontinent—the central US, western Europe, or east Asia. Zones are basically data centers within regions. This mapping between a zone and a data center is loose, and it's not really explicit anywhere, but that really is what a zone is.

These distinctions matter to use as an end users because regional and zonal resources are often billed and treated differently by the platform. You will pay more or less depending on the choices you make regarding these levels of scope access. The reason that you pay more or less is that there are some implicit promises made about performance within regions.

For instance, the Cloud Docs tell us that zones within the same region will *typically* have network latencies in the order of less than 5 milliseconds. What does *typical* mean? Well here, it is the 95 percentile delay latency, that is, 95% of all network traffic within a region will have latency of less than 5 ms. That's a fancy way of saying that within a region, network speeds will be very high, whereas across regions, those speeds will be slower.

Cost and latency are two reasons why these geographical choices are important to you, another has to do with failure locations. Zones can be thought of as single failure domains within a region. Now common sense says that, basically, it is a data center, so you might want to create different versions of resources situated in different zones or even in regions depending on your budget and your user base. That's because a zone is a single failure domain. Zones reside inside regions, and they are identified using the name of the corresponding region as well as a single lowercase letter, `asia-east1-a` for instance. A zone is a single point of failure in Google's data center network. Zones are analogous to Availability Zones in AWS. If you replicate resources across different zones, such architecture can legitimately be termed as **high-availability architecture**.

If a resource is available globally, it's known as a global or a multiregional resource. These multiregional resources tend to be the most expensive, the most available, and also the most widely replicated and backed up kind of resources. One level down come regional resources; these only need to be backed up to different data centers within the same region and then at the bottom of this access hierarchy are the zonal resources. These only need to be replicated within the same data center.

There are lots of examples in each of these categories, for instance, tools such as Cloud Storage, DataStore, and BigQuery. All of this can be global or multiregional; this makes sense intuitively, as we expect storage technologies to be global rather than regional (Cloud SQL and BigTable are regional; however, Cloud Spanner can be either regional or multiregional).

On the other hand, compute tends to be regional or zonal. AppEngine is regional, whereas VM instances are zonal. Disk storage that takes the format of either persistent ordinary hard disks or persistent SSD disks is zonal as well. Disks need to be local, and they need to be in the same zone as the corresponding virtual machine instance they are used by:

Region	Location	Zone
Northamerica-northeast1	Montreal, Canada	Northamerica-northeast1-a
		Northamerica-northeast1-b
		Northamerica-northeast1-c
Us-central1	Iowa, USA	Us-central1-a
		Us-central1-b
		Us-central1-c
		Us-central1-f
Us-west1	Oregon, USA	Us-west1-a
		Us-west1-b
		Us-west1-c
Us-east4	Virginia, USA	Us-east4-a
		Us-east4-b
		Us-east4-c
Us-east1	South Carolina, USA	Us-east1-b
		Us-east1-c
		Us-east1-d
Southamerica-east1	Sao Paulo, Brazil	southamerica-east1-a
		southamerica-east1-b
		southamerica-east1-c

Europe-west1	St. Ghislain, Belgium	Europe-west1-b
		Europe-west1-c
		Europe-west1-d
Europe-west2	London, England	Europe-west2-a
		Europe-west2-b
		Europe-west2-c
Europe-west3	Frankfurt, Germany	Europe-west3-a
		Europe-west3-b
		Europe-west3-c
Europe-west4	Eemshaven, Netherlands	Europe-west4-a
		Europe-west4-b
		Europe-west4-c
Asia-south1	Mumbai, India	Asia-south1-a
		Asia-south1-b
		Asia-south1-c
Asia-southeast1	Jurong, Singapore	Asia-southeast1-a
		Asia-southeast1-b
		Asia-southeast1-c
Asia-east1	Changhua, Taiwan	Asia-east1-a
		Asia-east1-b
		Asia-east1-c
Asia-northeast1	Tokyo, Japan	Asia-northeast1-a
		Asia-northeast1-b
		Asia-northeast1-c
Australia-southeast1	Sydney, Australia	Australia-southeast1-a
		Australia-southeast1-b
		Australia-southeast1-c

Accessing the Google Cloud Platform

Now that we understand some of the hardware and software choices that are available to us in the Google Cloud Platform buffet, we also should know how we can go about consuming these resources. We have multiple following choices:

- One really handy way is using the GCP console, also known as the web console; simply access this from a web browser at `https://console.cloud.google.com/`
- Another is by making use of a command-line interface using command-line tools. There are four command-line utilities that you might encounter while working with the GCP:
    - `gcloud`: This is for pretty much everything other than the specific cases mentioned later
    - `gsutil`: This is for working with cloud storage buckets
    - `bq`: This is for working with BigQuery
    - `kubetcl`: This is for working with Kubernetes (note that `kubectl` is not tied to GCP. If you use Kubernetes on a competing cloud provider such as Azure, you'd use `kubectl` there as well)
- Another way is to programmatically access GCP resources is from various client libraries. These are available in a host of languages, including Java, Go, and Python.

Projects and billing

Let's also really quickly talk about how billing happens on the Google Cloud Platform. At heart, billing is associated with projects. Projects are logical units which consumes a bunch of resources. Projects are set up within organizations, and we will get to that hierarchy later on in the course. Projects are associated with accounts and accounts with organizations. However, billing really happens on a per project basis. Each project can be thought of as **Resources** + **Settings** + **Metadata**. So, if GCP is a lunch buffet, a project can be thought of as a meal. You select what you would like to consume, how you would like to consume it, and associate all of that information inside this one unit that should then pay for it.

Extending that analogy just a little further: just as you can mix and match food items within a meal, you can easily have resources within a project interact with each other. And so in a sense, a project can be thought of as a namespace. If you have various name resources for instance, those names typically only need to be unique within the project. There are some exceptions to this, which we will discuss later, Google Cloud Storage buckets for instance.

A project is really associated with or defined by three pieces of metadata—the name, ID, and the number. The project ID is unique and permanent. Even if you go ahead and delete a project that ID will not be available for use for other projects in the future.

Setting up a GCP account

Execute the following steps to set up a GCP account:

1. Go to `https://console.developers.google.com/` and sign in to continue using Google Cloud Platform.
2. If you already have a Gmail account that's what you will use to sign in here. If you don't, get a Gmail account before you sign in to Google Cloud Platform.
3. If you are doing this for the very first time, it will take you to a page where it will ask you for a bunch of personal information.

This is where you get access to all GCP products. Google currently enables a free trial for everyone and gives you 300 US Dollars of free credit. So even if you are going to upgrade to a paid account, you won't shell out any money until you reach the 300 dollar limit. In addition, if you consume resources worth more than 300 USD, all your resources will be shut down, so you don't inadvertently end up paying a large bill because you forgot to turn down VM or shut down a BigTable instance. Google is considerate that way. You will need to provide a credit card number in order to use the free trial, but you won't be charged though.

Your Google Cloud account has been created. You will automatically be taken to a page that is the dashboard for your account:

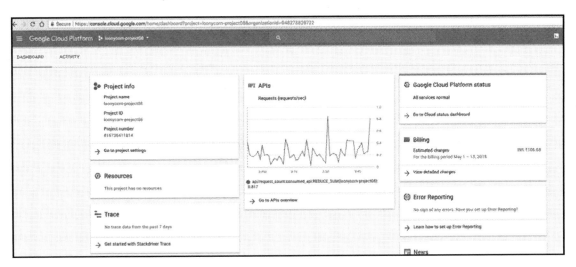

The first thing is to create a new project. Click on the drop-down icon right up top next to the three horizontal lines (that is, the **Products & Services** menu, also colloquially known as the hamburger). Here, we already have a project; the name of that project is `loonycorn-project08`:

If you click on the arrow next to the project name, a new dialog will open up, allowing you to create a new project, or select an existing one:

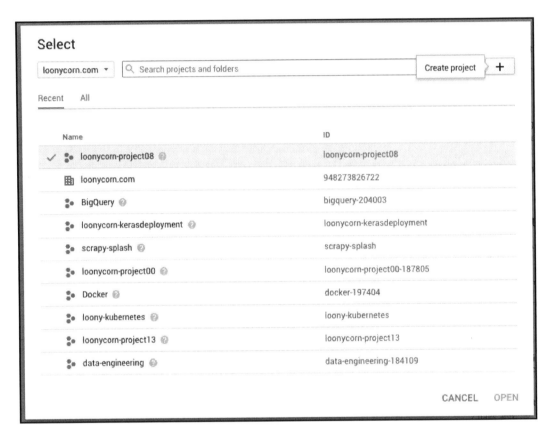

The projects associated with your Google Cloud Account are your top level billing instances. All of the GCP resources are provisioned under some or another project. You can choose between having a common billing account for each project or separate ones accordingly. All projects and billing accounts can be linked to a common organization, which will be linked to your Google Cloud account. Billing accounts encompass source of payment (for example, credit card details). Thus via different billing accounts you can ask different people to pay for different resources (for example, different teams of your organization).

Every project has a unique name which you specify as well as an ID generated by Google. The project ID contains the project name which we have specified and a string of numbers which makes it unique across GCP globally.

Let's orient ourselves on the dashboard page. At the very top, you can see what project this dashboard is associated with. There is also a dropdown to allow you to switch between projects easily. The very first card gives us the details of the projects such as its name and the associated project ID. There is also a quick link to your project settings page where you can change your billing information and other project-related details. The compute engine card shows you a summary of your compute instances. We have no instances; therefore, this card is currently empty. We get a quick status check on the right indicating that all our services are green. We can see the billing details of the project at a glance.

Now we are at the Google Cloud dashboard that shows how we get all the services that Cloud Platform makes available to us. You will use this three-line navigation button at the top left. This is the most important button that you will find that while reading this book and using the platform:

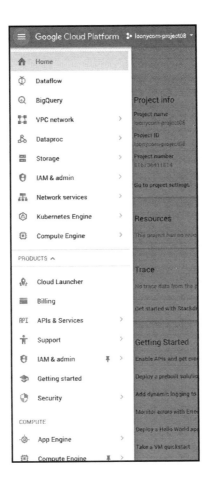

You will be navigating here over and over again. Click on the hamburger menu, open up the navigation menu, and you will see all Cloud Platform services and products available to you. Take the time and explore this menu as there is a lot of interesting stuff out there. But what are we going to work on? First is to create a VM instance, an instance of the compute engine. Go to the compute engine menu and click on **VM instances**:

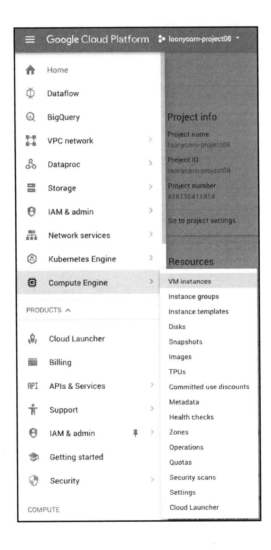

This will take us to a page where we can create our very first virtual machine instance on Google Cloud. You also now know that all Google Cloud resources or services or products that you use are built to a top-level projects. You can set up different projects for different teams in your organization.

Using the Cloud Shell

Before we jump into the compute options on GCP and create our first VM instance, let's understand the Cloud Shell. A Cloud Shell is a machine instance that runs on the Google Cloud which serves as your command line. All GCP accounts have a Cloud Shell that they can use to access resources on the Google Cloud Platform. You can access the Cloud Shell by clicking on a button to the top right of the navigation ribbon:

The great thing about the Cloud Shell is that it provides a complete environment for you to connect to various resources in the Cloud. Also, it is worth noting that the Cloud Shell is completely free for usage. The cool thing about it is that you can directly use the `gcloud` command-line tools to connect to resources in the cloud, create resources, provision it, and so on. You don't need to install and set up anything. The Cloud Shell is what you would use if, say, your organization does not allow you to download software on your local machine. It is a great alternative in that case, which just works. When you first connect to the Cloud Shell or `gshell`, Google has to spin up an active instance to use for this. It might take a little while, so be patient:

The figure that follows is our provisioned Cloud Shell and you will notice that it is associated with the same project which we mentioned earlier. Let's take the `gcloud` command-line tool for a test run. Remember that the Cloud Shell is just a terminal session on an ephemeral VM. This session will get disconnected after 30 minutes of inactivity. Also, when you are in the Cloud Shell, you are in a `home` directory with 5 GB of space, and this `home` directory will remain constant across all Cloud Shell sessions in the project and will be deleted after 120 days of inactivity:

```
 ⊞   🔧      loonycorn-project08 ×     +
Welcome to Cloud Shell! Type "help" to get started.
vitthal@loonycorn-project08:~$ pwd
/home/vitthal
vitthal@loonycorn-project08:~$ ▮
```

Let's explore the Cloud Shell further. The `gcloud` is Google's main command-line tool that allows you to work with resources and to a whole bunch of operations. It's especially useful if you want to script operations and just run a script rather than perform it manually over and over again.

You can view what the current default project is by typing out the `gcloud config list` command:

```
vitthal@loonycorn-project08:~$ gcloud config list
[component_manager]
disable_update_check = True
[compute]
gce_metadata_read_timeout_sec = 5
[core]
account = vitthal@loonycorn.com
disable_usage_reporting = False
project = loonycorn-project08
[metrics]
environment = devshell

Your active configuration is: [cloudshell-25365]
```

You can see that `loonycorn-project08` is the default. If you need help with what commands are available with `gcloud`, simply type `gcloud -h`, and you will see a whole bunch of information. The `gcloud config list` command shows you what properties have been set so far in the configuration. This will only display those properties that are different from the defaults. For example, you can see here that the account has been set to `vitthal@loonycorn.com` and the project is `loonycorn-project08`:

```
vitthal@loonycorn-project08:~$ gcloud -h
Usage: gcloud [optional flags] <group | command>
  group may be            alpha | app | auth | beta | components | compute |
                          config | container | dataflow | dataproc | datastore |
                          debug | deployment-manager | dns | domains |
                          endpoints | firebase | iam | iot | kms | logging | ml |
                          ml-engine | organizations | projects | pubsub |
                          services | source | spanner | sql | topic
  command may be          docker | feedback | help | info | init | version

For detailed information on this command and its flags, run:
  gcloud --help
```

If you need help for a particular command, let's say it's the `compute` command, you can simply say `gcloud compute --help`:

```
vitthal@loonycorn-project08:~$ gcloud compute --help
```

This essentially throws up the main page for that particular command. In other words, `gcloud` has context-sensitive help, and that is a great way to go about building the commands you need:

```
NAME
    gcloud compute - create and manipulate Google Compute Engine resources

SYNOPSIS
    gcloud compute GROUP | COMMAND [GCLOUD_WIDE_FLAG ...]

DESCRIPTION
    The gcloud compute command group lets you create, configure and manipulate
    Google Compute Engine virtual machines.

    With Compute Engine you can create and run virtual machines on Google
    infrastructure. Compute Engine offers scale, performance, and value that
    allows you to easily launch large compute clusters on Google's
    infrastructure.

    More information on Compute Engine can be found here:
    https://cloud.google.com/compute/ and detailed documentation can be found
    here: https://cloud.google.com/compute/docs/

GCLOUD WIDE FLAGS
    These flags are available to all commands: --account, --configuration,
    --flatten, --format, --help, --log-http, --project, --quiet, --trace-token,
    --user-output-enabled, --verbosity. Run $ gcloud help for details.

GROUPS
    :
```

Everything you need is right there on the screen.

In a nutshell, the Google Cloud Shell is a great tool for quick work on the console. Remember, again, though, that it is a short, time-limited session on an ephemeral VM. So, if you are going to be intensely developing on the Google Cloud and you can download software, it's better to download the Google Cloud SDK and use that instead. This offers a permanent connection to your instances on the cloud instead of a temporary VM instance that has to be spun up in order to use Cloud Shell.

Summary

You learned about the distinction between global, regional, zonal resources, and the SLAs provided by Google for network traffic and availability within regions and zones. We got started with GCP by exploring the GCP web console. We also made use of the Google Cloud Shell and typed out a few basic commands using the `gcloud` command-line utility.

Compute Choices – VMs and the Google Compute Engine

3

In the cloud world, the most hands-on of these approaches is not really an option—you are not going to actually own the machines, and physically maintain them. That is the whole point of switching to the cloud—that the cloud provider manages scaling for you and allows you to pay as you go. But a cloud equivalent of this approach still exists—you could provision a large number of virtual machines (again, these machines are virtual, not physical), and run your app on all of these. You'd be able to log in to these machines, and you'd have to manage scaling up or down (by provisioning more or less VMs). The cloud provider is still providing you with very valuable services—you can autoscale your groups of VMs, you can have your VMs stay live during system maintenance, and so on. These services are collectively called **Infrastructure-as-a-Service (IaaS)**.

In this chapter we will:

- Explore **Google Compute Engine (GCE)** which serves as Infrastructure as a Service provision of GCP.
- Learn how to create and manage GCE VMs along with its various aspects like disk type and machine types.

- Demonstrate using GCE VMs via running a webserver on it.

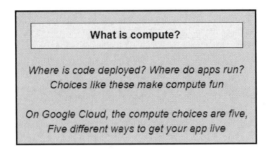

You could also easily go further. You might decide that you just want to write code—not deal with any provisioning of machines or networking or Ops. The cloud provider will allow you to write your code and deploy it without worrying about the underlying systems—virtual or physical. All that you know is that your app is available as a service—most likely as an HTTP endpoint that clients can hit using RESTful API calls. The cloud provides complete isolation from the infrastructure autoscaling, load-balancing, traffic-splitting—all of this is managed for you. Such a service is basically a platform on which you write your code, and forget about the rest. These services are collectively called **Platform-as-a-Service (PaaS)**.

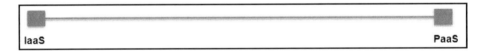

Let's draw a line with IaaS at one end, and PaaS at the other. The leading cloud providers—Amazon AWS, Microsoft Azure, and Google Cloud Platform—all offer the entire range of compute options, from IaaS to PaaS.

In addition to these, there are a couple of other approaches worth discussing—containers and SaaS:

- Containers lie somewhere in between IaaS and PaaS and involves the use of portable, lightweight images of your app—these lightweight images are called **containers**. Docker is a pretty common container format, and the GCP has a great orchestration framework called **Google Kubernetes Engine (GKE)** to run app containers on managed clusters. But that will be dealt in more detail in the later chapter.

- Another approach, further to the right of PaaS, would be **Software-as-a-Service (SaaS)**. In our preceding web app example, Heroku acted as an example of a PaaS offering, while Shopify was an SaaS offering. It probably is fair to say that Microsoft Azure is currently far ahead of the other two in SaaS, because it makes very powerful software such as Office 365 available to users. IaaS reduces the burden of DevOps, PaaS virtually eliminates it, and SaaS reduces the burden of development.

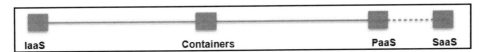

The preceding line is a general representation of the compute choices out there, but on the GCP, there actually are five specific options. None of these really involve SaaS, except for very limited use cases, so let's leave that out for now. The offerings on the GCP are shown as follows:

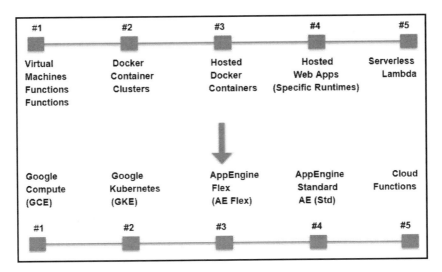

If you have an infra background, these five choices might make perfect sense to you, but even if you do not, never fear, we'll talk about each of them. Throughout the course of this chapter and the next, we will describe each of these five compute options. This chapter focuses on the first—**Google Compute Engine (GCE)**, which is basically a service to provision and work with virtual machines on the cloud.

GCE is a prototypical IaaS use case. What you need is a set of machines, placed at your disposal to set up in exactly the way you want. Configuration, administration, and management would all then be your responsibility. While this might sound like an on-premise data center, there are two crucial differences:

- The VMs are not running on hardware bought by you—rather, you just provision them whenever you need them and delete them when you're done.
- Several powerful infra services—autoscaling groups of VMs, load-balancing, the importing of external images, and so on—are provided by the cloud platform. This is why GCE is an IaaS solution.

In this chapter, we will get you familiar with GCE by covering the following topics:

- Creating, customizing, and modifying VM instances
- Block-based storage (local SSDs and persistent storage), which can be attached to your VMs
- Load balancing, start up scripts, and disk images that allow you to make optimal use of your VM instances

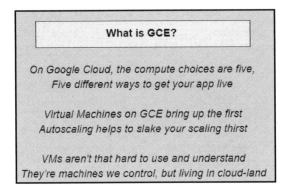

What is GCE?

On Google Cloud, the compute choices are five,
Five different ways to get your app live

Virtual Machines on GCE bring up the first
Autoscaling helps to slake your scaling thirst

VMs aren't that hard to use and understand
They're machines we control, but living in cloud-land

Google Compute Engine – GCE

Google Compute Engine is the IaaS component of the GCP that lets you create and run VM on Google infrastructure. Each VM is called a Compute Engine instance. A Compute Engine instance can run Linux and Windows server images provided by Google or any customized versions of these images. You can also build and run images of other operating systems.

You can choose the machine properties of your instances, such as the number of virtual CPUs and the amount of memory, by using a set of predefined machine types or by creating your own custom machine types.

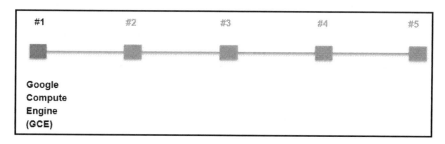

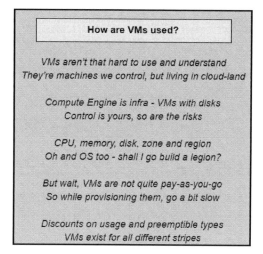

Creating VMs

This section will walk you through creating a VM instance. There are several ways to create a VM instance in GCE:

- Through the web console
- The `gcloud` command-line tool from Cloud Shell
- Using API calls

There actually is a fourth way as well—that's an **Infrastructure as Code (IaC)** approach relying on the Deployment Manager. Infrastructure automation is a big deal these days, and we'll get to this approach—but in a later chapter.

Creating a VM instance using the web console

The web console will allow you to view all the available options when configuring a VM. This is probably the best way to get started with provisioning VMs on GCP:

1. Start with the hamburger (three horizontal bars on the top left).
2. Click on **Compute**, and then on **VM instances**.
3. Click on **Create a new instance**. A form will pop up.
4. Enter a name for your instance.

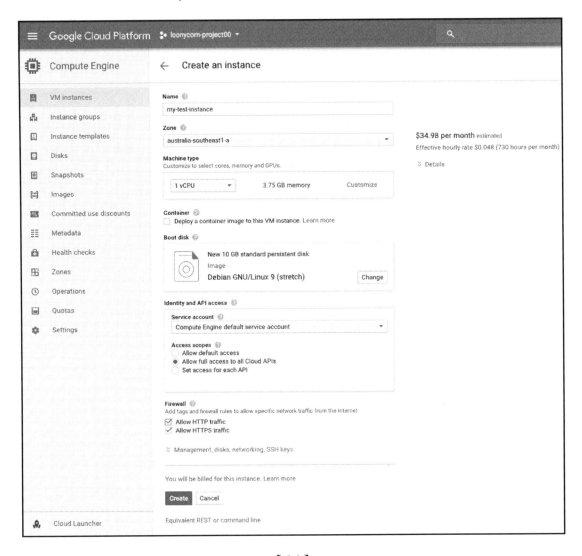

5. Pick a **Zone**. Note that some zones are more expensive than others, probably based on the resources available in it. There are a number of factors that matter when deciding the right zone. For instance, if you expect most of your traffic to be from Asia, it's preferable to pick a zone in Asia.

6. Choose a **Machine type** from the drop-down list. If you are not going to run something very computation-heavy, you can choose a micro instance that has one shared virtual CPU and very little memory. We will choose the same for the purpose of this tutorial as it is the most economical option in this case. The cost of the VM will depend on the machine type as well, if you recall our discussions from the previous section.

7. By default, the instance has a **10 GB standard persistent disk**. You can choose to change this, if you so desire, by clicking on the **Change** button. We are keeping the default since that's the minimum requirement to keep Debian smoothly running.

> As this is the root disk for the instance, we recommend the readers to stick with the default (Debian) as a lot of the examples later on rely on this being a Linux VM.

8. Choose how you want to restrict your instance, such as whether or not it should have access to cloud APIs, or serves HTTPS traffic and so on. Since we would be using this instance to install applications (like Apache webserver) via internet which serve HTTP/HTTPS traffic. We'd recommend keeping both options checked. And it is also recommended to have access to complete GCP Cloud APIs in case we make this VM interact with other GCP provisions.

9. Note the link that says management, disks, networking, and SSH keys. Clicking on this will give you advanced configuration options. But it is alright to keep them as default for now.

10. Once you've made your design choices, click **Create**. The preceding screenshot shows a sample set of choices. The design creation will take a few minutes.

Once it's complete, you can SSH directly into the instance to set up the software you want on it. This can be done in several ways:

- Directly through the browser by clicking on **SSH**
- You can also use your Cloud Shell and the `gcloud` command within it to SSH to this instance

  The command would go as follows:

  ```
  gcloud compute ssh [INSTANCE NAME]
  ```

- You can connect from an SSH client on your local machine, such as a terminal window on Mac or Linux, or the PuTTY program in Windows.

If you choose **Open in browser window**, and if you have pop-ups blocked on your machine, you will find an error message to the top right of your browser. Once you enable pop-ups, the SSH client will open up in a new browser window.

You can tell it's your VM instance from the prompt that displays the name you'd given in step two. Run a few commands to see what software has been pre-installed, as shown in the following screenshot:

```
Connected, host fingerprint: ssh-rsa 2048 52:86:23:0C:CC:68:6E:D7:43:BB:2A:9A:AE:
Linux my-test-instance 4.9.0-4-amd64 #1 SMP Debian 4.9.51-1 (2017-09-28) x86_64

The programs included with the Debian GNU/Linux system are free software;
the exact distribution terms for each program are described in the
individual files in /usr/share/doc/*/copyright.

Debian GNU/Linux comes with ABSOLUTELY NO WARRANTY, to the extent
permitted by applicable law.
vitthal@my-test-instance:~$ sudo apt-get update
Get:1 http://security.debian.org stretch/updates InRelease [63.0 kB]
```

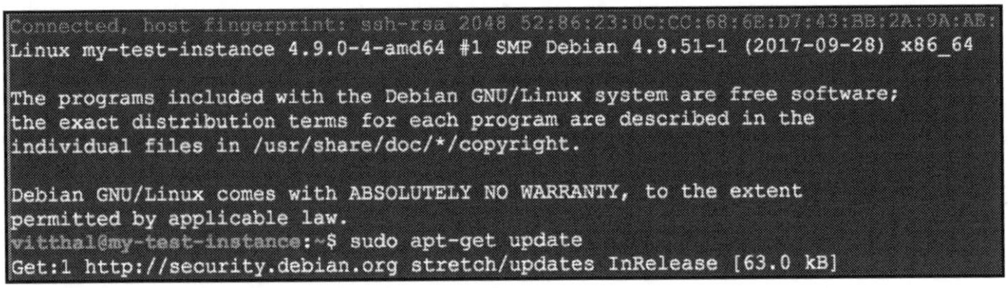

As this is a Linux machine, you can use Linux commands to install, download, or update. Run the `exit` command to quit the SSH window. On your **VM instance details** page, click on the VM name to get to the **VM instance details** page where you'll now be able to see a spike in the graph.

Creating a VM instance using the command line

An easy way to get the right command line is to piggyback on the web console—it has a neat little way to get the command line corresponding to a particular UI operation:

1. As before, start with the hamburger (three horizontal lines).
2. Navigate to **Compute**, and then to **VM instances**.
3. Click on **Create a VM instance** in the **VM instances** page and you'll get the UI to set up the configuration for this virtual machine.
4. Specify the configuration parameters using this console, as we saw in the previous section. At the very bottom of this form, you can find the **Equivalent REST** or **command line** option.
5. Click on both of these to get the **Equivalent REST** and `gcloud` commands respectively to set up the VM with the exact settings specified. The `gcloud` command is what you can use within scripts in order to create multiple VM instances with the same configuration.

6. Click on the icon with ≥ sign on the top-right side beside search bar. Open up your Cloud Shell from the console, which is completely free to use, and paste the `gcloud` command and hit *Enter* to create a new VM instance. Refresh the browser to see the new VM listed in the **VM instances** page.

---

gcloud command line

This is the gcloud command line with the parameters you have selected.

```
gcloud beta compute --project "loonycorn-project00" instances create "instance-1" --zone "us-east1-b" --machine-ty
pe "f1-micro" --subnet "default" --maintenance-policy "MIGRATE" --service-account "926633837560-compute@developer.
gserviceaccount.com" --scopes "https://www.googleapis.com/auth/devstorage.read_only","https://www.googleapis.com/a
uth/logging.write","https://www.googleapis.com/auth/monitoring.write","https://www.googleapis.com/auth/servicecont
rol","https://www.googleapis.com/auth/service.management.readonly","https://www.googleapis.com/auth/trace.append"
 --min-cpu-platform "Automatic" --image "debian-9-stretch-v20171025" --image-project "debian-cloud" --boot-disk-si
ze "10" --boot-disk-type "pd-standard" --boot-disk-device-name "instance-1"
```

☑ Line wrapping

gcloud reference

CLOSE   RUN IN CLOUD SHELL

Running `help` on this `gcloud` compute instance `create` command should show you all the options that you have available and you can use these to create custom instances from the Cloud Shell. But if you want to customize your instance with a lot of parameters, it's better to specify them on the web console, generate the corresponding command-line command, and use that:

```
gcloud compute instances create --help
```

You can further set up some default values in your configuration file so that any new instances that you create will use this default value. For example, if you set the default zone to be us-central1-a, all new instances will be created in this zone:

```
gcloud config set compute/zone us-central1-a
```

Note that if you wish to SSH into an instance that is not in the default zone from the Cloud Shell, you'll need to explicitly specify the zone using the zone parameter in the SSH command.

Now we know that if we wanted to automate the creation of virtual machines with specialized configurations, we can simply write a script with the required gcloud command, which is easily obtained by setting up the configuration on our web console and clicking on the **Equivalent REST** or **command line** link at the very bottom.

VM customization options

In the preceding process, while creating VMs, we encountered several customization options–some of these are pretty important to understand, so let's break down what we just did.

Operating system

The first choice you have to make is that of the operating system. There are public images available for Linux and Windows servers that come from Google. In addition, if you decide that you require some exotic operating system, you can use private images that you create or that you import into Compute Engine. Compute Engine uses operating system images to create the root persistent disks for your instances. You specify an image to be used as this root disk when you create an instance. Images contain a boot-loader, an operating system, and a root filesystem.

Lift-and-shift: The process of importing an external VM via a custom image is complex and not for the fainthearted, but this **lift-and-shift** is a rite of passage for most organizations getting onto the cloud. Do check out third-party tools that help, particularly CloudEndure—a free third-party service that is trusted by Google and has pretty good word-of-mouth.

Compute zone

A zone in which your VM will reside is a required choice when creating a VM. Compute Engine resources live in regions or zones. Recall that a region is a specific geographical location where you can run your resources and each region has one or more zones. Resources that live in a zone, such as instances or persistent disks, are referred to as zonal resources. Other resources, such as static external IP addresses, are regional. Regional resources can be used by any resources in that region, regardless of zone, while zonal resources can only be used by other resources in the same zone. The compute zone will decide the billing for your VM along with the machine type. Distributing multiple VMs across multiple zones is recommended for higher availability. The following screenshot lists some of the zones available to us on GCP:

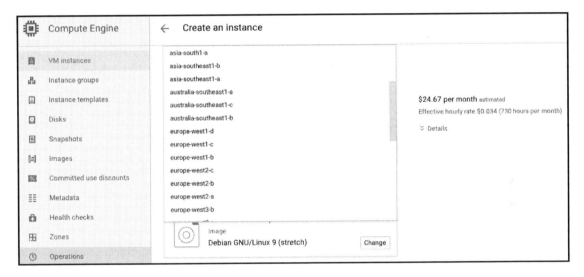

Machine type

You can choose the machine properties of your instances, such as the number of virtual CPUs and the amount of memory, by using a set of predefined machine types or by creating your own custom machine types. There is a varied set of machine types available to you, as can be seen in the preceding screenshot. There are standard machine types as well as machine types optimized for high memory usage and also something known as shared-core machine types.

These are small and are used for non-resource intensive jobs. With the advent of machine learning, GPUs have become increasingly important as well and the machine type choices include the ability to attach GPUs to our instances in some zones. Predefined machine types have preset virtualized hardware properties and a set price, while custom machine types are priced according to the number of vCPUs and memory that the virtual machine instance uses.

Networks – aka VPCs

We will discuss networks in detail in a later chapter, but for those who are already familiar with the idea of VPCs, each VM must belong to exactly one VPC.

As an aside, networking on the GCP is pretty different from that in either AWS or Azure, so definitely do read the chapter on networking if you are planning on creating custom VPCs or tinkering with any of their properties.

Storage options

This is an important enough topic to require a section of its own—which follows next.

Persistent disks and local SSDs – block storage for GCE

Persistent disk is the term used by Google to identify block storage. It can either be **Hard Disk Drive (HDD)** or **Solid State Drive (SSD)**. They can be used as non-volatile storage for GCE VMs.

Understanding persistent disks and local SSDs

Standard HDD persistent disks are efficient and economical for handling sequential read/write operations, but are not optimized to handle high rates of random **input/output operations per second (IOPS)**.

If your applications require high rates of random IOPS, use SSD persistent disks. Persistent disks can be attached to multiple instances in read-only mode for data sharing.

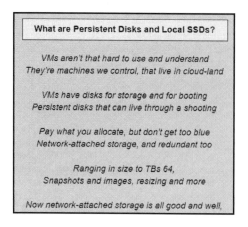

One might get confused between Persistent Disks and Cloud Storage Buckets (which we will explore later in this book) since both are cloud storage technologies accessible via a network. But it is important to remember that persistent disks are created for Compute Engine instances via Compute Engine APIs and are accessed via `gsutil` command line tool not `gcloud`. Further differences can be noticed in the following table:

Parameter	Standard Persistent Disks	SSD Persistent Disks	Local SSD	Cloud Storage Buckets
Storage cost (per GB per mo)	4-5 cents	15-20 cents	20-30 cents	0.7-2.5 cents
Maximum storage space per instance	64 TB	64 TB	3 TB	Unlimited
Scope of Access	Zone	Zone	Instance	Global
Data Redundancy	✓	✓	X	✓
Encryption at rest	✓	✓	✓	✓
Custom Encryption Keys	✓	✓	X	✓
Supported Machine types	All	All	Most	All

Creating and attaching a persistent disk

As we discussed in the previous sections, a persistent disk is the storage option that is associated with the VM instances in GCE, by default. This section will walk you through creating and attaching a persistent disk.

Let's say we have already created a VM instance called `test-instance` in the US zone `central1-f`. We now want to expand the storage that is available to this VM instance, which can be done by creating a new persistent disk. We will use the command line for this:

```
gcloud compute disks create test-disk --size=100GB --zone us-central1-f
```

- `gcloud compute disks create` is the command
- `test-disk` is the name of our disk
- The size is `100GB`
- The zone is `us-central1-f`

The persistent disk that you set up has to be in the same zone as your instance. You can't create a persistent disk in another zone and attach it to an instance that lives in a completely different zone, because persistent disks have to be connected to the instance with really high-speed connections—and that is only possible in the same zone. Note that ideally when you are creating a persistent disk, there should be at least 200 GB in size for optimal read and write performance or you'll get a warning.

1. Click on your test instance VM to edit your settings and let's attach this particular disk to your VM instance.
2. Click on add item under **Additional disks** and, in the drop-down list, you will find **test-disk**, the standard persistent disk that we set up.

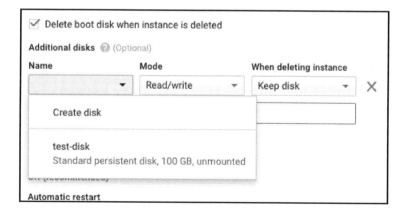

3. Let us use the command line to attach this disk to our instance. The command line is especially preferable if this is a repeated operation. Use the `gcloud compute instances attach-disk` command to specify the instance and the disk you want attached and the instance and the zone where they both live and hit *Enter*:

```
gcloud compute instances attach-disk test-instance --disk test-disk
--zone us-central1-f
```

4. Once the command has returned, hit **REFRESH** on your web console and go into the **test-instance** to see whether the disk has indeed been attached. Note that **test-disk** is now attached to this VM instance.

Boot disk and local disks

Name	Size (GB)	Type	Mode	
test-instance	10	Standard persistent disk	Boot, read/write	

☑ Delete boot disk when instance is deleted

Additional disks

Name	Size (GB)	Type	Mode	When deleting instance
test-disk	100	Standard persistent disk	Read/write	Keep disk

5. You can also SSH into your test instance to confirm that the disk is indeed part of the instance now. You can view all the hard disks that are associated with this instance by running `ls -l /dev/disk/by-id`. This will give you the list of hard disks attached. You will see an SCSI disk called `Google persistent disk-1`, which is the new disk that we just attached.

```
Debian GNU/Linux comes with ABSOLUTELY NO WARRANTY, to the extent
permitted by applicable law.
vitthal@test-instance:~$ ls -l /dev/disk/by-id
total 0
lrwxrwxrwx 1 root root  9 Nov 30 10:56 google-persistent-disk-1 -> ../../sdb
lrwxrwxrwx 1 root root  9 Nov 30 10:18 google-test-instance -> ../../sda
lrwxrwxrwx 1 root root 10 Nov 30 10:18 google-test-instance-part1 -> ../../sda1
lrwxrwxrwx 1 root root  9 Nov 30 10:56 scsi-0Google_PersistentDisk_persistent-disk-1 -> ../../sdb
lrwxrwxrwx 1 root root  9 Nov 30 10:18 scsi-0Google_PersistentDisk_test-instance -> ../../sda
lrwxrwxrwx 1 root root 10 Nov 30 10:18 scsi-0Google_PersistentDisk_test-instance-part1 -> ../../sda1
vitthal@test-instance:~$
```

6. Once the status of your disk creation is ready, the disk needs to be formatted.

Linux procedure for formatting and mounting a persistent disk

Newly created persistent disks do not have any filesystems on them. We must format them with the desired filesystem and the number of partitions we need. Here, we will format it with a single partition and ext4 filesystem. To do so:

1. Go to the **VM instances** page and access your instance through the browser using SSH.

2. One you are prompted to the Terminal, use the `lsblk` command to list the attached disks to your instance:

   ```
   sudo lsblk
   ```

3. To format disks, use the make filesystem (`mkfs`) command. You can also make the runtime and formatting faster by means of optional arguments to disable lazy initialization:

   ```
   sudo mkfs.ext4 -m 0 -F -E lazy_itable_init=0, lazy_journal_init=0,
   discard /dev/sda
   ```

4. Now, to mount the formatted disk, create a directory that will serve as your mounting point:

   ```
   sudo mkdir /mnt/my-mounting-dir
   ```

5. Use the `mount` command and provide the disk and mounting point as arguments. Also make sure that the discard option is enabled:

   ```
   sudo mount -o discard, defaults /dev/sda /mnt/my-mounting-dir
   ```

6. You can also configure read and write permissions for users. We will provide write access to all users:

   ```
   sudo chmod a+w /mnt/my-mounting-dir
   ```

Again, if you are attaching a persistent disk to your VM, the disk and the VM have to be in the same zone. Your VM instance and the persistent disk cannot be in different zones.

Sharing a persistent disk between multiple instances

You can also share a non-bootable persistent disk between multiple VM instances with a condition that it remains read-only in all of them. This occupies less overall storage in a multi-instance application and also saves the replication exercise. It also reduces billing since we use less storage. To do so, use the `instances attach-disk` command with `gcloud` and provide an instance name as well as a disk name:

```
gcloud compute instances attach-disk test-instance --disk sdb --mode ro
```

Repeat this operation for each attachment.

Resizing a persistent disk

Resizing the disk does not configure the filesystem to use additional space automatically. We have to do it ourselves. If our persistent disk has both a filesystem and partition table, we must edit both:

1. We can use the `gcloud` command-line tool for this purpose.

   ```
   gcloud compute disk resize [DISK NAME] —size [DISK_SIZE]
   ```

2. Get access of your persistent disk using SSH and determine the partition that you want to modify. You can use `lsblk` to have a list of your disks and partitions. If your picked partition has a partition table, then we must grow the partition before resizing it:

   ```
   sudo growpart /dev/sda [PARTITION NUMBER]
   ```

3. Now, extend the filesystem and provide a disk name or partition name:

   ```
   sudo resize2fs /dev/sda/[PARTITION_NUMBER]
   ```

4. You can use the `df -h` command to verify your resizing.

More on working with GCE VMs

In this section, we will explore the various features that the GCE offers. Each one of the features described is important, so do stay tuned.

Rightsizing recommendations

In the on-premise world, it pays to over-provision. If you need a server of capacity X today, you're best off buying one with a capacity of 1.5X—if only to not have to deal with finance and procurement all over again in a year's time.

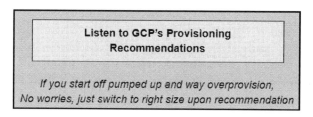

When you switch to the cloud though, if you don't adjust that mindset, you might end up with sticker shock. On the cloud, remember that you can scale both up and down.

That's where the recommendations from GCE come in handy. Compute Engine provides machine type recommendations to optimize the resource utilization and minimize expenses of your virtual machine instances. These recommendations are generated automatically based on system metrics such as the CPU and memory utilization, gathered by the Google Stackdriver, which is a suite of GCP tools for **Logging and Monitoring** services over the last eight days.

You can then use these recommendations to resize your instance's machine type to more efficiently use a machine type's resources.

```
micro (1 shared vCPU)
0.6 GB memory, f1-micro

small (1 shared vCPU)
1.7 GB memory, g1-small

✓ 1 vCPU °
3.75 GB memory, n1-standard-1

2 vCPUs
7.5 GB memory, n1-standard-2

4 vCPUs
15 GB memory, n1-standard-4

8 vCPUs
30 GB memory, n1-standard-8

16 vCPUs
60 GB memory, n1-standard-16

32 vCPUs
120 GB memory, n1-standard-32

64 vCPUs
240 GB memory, n1-standard-64

2 vCPUs
13 GB memory, n1-highmem-2

4 vCPUs
26 GB memory, n1-highmem-4
```

Availability policies

When maintenance events such as hardware or software updates require your VM to be moved to a different host machine, the Compute Engine automatically manages the scheduling behavior for your instances.

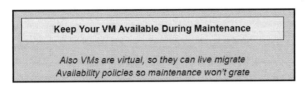

Keep Your VM Available During Maintenance

Also VMs are virtual, so they can live migrate
Availability policies so maintenance won't grate

If you configure the instance's availability policy to use live migration, which is a very powerful feature, exclusive to GCP. Compute Engine will live migrate your VM instances, which prevents your applications from experiencing disruptions during maintenance. Alternatively, you can choose to terminate your instances during these events.

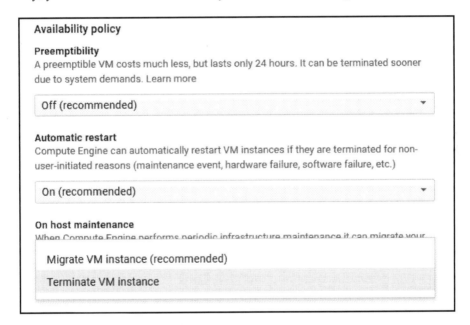

Availability policy

Preemptibility
A preemptible VM costs much less, but lasts only 24 hours. It can be terminated sooner due to system demands. Learn more

Off (recommended)

Automatic restart
Compute Engine can automatically restart VM instances if they are terminated for non-user-initiated reasons (maintenance event, hardware failure, software failure, etc.)

On (recommended)

On host maintenance
When Compute Engine performs periodic infrastructure maintenance it can migrate your

Migrate VM instance (recommended)

Terminate VM instance

When viewing the instance details in the console, you will see the option that is currently enforced under the section **Availability policies**. One example of the VM configuration with the availability policy set to migrate the VM instance during maintenance is shown in the following screenshot:

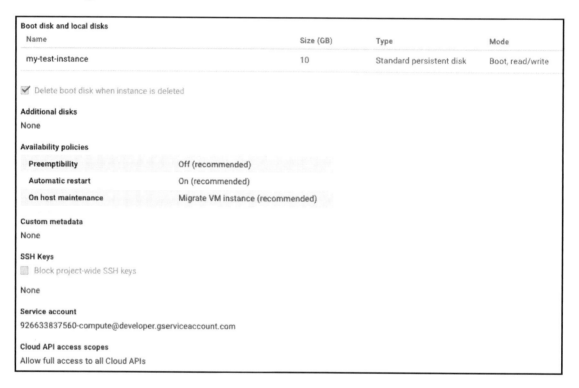

Boot disk and local disks

Name	Size (GB)	Type	Mode
my-test-instance	10	Standard persistent disk	Boot, read/write

☑ Delete boot disk when instance is deleted

Additional disks
None

Availability policies

Preemptibility	Off (recommended)
Automatic restart	On (recommended)
On host maintenance	Migrate VM instance (recommended)

Custom metadata
None

SSH Keys
☐ Block project-wide SSH keys

None

Service account
926633837560-compute@developer.gserviceaccount.com

Cloud API access scopes
Allow full access to all Cloud APIs

Auto-restart

Auto-restart refers to the behavior that the VM takes after a hardware failure or a system event. If set to auto-restart, the system will try launching a replacement VM.

Replacement VMs On Crashes

And if God forbid your VM crashes (or cracks)
Auto-restart can cover your tracks

However, auto-restart will not restart the VM if it was terminated due to a user event such as shutting down or terminating the VM.

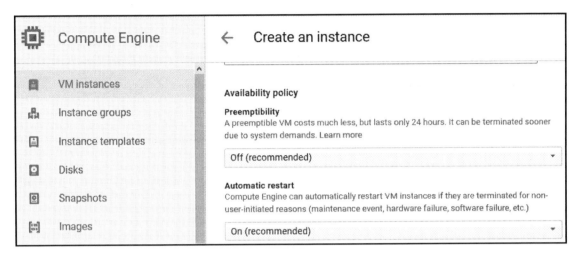

Preemptibillity

A preemptible instance is a VM instance type that is much cheaper than the regular Compute Engine machine types that we discussed in the previous section. The reason for this is that a preemptible instance uses spare resources in Google's infrastructure, but they might be terminated (that is, preempted) at any time if Google requires the resources held by this VM.

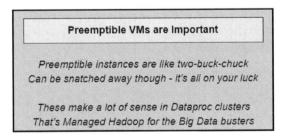

Preemptible instances cost only a fraction of what other VM instances do and so if you have a fault-tolerant application, for instance, a processing-only node in a Hadoop cluster, a preemptible instance might make a lot of sense and particularly so, if you are budget conscious.

Preemptible instances will definitely be terminated after running for 24 hours. Hence, do not ever use preemptible instances for long running jobs. When using a preemptible instance for relatively short jobs, the probability of termination is typically quite low. This probability of termination will vary based on the day, the zone, the network conditions, and other factors such as migrations and maintenance. Preemptible instances, unlike other VM types, cannot migrate; that is, they cannot stay alive during software updates and they will be forcibly restarted during maintenance. The first step in the preemption process is that the Google Cloud Platform or Compute Engine will send your instance a soft off signal where your machine has 30 seconds in which to clean up through a shutdown script and give up control. If it does not do so, Compute Engine will forcibly take control by sending a mechanical off signal. Therefore, if you use preemptible instances, do ensure that you have a well written shutdown script associated with the preemptible instance.

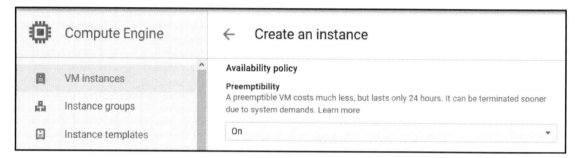

Load balancing

The GCP offers several load-balancing options, all of which work with virtual machines. A common usage pattern is to use an HTTP/HTTPS-based load balancer (which deals with web traffic), and wire this up as a frontend, with several groups of VM instances at the backend.

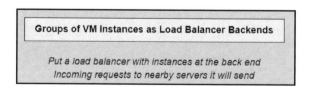

Those groups could be managed instance groups (see following section), or just unrelated sets of instances. The load balancer will then distribute the incoming web requests to VMs in the backend.

This is a common way to distribute traffic based on user proximity (users from Asia should hit backend servers in Asia, those in Europe should hit backend instances in Europe), as well as content type (folks requesting hi-def video get directed to one set of instances, while those requesting regular video go to another).

Autoscaling and managed instance groups

Compute Engine offers autoscaling to automatically add or remove virtual machines from an instance group based on increases or decreases in load. This allows your applications to gracefully handle increases in traffic and reduces cost when the need for resources is lower. All you have to do is define the autoscaling policy and the autoscaler performs automatic scaling based on the measured load.

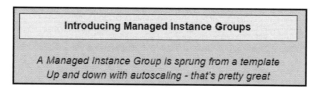

We will have a lot more to say about *managed instance groups* and load balancing in the chapters to come.

Billing

Google offers a very easy-to-use tool to estimate the cost of running your instance with a particular configuration.

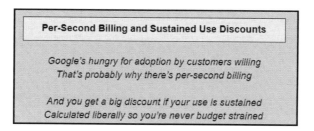

VMs range in price from pretty cheap to really expensive. In the following screenshot, you can see that a VM with **1 vCPU** and **2 GB** of memory is projected to cost $21.90 per month:

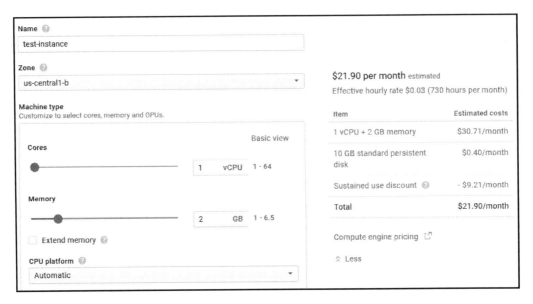

However, scaling this instance to **20 vCPU** cores and **170 GB** of memory will incur a hefty $830 per month, as seen in the following screenshot:

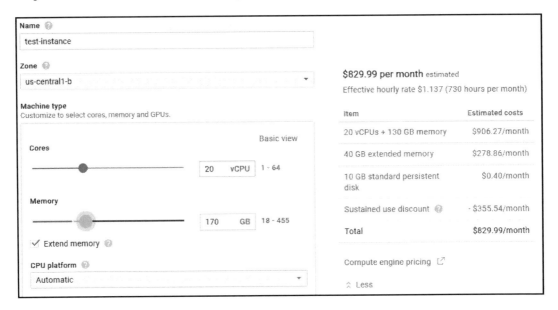

VMs are very transparent about their pricing, while when provisioning one, you are told what the base rate will be. This base rate varies with the specs and OS of the machine—as the preceding screenshots show, VMs could be either really cheap or really expensive, depending on how powerful you'd like them to be.

A natural question then is—how is this base rate going to be applied? All machines are charged for one minute at boot time, which is the minimum charge for a VM, after which, the per-second pricing begins. A bill is sent out at the end of each billing cycle, listing previous usage and charges.

The estimated costs of your instances and Compute Engine resources can be seen when you create them in the Google Cloud Platform Console or you can estimate your total project costs with the Google Cloud Pricing Calculator.

You should know that VMs are billed until they are deleted, and that charges accrue even when the VM is stopped. A stopped VM will not incur charges for CPU, but you will still be charged for attached disks and IPs.

There is some fine print around how exactly these sustained discounts are calculated. For predefined machine types, all VMs in the project within the same zone are grouped together into one inferred instance—this makes the discount much more generous of course. For custom machine types, the CPU and memory usage are separately pooled across all VMs in the same zone, and then a discount rate is applied separately to each.

% of Usage	% of base rate
First 25	100
Next 25	80
Last 25	60

Custom-type sustained use discount

% of month usage	% of base rate
0-25	100
25-50	80
50-75	60
75-100	40

Predefined-type sustained use discount

Labels and tags

Labels are a lightweight way to group together resources that are related or associated. For example, a common practice is to label resources that are intended for production, staging, or development separately, so you can easily search for resources that belong to each development stage when necessary.

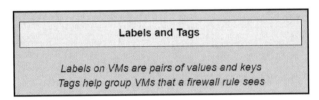

You could add labels to resources to form billing groups. You can apply labels to any of these resources—virtual machine instances, Forwarding rules (Alpha), Images, Persistent disks, Snapshots, Static external IPs, and VPN tunnels.

Labels are just key-value pairs and they correspond to tags in Azure; rather confusingly, GCP also has tags, but they apply only to VMs, and are used to specify which VMs in a network should be subject to a particular firewall rule and so on.

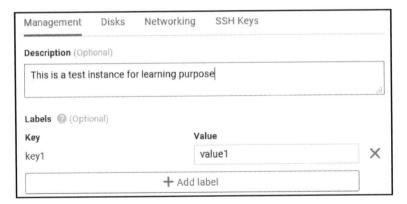

Startup scripts

We can run our own startup scripts from VM instances to perform automatic actions such as updating the system, and sending notifications and so on.

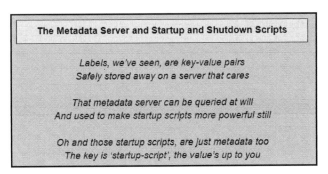

A startup script is specified using metadata keys through the metadata server and can be applied using the console or `gcloud` command line:

1. Once you have set the default region and zone for your instance, you can provide a startup script using the `gcloud` command line while creating an instance. The script is provided with a—`metadata` flag:

```
gcloud compute instances create example-instance --tags http-server
--metadata startup-script='#! /bin/bash
# Installs apache and a custom homepage
# Go to root directory
sudo su -
# For automatic Updates
apt-get update
# Install apache
apt-get install -y apache2
# Edit index.html file
cat <<EOF > /var/www/html/index.html
<html><body><h1>Hello World</h1>
<p>This page was created from a simple start up script!</p>
</body></html>
EOF'
```

2. For an already running instance, startup scripts can be added using the `add-metadata` flag as follows. The path can be a URL as well, which means that the script can also be located from a Cloud Storage bucket object:

```
gcloud compute instances add-metadata example-instance  --metadata-
from-file startup-script=path/to/file
```

Snapshots and images

Snapshots are used to back up data from persistent disks to Cloud Storage, but they are not visible in your buckets as they are managed by the snapshot service. Snapshot is not available for local SSD. They can be used to create new disks, which may be in another region or zone in the same project, and thus they form the basis of VM migration. But you cannot share snapshots across projects.

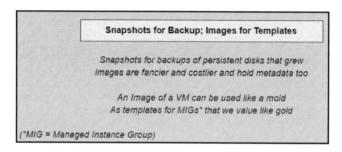

Snapshots do not back up VM metadata, tags, and so on. In this way, they are different from images—which are used primarily to create instances or configure instance templates. Snapshots can be created from persistent disks even while they are attached to running instances. Images, in turn, can be either public or custom, and are an important tool in creating managed instance groups to clone a given single instance.

Snapshots are incremental and can hence be used to create regular snapshots on a persistent disk faster and at a much lower cost than regularly creating a full image of the disk.

On Windows, you can enable **Volume Shadow Service** (**VSS**), which enables a disk to be backed up without having to be shut down. Snapshots are the size of the existing disk. They cannot be restored to a smaller disk or other disk types. Thus, *shrinking* a disk would be an OS copy process of data from one attached disk to a second smaller attached disk. Multiple copies of each snapshot are redundantly stored across multiple locations with automatic checksums to ensure the integrity of data.

How to snapshot a disk

Snapshots are used to back up persistent disks. They are different from backup disk images since they are created to be used periodically. If we create subsequent snapshots of persistent disk, only the first snapshot will back up the entire data of disk, while the other ones will only have reference to prior snapshots for the duplicate data and will contain updated data or newly added data with logs. This reduces total storage to be used and hence reduces the billing amount. To create a persistent disk snapshot, follow these steps:

1. Use the `gcloud compute disks snapshot` command and provide a disk name as an argument:

   ```
   gcloud compute disks snapshot sda
   ```

2. It returns a status flag result as READY or FAILED. To verify the snapshot creation, use the following:

   ```
   gcloud compute snapshots list
   ```

3. To restore data from the created snapshot, create a persistent disk larger than the size of the snapshot. Do this from the snapshot itself and make sure you are not doing it from the `root` directory:

   ```
   gcloud compute disks create sdb  --source-snapshot=test-instance-snapshot --size=600GB
   ```

4. Attach this persistent disk to an instance:

   ```
   gcloud compute instances attach-disk test-instance01 --disk=sdb
   ```

5. The preceding command is useful when snapshot and restoration disks are of the same type. For different types of disks, use a type argument and provide the disk type.

6. Finally, to delete the snapshot, use the following command:

   ```
   gcloud compute snapshots delete test-instance-snapshot
   ```

How to create an image of a disk

Custom disk images are different from public images managed by Google. These are local to your project. They are useful for creating one or more instances when you have customized your instance in a certain way. For example, you could have installed updates, some applications, or could have set up some environment to work on and you would not want to repeat the procedure over again. Unlike snapshots, custom images are to be backed up once per instance only. We can create multiple images as variants, but they will be complete backups of the instance and will result in more billing due to access storage:

1. To create the image, use the `gcloud compute instance create` command and provide an image name, source disk, the zone of the source disk, and the image family. The image family is an optional argument that specifies which OS we are using along with its version. In our case, it is Debian 9:

```
gcloud compute images create sda-image \
   --source-disk sda \
   --source-disk-zone us-east1-b \
   --family debian-9
```

2. For creating an image from another image, replace the source disk and source disk zone with the source image and source image project accordingly:

```
gcloud compute images create [IMAGE_NAME] \
   --source-image [SOURCE_IMAGE] \
   --source-image-project [IMAGE_PROJECT] \
   --family [IMAGE_FAMILY]
```

Cloud launcher

Google cloud launcher is a fast deployment services for software packages running on the resources of GCP (for example, a web server on compute engine VM). The sole purpose of this provision is to make sure that users who are new to GCP services can get started quickly with it and fulfil their purposes such as hosting a blog. The deployments can be scaled based on the requirements later on.

The best part is that all of these tasks can be achieved via simple user friendly GUI. This is how cloud launcher looks like:

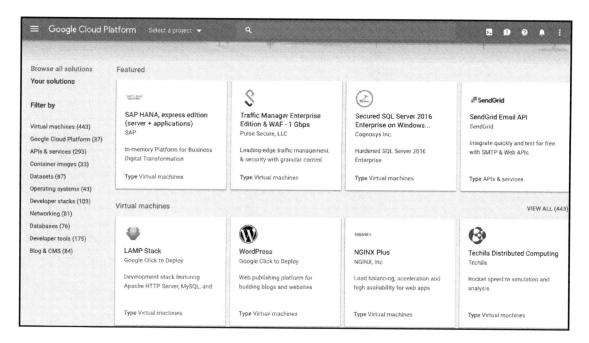

To deploy your complete application, you can choose and deploy your packages and provision resources according to your requirements and budget. Billing follows the patterns of the resources you selected.

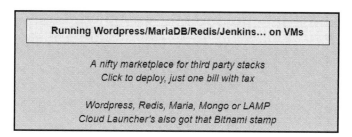

Deploying LAMP stack using GCE

Let's explore how we would set up a LAMP stack on a VM instance. LAMP is a stack of Linux, Apache, MySQL, and PHP:

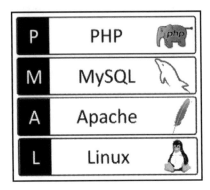

1. Connect to your Linux VM instance using SSH and update it. We will follow Debian 9 commands throughout this example:

   ```
   sudo apt-get update
   ```

2. Install Apache 2's PHP module:

   ```
   sudo apt-get install libapache2-mod-php php
   ```

3. To test the installation, enter your external IP address and you should see the **Apache test** page. You can copy the external IP from the list on the console page of VM instances. It should show the Apache starting page:

   ```
   http://[EXTERNAL_IP]
   ```

Apache2 Debian Default Page

debian

It works!

This is the default welcome page used to test the correct operation of the Apache2 server after installation on Debian systems. If you can read this page, it means that the Apache HTTP server installed at this site is working properly. You should **replace this file** (located at `/var/www/html/index.html`) before continuing to operate your HTTP server.

If you are a normal user of this web site and don't know what this page is about, this probably means that the site is currently unavailable due to maintenance. If the problem persists, please contact the site's administrator.

Configuration Overview

Debian's Apache2 default configuration is different from the upstream default configuration, and split into several files optimized for interaction with Debian tools. The configuration system is **fully documented in /usr/share/doc/apache2/README.Debian.gz**. Refer to this for the full documentation. Documentation for the web server itself can be found by accessing the **manual** if the `apache2-doc` package was installed on this server.

The configuration layout for an Apache2 web server installation on Debian systems is as follows:

```
/etc/apache2/
|-- apache2.conf
|          `--  ports.conf
|-- mods-enabled
|          |-- *.load
|          `-- *.conf
|-- conf-enabled
|          `-- *.conf
|-- sites-enabled
|          `-- *.conf
|
```

4. To verify that PHP and Apache are working together, edit the `phpinfo.php` file and access it with your VM instance external IP:

   ```
   sudo sh -c 'echo "[YOUR_PHP_CODE]" > /var/www/html/phpinfo.php'
   http://[YOUR_EXTERNAL_IP_ADDRESS]/phpinfo.php
   ```

5. If it fails, you will receive a 404 error.

6. Finally, to install MySQL and relevant components, use the following command:

   ```
   sudo apt-get install mysql-server php5-mysql php-pear
   ```

7. You now have a complete **Linux, Apache, MySQL, PHP (LAMP)** stack.

Modifying GCE VMs

You can choose to edit your virtual machine's settings. However, if the scope of the program that you run on this instance expands and it needs more resources, you will have to stop the instance and then re-configure your machine type and restart. Note that stopping the VM instance can have unintended side effects such as losing critical data in case of VM having been provisioned on local SSD:

1. Click on the name of the instance you wish to edit.

2. Navigate to the **VM instance details** page. Select your VM and click **STOP** to stop the VM.

3. Hit **EDIT** on the **VM instance details** page. The VM instance can now be reconfigured.

4. If you go to machine type, you can choose from the standard instances available in the drop down menu or if you click on **Customize**, you will see sliders that allow you to configure the number of CPUs on your machine, the amount of memory, and so on. Choose something that is sufficient for your needs.

5. Note that you can't change the zone once the instance has been created. If the original was Australia, it will continue to be Australia.

6. You can define labels and add resources to this instance to make billing groups.

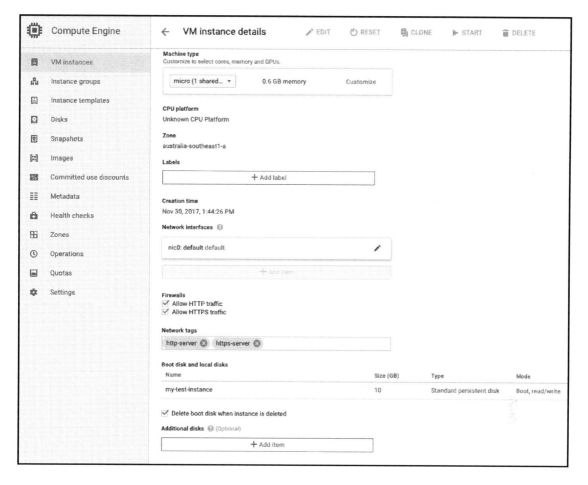

7. You can also add more disks to your instance, but this requires that you have set up additional hard disks earlier. If you haven't done so, you won't see any additional disks listed here. However, you can create a disk using the link provided right there.

8. Instead of allowing your instance access to all cloud APIs, you can set these permissions at a more granular level by specifying access for each API. It will list every API that has been enabled and you can individually configure permissions for each of them.

9. If you choose not to make any changes, click **Cancel**. You can delete your instance by clicking on the **Delete** button at the top of the **VM instance details** page. As soon as you are done with an instance, it is better to delete them, so it doesn't take up resources and add to your bill. Be mindful, however, that a deleted VM cannot be restored.

If you choose to restart the VM by clicking on the **Restart** button at the top of the VM details page, note that the external IP address will change. The **RESET** button is an option to stop the VM temporarily without losing the IP address.

Summary

In this chapter, we have seen that Google Compute Engine falls under the umbrella of IaaS, and have learned how that compares with PaaS and SaaS. The provisioning and configuration of VM instances, including the use of startup scripts, as well as machine types and their effect on costs should now be clear. Some of the additional features linked to VM instances such as load balancing and autoscaling have also been discussed. And finally, we have covered the forms of storage that can be attached to a VM, such as persistent disks and local SSDs, while also touching upon snapshots and images.

Now that we have looked at Google's IaaS offering with Compute Engine, we can now move toward the PaaS options by examining **Google Kubernetes Engine** (**GKE**) and **App Engine** (**AE**).

4
GKE, App Engine, and Cloud Functions

Let's go back to the conversation we had on compute options in general at the start of the preceding chapter. We had discussed that there is a range, from IaaS through to SaaS. We had also spoken about how the IaaS offerings on the cloud make provisioning infra really simple. PaaS offerings allow us to just focus on writing code, without having to deal with the infrastructure. The SaaS offerings go a step further and give us functionality without even writing code:

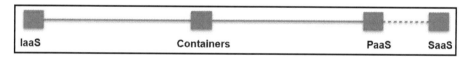

The GCP IaaS offering, which we discussed at length, is the **Google Compute Engine (GCE)**, which allows us to provision VMs really easily. In this chapter, we will discuss the remaining four compute options on the GCP, all of which range from IaaS through PaaS (there aren't really strong SaaS offerings on the GCP just yet). The topics we will touch upon include:

- Containers, Kubernetes, and the **Google Kubernetes Engine (GKE)**
- Using Google App Engine Flex

- Using Google App Engine Standard

#1	#2	#3	#4	#5
Virtual Machines Functions	Docker Container Clusters	Hosted Docker Containers	Hosted Web Apps (Specific Runtimes)	Serverless Lambda Functions
Google Compute (GCE)	Google Kubernetes (GKE)	AppEngine Flex (AE Flex)	AppEngine Standard AE (Std)	Cloud Functions

GKE

Kubernetes Engine is a managed, production-ready environment used for deploying containerised applications. It accelerates the TTM (Time To Market) by introducing the latest innovations in developer productivity, resource efficiency and so on.

Contrasting containers and VMs

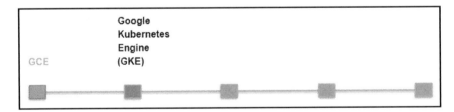

You might recall our short introduction of containers, and Kubernetes, at the start of the previous chapter. We had given the example of a simple web application, with a web app upfront and a database out back. We could start with these hosted on VM instances—but then, as the web app got complicated, we'd likely decompose the code into separate services. This move from a monolithic architecture to a service-oriented one, and finally, perhaps even to one based on microservices, is quite typical of the evolution of such app architectures.

The dependencies between these services would quickly get complicated to manage and, to simplify things, we'd probably decompose the services to rest on separate VMs. Then, at this point, we probably would want a **continuous integration/continuous delivery (CI/CD)** system, where code artifacts are built and deployed on an on-going basis. There would be little point in including the OS image inside each such artifact. That, in a nutshell, gets us to the idea of containers and their differences from VMs. The following diagram shows how containers are different from VMs:

How are containers different from VMs?

On Google Cloud, compute chioces are five,
Five different ways to make your app live

GKE, Kubernetes Engine, is our number two
Container clusters, and multi-cloud too

Kubernetes today is the flavor of the day,
Dockers containers run the right way

Apps on the OS on top of hardware
Simple and direct - that's bare metal-ware

Add a hypervisor as a layer of abstraction
Then VMs on top, that's got a lot of traction

Cool! but the VM has a guest OS inside
We could shrink the image if we really tried

No OS, just libraries and all the apps
That's the idea of Docker, hope you're still listening chaps

A container is a unit, quite like a jar
Portable enough to put in your car

Docker containers are a hybrid boon
Multi-cloud too - but don't rejoice too soon

Containerizing code is quite a hard one
Far often said, less often done

So Kubernetes manages your container cluster
Cluster orchestration like a skilled conductor

Kubernetes is open-source, but quite the source of pride
By Google, but runs on the other clouds and even client side

What is a container?

A container image is a lightweight, standalone, executable package that also encapsulates everything that is needed to run it. This would include code, the runtime, system tools, system libraries, and settings.

This definition comes from the website of Docker, which of course is a market-leading container firm. Consider a number of containers running on top of the same OS kernel. Each one of these containers will then, effectively, have its own little environment and executable files, as well as the entire runtime set up. Each one of these containers can be created by using a software such as Docker. Docker can be thought of as a kind of CD tool that takes in your code and outputs a container that can be carried around and run in its own little sandbox. Containers differ from VMs in some important ways, but the basic idea is fairly similar. Individual containers are often in the Docker file format.

In the case of containers, right below our individual containers lies Docker, which, as we know, is an open platform that allows folks to build and run distributed applications in the form of containers. The crucial bit though, is that Docker runs on top of the host OS, which means that each individual container does not abstract the OS. In contrast, in the case of VMs, we can see that each VM has its applications, libraries, and a guest OS. Beneath each of the VMs lies the VM monitor, or hypervisor as it is known. This is a piece of software that should be created by a company such as VMware for instance, which ensures that one or more VMs are able to run on the host machine and interact with the hardware and the other infrastructure:

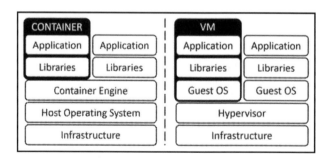

In effect, containers add one further level of indirection to your code. This makes them different from VMs because we virtualize the OS. For instance, in the previous block diagram, Docker was acting as a proxy between the container and the OS.

In a VM, on the other hand, every VM has its own OS that talks to the hypervisor and that hypervisor VM monitor is, in effect, virtualizing or abstracting the hardware. Now it's pretty clear that a VM needs to lug around its OS within it, which makes it a little less portable and a little bigger in size and slower to boot. In general, a virtual machine is definitely more heavyweight than a Docker container, because a VM contains the whole OS (including kernel) while the containers only contain an abstraction of the OS (while using shared kernel). For those of you who are not familiar with containers in general.

 You can visit this link from official Docker website: `https://www.docker.com/what-docker`

Hence, VMs tend to be an order or several orders of magnitude bigger than containers and they are also slower to deploy and get started with. Here is a quick comparison between the two–GCE and GKE.

GCE instances are VMs, like those on the right. GKE clusters host containers, like those on the left. This is an important distinction:

Containers	VMs
• Run atop container manager (for example, Docker)	• Run atop hypervisor (for example, KVM)
• Lightweight—no OS, only apps (image size in MB)	• Heavyweight—include OS (image size in GB)
• Quicker to boot	• Slower to boot

Docker containers and Kubernetes – complements, not substitutes

A common question that people have is - what exactly is the relationship between Docker and Kubernetes? Well, technically Docker is a container hosting and container runtime platform while kubernetes is a container orchestration platform. In other terms, containers run on Docker while they can be managed by kubernetes. There are other orchestrators as well, but they would go way out of the scope and relevance of this book. Kubernetes was earlier developed by Google to manage their own containers; that is, for internal use at Google. Many of the kubernetes orchestration techniques are derived from the results of Google's own struggle with handling containers on large scale. Some of these features include StatefulSets, Configmaps and most importantly High availability cluster configuration.

Going forward, Docker users can choose between Kubernetes and Swarm for scheduling, and Docker's enterprise edition will ship with Kubernetes. This will allow users to deploy containers directly to a Kubernetes cluster using a Docker stack file.

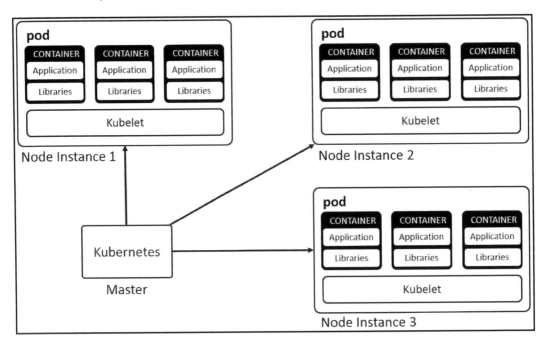

At the technology level though, the relationship between Docker containers and the Kubernetes orchestration system is complementary. If you decide to go down the container path in the GCP, you'll most likely run a Kubernetes container cluster (although there are two other options as well—App Engine Flex and containers on a VM. More details will follow). Schematically, here is what a container cluster would look like.

These containers run in a container cluster, which is managed using software known as Kubernetes. Kubernetes is an open-source system for automating deployment, scaling, and management of containerized applications that was originally designed by Google and donated to the **Cloud Native Computing Foundation (CNCF)**:

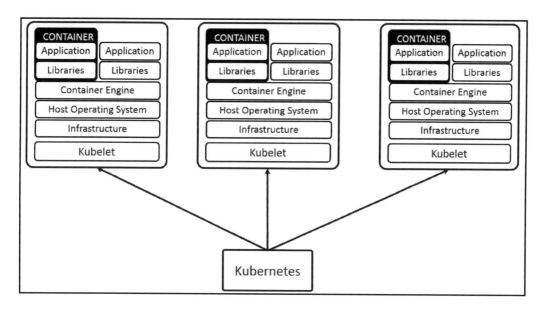

Notice how in the cluster, we have one supervising machine, which is the block at the bottom running Kubernetes, known as the master endpoint. This master endpoint is in touch with a number of individual container machines, each running containers and each talking or communicating with the master using a piece of software known as a **Kubelet**. In the world of the GKE, that coordinating machine is known as the master node, running Kubernetes. Each of the other VMs in the cluster is known as a node instance. Each node instance has its own Kubelet talking to the master and atop, which runs a pod. A Pod is the atomic unit of kubernetes cluster orchestration. Inside each pod there can be one or multiple containers. This is important, as the master talks to node instances, which in turn contain pods and those pods contain the containers.

GKE

Note that Kubernetes is not, by itself, a part of the GCP. You could run Kubernetes clusters on GCP, AWS, Azure, or even on-premise. That's the big appeal of Kubernetes. GKE is merely a managed service for running Kubernetes clusters on the Google Cloud.

So to clarify, GKE is a management and orchestration system for Docker container and container clusters that run within Google's public cloud services and GKE runs Kubernetes.

As we have already discussed, these GKE clusters have a master node running Kubernetes that controls a set of node instances that have Kubelets and inside those Kubelets are individual containers. Kubernetes can be considered an abbreviation for all of the container functionality available on GCP. Kubernetes is the orchestrator that runs on the master node, but really depends on the Kubelets that are running on the pods. In effect, a pod is a collection of closely coupled containers, all of which share the same underlying resources. For instance, they will all have the same IP address and they can share disk volumes. They may be a web server pod for instance, which could have one container for the server and then containers for the logging and the matrix infrastructure. Pods are defined using configuration files specified either in JSON or YAML. Each pod is, in effect, managed by a Kubelet, which is, in turn, controlled by the master node.

The VM instances that are contained in a container cluster are of two types, as we have already seen. There is one special instance that is a master, the one that run Kubernetes, and the others are node instances that run Kubelets.

As we have already seen, these node instances are pretty similar to each other. They are managed from the master to run the services that are necessary to support the Docker containers that contain the actual code that's being executed. Each node runs the Docker runtime and also holds the Kubelet agent that manages the Docker runtime, while also ensuring that all of the Docker containers that are scheduled on the host are running successfully. Let us further understand both these types in a little more detail.

The master endpoint runs the Kubernetes API server, which is responsible for servicing REST requests from wherever they come in, scheduling pod creation and deletion, and synchronizing information across different pods.

Are all instances in the cluster necessarily identical to each other? Actually, no. Within your container cluster, you might want to have groups of different instances that are similar to each other. Each of these are known as **node pools**. A node pool is the subset of machines within a cluster that shares the same configuration. As you might imagine, the ability to have different node pools helps with customizing instance profiles in your cluster, which, in turn, can become handy if you frequently make changes to your containers. However, you should be aware that it should be possible to run multiple Kubernetes node versions on each node pool in your cluster and have each of those node pools independently listen to different updates and different sets of deployments. Node pools are the most powerful way of customizing the individual instances within the clusters.

The GCP also has its own container builder. This is a piece of software that helps to execute container image builds on the GCP's infrastructure. Dockerfiles (text files) are turned into Docker images which can be stored into docker/container registry, downloaded and run on any machine having Docker installed.

Creating a Kubernetes cluster and deploying a WordPress container

This section will walk you through setting up Docker containers in the cloud using Google Compute VM instances. We will also see what you need to do to expose your pod to external traffic. Let's see how we can set up a Kubernetes cluster running on the GKE.

First, we need to set up some default configuration properties before we create our container cluster:

1. Set the default compute zone and the compute region as appropriate.

   ```
   gcloud config set compute/zone ZONE
   gcloud config set compute/region REGION
   ```

2. Use the `gcloud container clusters create` command to create a cluster running the GKE. The name of our cluster is `my-first-cluster` and we want this cluster to have exactly one node. This will be set up in the default zone and the default region that we specified in our configuration, that is, `us-central1-a`:

   ```
   gcloud container clusters create my-first-cluster --num-nodes 1
   ```

3. The confirmation message on the command line that says we have one node in this cluster and its current status is running. You can use the `gcloud compute instances list` command to see the list of clusters and VM instances that you have running. Also, note that with just one command GKE provisioned a fully-functional Kubernetes cluster. This saves a lot of time and efforts of manually configuring and spinning-up *k8s* clusters.

4. Now that we have a cluster up and running, we will deploy WordPress to it. WordPress is simply a content management system used for applications like blogging. We will deploy a WordPress Docker container on our cluster. This WordPress Docker container is publicly available as an image and can be accessed using `--image=tutum/wordpress`.

5. Use the command-line equivalent for working with Kubernetes clusters: the `kubectl` command. We want this container with the WordPress application to run on port `80`. This WordPress image contains everything needed to run this WordPress site, including a MySQL database:

```
kubectl run wordpress --image=tutum/wordpress --port=80
```

Having deployed this container to your cluster, what you have created on your cluster is a **pod**. A pod is basically one or more containers that go together as a group for some meaningful deployment. In this case, for our WordPress container, there is one container within this pod.

You can use the `kubectl get pods` command to see the status of the pods that you have running. We have one pod that starts with the term `wordpress`. There are zero out of one (`0/1`) pods running and its current status is `ContainerCreating`, as shown in the following screenshot:

```
vitthal@loonycorn-project00:~$
vitthal@loonycorn-project00:~$ gcloud config set compute/zone us-central1-a
Updated property [compute/zone].
vitthal@loonycorn-project00:~$ gcloud container clusters create my-first-cluster --num-nodes 1
Creating cluster my-first-cluster...done.
Created [https://container.googleapis.com/v1/projects/loonycorn-project00/zones/us-central1-a/clusters/my-first-cluster].
kubeconfig entry generated for my-first-cluster.
NAME              ZONE            MASTER_VERSION  MASTER_IP       MACHINE_TYPE   NODE_VERSION  NUM_NODES  STATUS
my-first-cluster  us-central1-a   1.7.8-gke.0     35.202.192.175  n1-standard-1  1.7.8-gke.0   1          RUNNING
vitthal@loonycorn-project00:~$ kubectl run wordpress --image=tutum/wordpress --port=80
deployment "wordpress" created
vitthal@loonycorn-project00:~$ kubectl get pods
NAME                        READY   STATUS              RESTARTS   AGE
wordpress-2644474461-qjr06  0/1     ContainerCreating   0          34s
vitthal@loonycorn-project00:~$
```

It's not ready yet. You can run the command another couple of times to see how the status is updated. At some point, you should see the status as running and it will also show as one out of one (`1/1`). Your pod is now ready with your Docker container running successfully on it.

6. When you first create a pod, its default configuration only allows it to be visible to other machines within the cluster. We don't want just the internal machines to access this spot. We want it to be made available to external traffic. This can be done by exposing the pod as a service so that external traffic can access your WordPress site. `kubectl expose pod` is the command that is used for this. Specify the name of your container, which is `wordpress-`, followed by a string of numbers and letters. The name that you want to specify for your containers is `wordpress` and the type of service to set up is a load balancer:

```
kubectl expose pod wordpress-2644474461-qjr06 --name=wordpress
--type=LoadBalancer
```

This load balancer creates an external IP address that this port can use to expect traffic. This is what makes your WordPress site available to external users as a service. Kubectl expose creates a service, the forwarding rules for the load balancer, and the firewall rules that allow external traffic to be sent to the pod. While exposing the pod, we named a service `wordpress` and you can now use this name in order to check the services that we have available.

7. You can use the `kubectl describe services` command, followed by the service name, to see information about your WordPress service. At the very bottom here, beneath the title events, you can see the series of events that have occurred on this cluster. The very first thing that we did was to create a load balancer. Run the command to describe the services again until you notice a couple of changes. The load balancer has finished creation and it now has an ingress IP address that you can use to direct external traffic tools. This added a new event:

```
vitthal@loonycorn-project00:~$ kubectl expose pod wordpress-2644474461-qjr06 --name=wordpress --type=LoadBalancer
service "wordpress" exposed
vitthal@loonycorn-project00:~$ kubectl describe services wordpress
Name:                     wordpress
Namespace:                default
Labels:                   pod-template-hash=2644474461
                          run=wordpress
Annotations:              <none>
Selector:                 pod-template-hash=2644474461,run=wordpress
Type:                     LoadBalancer
IP:                       10.43.244.95
LoadBalancer Ingress:     35.202.217.162
Port:                     <unset>  80/TCP
TargetPort:               80/TCP
NodePort:                 <unset>  30854/TCP
Endpoints:                10.40.0.10:80
Session Affinity:         None
External Traffic Policy:  Cluster
Events:
  Type    Reason                Age   From                Message
  ----    ------                ----  ----                -------
  Normal  CreatingLoadBalancer  4m    service-controller  Creating load balancer
  Normal  CreatedLoadBalancer   3m    service-controller  Created load balancer
vitthal@loonycorn-project00:~$
```

8. Let's use this `LoadBalancer` ingress IP address to view our WordPress site running on the Kubernetes cluster. You will see the starter page to set up your WordPress site. If you have created a site on WordPress before, this should be very familiar to you. Click on the `Continue` button and you can then walkthrough the steps of actually creating a WordPress site if you want to:

9. If you switch back to the compute engine VM instances page and click through the cluster, the single node Kubernetes will show some activity because we deployed a WordPress Docker image to it and launched a site. You can explore the additional settings and config values that are associated with this Kubernetes cluster.

my-first-cluster

Details   Storage   Nodes

Cluster

Master version	1.8.10-gke.0	Upgrade available
Endpoint	199.223.236.78	Show credentials
Client certificate	Enabled	
Kubernetes alpha features	Disabled	
Total size	1	
Master zone	us-central1-a	
Node zones	us-central1-a	
Network	default	
Subnet	default	
VPC-native (alias IP)	Disabled	
Container address range	10.40.0.0/14	
Stackdriver Logging	Enabled	
Stackdriver Monitoring	Enabled	
Private cluster	Disabled	
Master authorized networks	Disabled	
Network policy	Disabled	

In this section, we learned what containers are and how they differed from VM instances. We have examined the architecture of container clusters in the GCP, the basic building blocks such as pods, and the underlying concepts such as Kubernetes that power the GKE. We now know that we need to run an explicit `kubectl` command in order to expose our pods to our external traffic and set up a load balancer, where our external traffic can be directed.

You can look into official kubernetes documentation for further reference on `kubectl` command line and various methods of operating objects and cluster: `https://kubernetes.io/docs/reference/kubectl/overview/`

Using the features of GKE

Apart from rapidly deploying kubernetes cluster and allowing it to get managed from cloud shell, GKE leverages many advantages of being under a full-fledged public cloud platform. Let's start with storage.

Storage and persistent disks

Recall that while working with Compute Engine instances, we had to choose from many storage options, which included persistent disks that could either be ordinary or SSD, local SSD disks, and Google Cloud Storage. Storage options on Kubernetes engine instances are not all that different, but there is, however, one important subtlety. This has to do with the type of attached disk. Recall that when you use the Compute Engine instance that comes along with an attached disk, the link between a Compute Engine instance and the attached disk will remain for as long as the instance exists and the same disk volume is going to be attached to the same instance until the VM is deleted. This will be the case even if you detach the disk and use it with a different instance.

However, when you are using containers, the on-disk files are ephemeral. If a container restarts for instance, after a crash, whatever data that you have had in your disk files is going to be lost. There is a way around this ephemeral nature of storage option, and that is by using a persistent abstraction known as GCE persistent disks. If you are going to make use of Kubernetes engine instances and want your data to not be ephemeral, but remain associated with your containers, you have got to make use of this abstraction or your disk data will not be persistent after a container restarts.

Dynamically provisioned storage classes use HDD by default but we can customize it and attach an SSD to a user defined storage class. Notice the kind of the file as `StorageClass`. Here, GCE's persistent disk is the provisioner with the type SSD.

1. You can save it with the name `ssd.yaml` or something convenient for you:

```
nano ssd.yaml
apiVersion: storage.k8s.io/v1
kind: StorageClass
metadata:
 name: ssd
provisioner: kubernetes.io/gce-pd
parameters:
 type: pd-ssd
```

2. Once it is saved, you can create a PVC (`PersistentVolumeClaim`). Let's name it `storage-change.yaml`. Notice that it has the name of our previously created storage class in the `StorageClassName`:

```
nano storage-change.yaml
kind: PersistentVolumeClaim
apiVersion: v1
metadata:
 name: storage-change
spec:
 accessModes:
 - ReadWriteOnce
 storageClassName: ssd
 resources:
 requests:
 storage: 1Gi
```

3. Apply the storage change by running the following command. Make sure to run them under the sequence given below since the storage class itself needs to be created first before PVC:

```
kubectl apply -f ssd.yaml
kubectl apply -f storage-change.yaml
```

Load balancing

Load balancing is yet another area where working with Kubernetes Engine instances is rather more complicated than working with Compute Engine VMs. With the Kubernetes Engine, you can make use of network-level load balancing, which works just out of the box. However, remember that the higher up the OSI stack you go, the more sophisticated your load balancing becomes. Extending that logic, the most sophisticated form of load balancing is going to be HTTP load balancing. This is something that does not work all that simply with Kubernetes Engines. If you want to use HTTP load balancing with container instances, you are going to have to do some interfacing of your own with the Compute Engine load balancing infrastructure:

1. First of all, deploy a single replica `nginx` server by running its Docker image on port `80`:

   ```
   kubectl run nginx --image=nginx --port=80
   ```

2. Create a service resource to access `nginx` from your cluster. The `NodePort` type allows Kubernetes Engine to make your service available on a random high port number:

   ```
   kubectl expose deployment nginx --target-port=80 --type=NodePort
   ```

3. You can also verify the service creation. The following command should show you the name of the service and the port number it has been assigned:

   ```
   kubectl get service nginx
   ```

4. Now you need to create and save an ingress resource that will contain rules and configurations of HTTP traffic:

   ```
   nano basic-ingress.yaml
   apiVersion: extensions/v1beta1
   kind: Ingress
   metadata:
    name: basic-ingress
   spec:
    backend:
    serviceName: nginx
   ```

5. This will create an HTTP load balancer. Run the file using the following command:

```
kubectl apply -f basic-ingress.yaml
```

6. Now you can find out the external IP address of your load balancer by calling ingress service:

```
kubectl get ingress basic-ingress
```

7. To remove this load balancer, use the following command:

```
kubectl delete ingress basic-ingress
```

Auto scaling

There are two possible levels at which Kubernetes clusters can be autoscaled—nodes (VMs) and pods.

Scaling nodes with the cluster autoscaler

For automatic resizing of your clusters based on nodes, you need to use something known as the cluster autoscaler. This will periodically check and optimize the size of your cluster, either increasing or reducing the number of instances. Let's say that your container cluster is larger than it needs to be and there are nodes that do not have any pods scheduled, those nodes will be deleted by the cluster autoscaler. On the other hand, if your cluster container is too small and if you have pods that are facing inordinate delays before they are run, the cluster autoscaler will add nodes and scale up your cluster:

```
gcloud container clusters create [CLUSTER-NAME] --num-nodes=5 \
--enable-autoscaling --min-nodes=3 --max-nodes=10 [--zone=[ZONE] \ --
project=[PROJECT-ID]]
```

Notice how the scaling of nodes is carried out using gcloud (not kubectl).

Scaling pods with the horizontal pod autoscaler

It is also possible in recent versions of Kubernetes to scale pods (rather than nodes). This also allows us to scale down to a node pool of zero, that is to scale down to zero if there is no demand for the service while also retaining the ability to scale up with demand.

Combining the two, that is, scaling in both directions allows you to make your application truly elastic. Remember that pods are a Kubernetes concept, so unsurprisingly, such autoscaling is carried out using `kubectl` rather than `gcloud`:

1. To do this, you need to apply a **Horizontal Pod Autoscaler (HPA)** by using the `kubectl autoscale` command. The `max` flag is mandatory, while the `min` flag is optional. The `cpu-percent` indicates total CPU utilization:

```
kubectl autoscale deployment my-app --max=6 --min=4 --cpu-percent=50
```

2. To check any HPA, use the `kubectl describe` command:

```
kubectl describe hpa [NAME-OF-HPA]
```

3. Similarly, use the `kubectl delete` command to remove HPAs:

```
kubectl delete hpa [NAME-OF-HPA]
```

Multi-zone clusters

When you enable multi-zone container clusters, the container resources are replicated in the additional zones within your nominated region, and work is scheduled across all of them. If one zone fails, the others can pick up the slack. In this case, any single zone is capable of running the entire application.

All of the zones are within the same region. The following diagram demonstrates this concept:

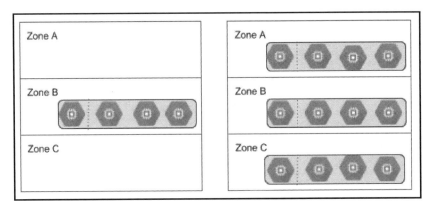

Cloud VPN integration

GKE allows you to reserve an IP address range for your container cluster, thus enabling your cluster IPs to coexist with private network IPs through Google Cloud VPN.

Rolling updates

You can also perform rolling updates. The updates can be container images, configurations, annotations, labels or resource allocation. The term rolling indicates the process's incremental nature to replace one pod at a time (no matter how fast it may be). The reason is to avoid server downtime while distributing updates.

Rolling updates involve updating the workloads of Kubernetes:

1. We will use the `kubectl set` command to perform manual updates. We will update `nginx` from version `1.10` to `1.12.2`:

   ```
   kubectl set image deployment nginx nginx=nginx:1.12.2
   ```

2. The `kubectl set` command updates one pod at a time. To control resource allocation for the updates, you can also provide the following flags:

   ```
   kubectl set resources deployment nginx --
   limits=cpu=400m,memory=1024Mi --requests=cpu=200m,memory=512Mi
   ```

3. Manually updating each and every application would be tiresome and time consuming. Kubernetes also allows us to roll out automatic updates:

   ```
   kubectl rollout status deployment nginx
   ```

4. The rollout can also be paused or resumed by using the following command:

   ```
   kubectl rollout pause deployment nginx
   kubectl rollout resume deployment nginx
   ```

5. In case of a misfire, the rollout of an update can also be rolled back to a stable previous version:

   ```
   kubectl rollout undo deployment nginx --to-revision=3
   ```

6. In addition to this, the update rollout history can also be viewed by using the following command:

```
kubectl rollout history deployment nginx
```

The container registry

The container registry provides secure, private Docker image storage on GCP. It can be thought of as a way to access, that is, to push, pull, and manage Docker images from any system, whether it's a Compute Engine instance or your on-premise hardware through a secure HTTPS endpoint. In a sense, this is a very controlled and regulated way of dealing with container images. You should be aware that it is possible to hook up Docker and the container registry so that they talk to each other directly. In this way, by using the Docker command line, which is the credential helper tool, you can authenticate Docker directly from the container registry. Since this container registry can be written to and read from pretty much any system, you could also use third-party cluster management or CI/CD tools and even those that are not on GCP. While Docker provides a central registry to store public images, you may not want your images to be accessible to the world. In this case, you must use a private registry:

1. To configure the container registry in GCP, first of all, you need to tag a built image with a registry name. The registry name format follows `hostname/project_ID/image` format. The hostname is your Google container registry hostname. For example, `us.gcr.io` stores your image in the US region:

```
docker tag nginx us.gcr.io/loonycorn-project-08/nginx
```

2. Then you need to push the image to the Docker container registry using the `gcloud` command line:

```
gcloud docker -- push us.gcr.io/loonycorn-project-08/nginx
```

3. To test your registry, you can try pulling your image with the same registry tag format:

```
gcloud docker -- pull us.gcr.io/loonycorn-project-08/nginx
```

4. Finally, to delete it from the container registry, use the following command:

```
gcloud container images delete us.gcr.io/loonycorn-project-08/nginx
```

5. Now, if you are using Kubernetes, it has a built-in container registry to run with `kubectl` so you can use public or private container images as well:

```
kubectl run nginx --image=us.gcr.io/loonycorn-project-08/nginx
```

Federated clusters

Cluster federation enables clusters across multiple regions, including other cloud providers or on-premise Kubernetes installations. It is useful for super high availability or for super scalability. With IP aliases, Kubernetes Engine clusters can allocate pod IP addresses from a CIDR block known to GCP. This allows your cluster to interact with other cloud platform products and entities, and also allows more scalable clusters. Cluster federation is useful when you want to deploy resources across more than one cluster, region, or cloud provider. You may want to do this to enable high availability, offer greater geographic coverage for your app, use more than one cloud provider, combine cloud provider and on-premise solutions, or for ultra-high scalability. Cluster federation is also helpful when you want resources to be contactable in a consistent manner from both inside and outside their clusters, without incurring unnecessary latency or bandwidth cost penalties, or being susceptible to individual cluster outages. Although it is an external topic from GCP so it goes out of the scope.

Google App Engine – flexible

Google App Engine is the most flexible and no-ops part of hosting your application.

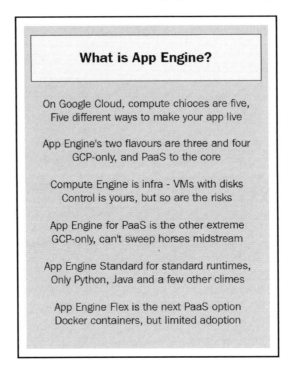

What is App Engine?

On Google Cloud, compute chioces are five,
Five different ways to make your app live

App Engine's two flavours are three and four
GCP-only, and PaaS to the core

Compute Engine is infra - VMs with disks
Control is yours, but so are the risks

App Engine for PaaS is the other extreme
GCP-only, can't sweep horses midstream

App Engine Standard for standard runtimes,
Only Python, Java and a few other climes

App Engine Flex is the next PaaS option
Docker containers, but limited adoption

Hosted Docker containers with App Engine Flex

Both VMs and containers require a fair amount of low-level intricacies and ops. *What if you decided that you didn't want to deal with any of that? What if you would rather use a standard PaaS web development tool or technology such as Heroku or Engine Yard?* Both of these are classic web development platforms that you could choose to leverage. Well, the GCP equivalent of doing this is making use of the Google App Engine:

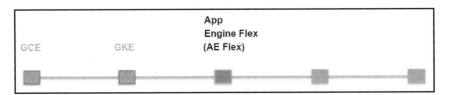

GCE　　　　GKE　　　App Engine Flex (AE Flex)

Using App Engine, you could set up a pretty complex web app with very little effort, focusing on just writing the code. One little note—at the time of writing (January 2018), App Engine is regional, not global. So, if your users are from all over the world, you might find that they experience latency issues. There is a great deal of clamor for multi-region support with global load balancing in App Engine, however, so presumably that will be rolled out at some point.

App Engine is available in two environments:

- Standard environment
- Flexible environment

The App Engine Standard environment is preconfigured with a few specific runtimes, such as Java 8, Python 2.7, Go, and PHP. This runtime really is a container, a Google-proprietary container, inside which you can write and deploy your code. This is a standard environment in which you can't change a thing. Thus, when you run your code in an App Engine standard environment, what you are really doing is making use of a Google-specific container.

In contrast, App Engine Flex offers a range of choices where you can tweak stuff and customize it. For instance, you might choose to make use of Python 3.x, .NET, or some other environment that is not available under App Engine Standard. We can then use App Engine Flex, which basically relies on Docker containers to allow any sort of custom runtime. To do so, all you need to do is specify your own Docker files, which can contain your own runtime and the OS image that you would like to use.

App Engine Flex is a PaaS way to run Docker containers, but it probably has been eclipsed in popularity and adoption by GKE. *Why?* Probably because the whole point of containerizing your workloads is to make them portable, and use them in multi-cloud environments. This is far easier and more practical to do with GKE than with App Engine Flex, where we'd end up using Google-specific services and getting tied to GCP, defeating the whole point of containerization. However, if you want to run a single container in a managed deployment without having to set up a Kubernetes cluster with GKE, App Engine might make sense for you.

Running a simple Python application with App Engine Flex

To try this Python example in the App Engine Flex environment, for the context of this tutorial, it would be convenient to use Cloud Shell.:

1. Once you have `git` installed, clone the following directory:

   ```
   git clone
   https://github.com/GoogleCloudPlatform/python-docs-samples
   ```

2. Now, Python sample codes can be found in the following sub-directory:

   ```
   cd python-docs-samples/appengine/flexible/hello_world
   ```

3. Now, run the application with the following:

   ```
   python main.py
   ```

4. You can also view the output on your browser's localhost:

   ```
   http://localhost:8080
   ```

5. From this directory, we can run Python code. But before that, if you don't have virtual environment installed, do it with the following command:

   ```
   sudo pip install virtualenv
   ```

6. In this virtual environment, create a dedicated Python environment along with its dependencies:

   ```
   virtualenv env
   source env/bin/activate
   pip install -r requirements.txt
   ```

7. Now, we can deploy this app by running the following command in the hello world directory:

   ```
   gcloud app deploy
   ```

8. Of course, the `gcloud` command only works if you have Google Cloud SDK installed on your local machine. We can view the deployed app's result with the following command. It will open a browser window and the address bar will contain an address having an `http//PROJECT_ID.appspot.com` pattern:

```
gcloud app browse
```

Cron Jobs with App Engine Flex

The App Engine Cron service takes you one step closer to automation by allowing you to schedule tasks at certain times or at regular intervals. Such tasks are known as cron jobs. These can invoke a URL by using an HTTP GET request. To use cron, you need to put a `cron.yaml` file in the root directory of your application, which might look something as follows:

```
cron:
- description: "daily task"
url: /tasks/daily
  schedule: every 24 hours
- description: "weekly task"
 url: /mail/weekly
 schedule: every monday 09:00
 timezone: Australia/NSW
 target: beta
```

As can be seen in the example, URL and schedules are mandatory jobs of cron files, whereas description, timezone, target, and so on are optional ones.

The schedule syntax has the following format:

```
every N (hours|mins|day of week) ["from" (time) "to" (time)]
```

Where `N` is the number and `time` is in HH:MM format (24 hours).

If you want your job to be rerouted, you can also add a `dispatch.yaml` file alongside `cron.yaml`, which might look as follows. With the dispatch file, the job will be re-routed to `service2` even though the target is beta:

```
dispatch:
- url: '*/tasks/weekly'
  service: service2
```

Finally, run following command on Cloud Shell to deploy the app on App engine.

```
gcloud app deploy cron.yaml
```

Advantages of GKE over Docker on VMs or App Engine Flex

Now, there are several different ways of deploying Docker containers on the GCP. We could use App Engine Flex, or even simply deploy them on VMs. But choosing either of these options would cause us to lose out on the power of Kubernetes. That is a pretty big loss, because we'd need to manage creating, managing, and scaling our deployments ourselves. It would also tie us to a specific platform—neither Docker on GCP VMs, nor App Engine Flex, would generalize easily to a non-GCP cloud, or to on-premise. Following are the parameters to keep in mind while making a choice between GKE or App Engine Flex.

- **Control**: The argument is simple here. Containers give a LOT more control and portability. From resource allocation to backend storage provision, everything can be customised with containers which is not the case with App Engine due to it being managed by Google.
- **Scaling:** Take deployment or scaling, App engine is always faster than GKE cluster specially for the tasks like autoscaling. On the other hand, if HPA (Horizontal Pod Autoscaler) is not employed, scaling on kubernetes can take significantly more time and efforts.
- **Cost:** Since App Engine Flex still uses managed VMs as its backend, GKE saves a lot of resources (the difference becomes more significant with large deployments) and so is more economic.
- **Service:** Both App Engine Flex and GKE use GCP's HTTP(s) load balancing so you can expect similar throughputs apart from the times where

Google App Engine – standard

Google App Engine (Standard) is the way to go for building and deploying data-rich and heavy load applications in a secure and reliable fully managed environment.

Hosted web apps with App Engine Standard

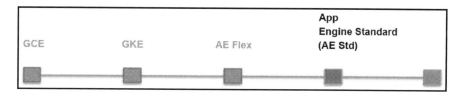

We've already introduced App Engine Standard previously—it is a PaaS compute offering in which we can deploy code in a few specific runtimes (Java 8, Python 2.7, Go, and PHP at the time of writing), into Google-proprietary containers. The advantage of App Engine Standard is that you just write the code—you don't bother with ops, containerization, or anything else.

If you are developing GCP first and are quite confident that your app is going to be GCP-only, then App Engine Standard is a great choice. It offers the following:

- Very fast autoscaling (order of milliseconds to autoscale your app)
- Several very handy Google-specific APIs that you can use (Memcache, datastore, task queues)
- Attractive pricing
- Ease of deployment for performing A/B testing, blue/green deployments, and canary releases.

You should be mindful though, that if you go with App Engine standard, you really are quite locked to the GCP. Moving to other clouds, or to a hybrid solution where you combine on-premise and the cloud, will all be quite difficult.

Typical App Engine architecture

The following diagram is a fairly typical architecture of an App Engine application and it illustrates the integration of App Engine with some other GCP services, notably memcache, and task queues.

Using App Engine, you can support different clients whether they are Android or IOS or even desktop apps. You would have load balancing in front of your app and use Google's Cloud DNS. App Engine could use memcache and other backends and whatever storage technologies that were required. For instance, it might have Cloud Storage or Cloud SQL or Cloud Datastore, or any of these things stacked up one after the other, and culminate finally in yet another bit of App Engine functionality, that is, autoscaling. This is how hosting on Google App Engine works:

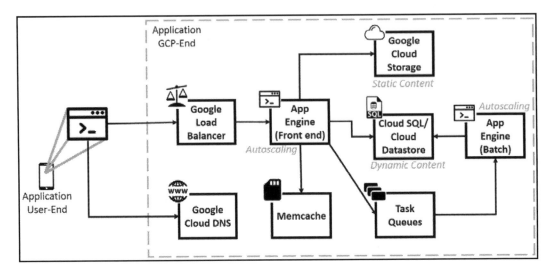

Memcache is a distributed in-memory data cache mostly used by scalable high-performance web applications. App engine also provides a memcache service. Memcache can be activated from App Engine's GCP console page where it has a dedicated tab for itself. There are two types of memcache available:

- **Shared memcache**: It is free and the storage space it can allocate is uncertain, hence, you hold a high risk of not caching important and frequent data. It is not recommended for mission critical applications.
- **Dedicated memcache**: It costs $0.06 per GB per hour. Here, we get up to 20 GB worldwide, whereas up to 100 GB in US-central regions as dedicated storage space. It also guarantees up to 10,000 reads and 5,000 writes per second.

One rule of thumb though is that cached data should be less than 1 MB and the optimum size is 1 KB. In case of multi-batch operations, the total size of cached data should not increase above 32 MB. Also, a null byte cannot be cached (since it can be handled through application programming itself). In general, read and write operations cannot reach their maximum throughput simultaneously. The number of read operations will affect the maximum possible number of write operations at a time, and vice versa.

The task queue API schedules background applications to be executed sequentially (in a queue) by worker services. There are two types of task queues—**push** and **pull**. As their names would indicate, push queues dispatch requests at a reliable, steady rate. They guarantee reliable task execution. Since we are controlling the rate at which tasks are sent from the queue, you can control the workers' scaling behavior and hence your costs. These are useful for slow operations such as social network notifications. Pull queues do not dispatch the tasks. They depend on other worker services to *lease* tasks from the queue on their own initiative. They provide more control over when and where tasks are processed, but they also require you to do more process management. When a task is leased, the leasing worker declares a deadline. By the time the deadline arrives, the worker must either complete the task and delete it, or the task queue service will allow another worker to lease it. Pull queues are useful for batch tasks that need to run simultaneously.

Deploying and running on App Engine Standard

This section will walks you through creating and deploying a very simple App Engine app on your GCP. Google App Engine helps you create applications out of the box, you simply code up the program that you want to run on GCP, use the right SDKs and the right libraries to deploy it, and you are good to go. There are no clusters to maintain and no VM instances to worry about. Here, we will create a simple Python application, test it locally, and then deploy it to App Engine and see it accept external traffic. Throughout this tutorial we shall be using Cloud Shell for convenience:

1. Use the `gcloud` command-line tool to set up the default value for the zone and region that you want to use. If you are using your local machine to connect to the cloud, you don't need to keep setting these config properties. But if you are using Cloud Shell, as shown here, because these instances are ephemeral and might change once your session is disconnected and you reconnect, you might have to set these properties afresh for each session.

2. Typically, you would perform app development on your local machine and simply deploy it to the server. Here, we will create the app on the cloud shell itself. We create a new directory on the Cloud Shell to hold the code for our app.

3. Move into this directory and then use an editor to create your Python file that holds your application. All the code in your application will be present in this one file. Here, it's titled `my_first_app`:

```
import webapp2

class MainPage(webapp2.RequestHandler):
    def get(self):
        self.response.headers['Content-Type'] = 'text/plain'
        self.response.write('Hello, World! From the folks at Loonycorn!')

app = webapp2.WSGIApplication([
    ('/', MainPage),
], debug=True)
```

4. We use the `webapp` package, which is simply a lightweight Python web framework that allows you to develop web apps very quickly. It's compatible with Google App Engine and is an easy way for you to get up and running with your website.

5. Set up a class named `Homepage`, which is derived from `webapp2.RequestHandler` and, within that, the get method holds the content of your web page. The response property of this class contains the response that we will send down to the client browser.

6. Set the content type header to be `text/html`, indicating that it is an HTML response. Write out a simple `hello world` response message in HTML. Set up a **Web Server Gateway Interface** (**WSGI**) application that receives a request and directs it to the appropriate page. Here, we only handle the /, which is sent to the home page. We have written our very first Python application on the App Engine.

7. Save the file. Exit from the editor and ensure `my_first_app` is present in your local directory

8. App Engine settings are specified in a file called `app.yaml`. Open up an `app.yaml` file in an editor and specify the configuration for your first App Engine project. The API version is 1. The `app.yaml` files contain the handlers that contain the mapping from URL paths to static files and the request handlers. Here, we want the URL to map to `my_first_app.app`, which is the Python module that we just created. Save this file. Now we are ready to test this instance of our site:

```
runtime: python27
api_version: 1
threadsafe: true

handlers:
- url: /.*
  script: helloworld.app
```

9. Kick-start the deployment instance of the application server by calling `dev_appserver.py ./` Point to where the Python module is, which is in the current directory for us.

10. Our application is now running in your development mode and you can preview this by clicking in the top-left corner of your cloud shell and choosing preview on port `8080`. Any changes that you make to your App Engine will be immediately available without you having to restart your deployment server:

11. What we saw so far is just the preview or development mode. Now, let's deploy this to production. This is done by using the `gcloud` command: `gcloud app deploy app.yaml`. This will ask you to choose the region where you want your app to be deployed. If your customers happen to be in Asia, choose the Asia region. Once this command runs through, we are done. You can view your application in the URL that is displayed on the command line in the output from the command you just ran. Copy this URL and view it in a browser to see your first App Engine app. If you want to see logs of your site, simply tail your logs using the commands that you can see on the screen `gcloud app logs tail -s default`:

```
Beginning deployment of service [default]...
Some files were skipped. Pass `--verbosity=info` to see which ones.
You may also view the gcloud log file, found at
[/tmp/tmp.HRPLCZnNjZ/logs/2017.12.02/19.42.53.874540.log].

├─ Uploading 2 files to Google Cloud Storage

File upload done.
Updating service [default]...done.
Waiting for operation [apps/loonycorn-project00-187805/operations/f2f9fe3b-31ef-4ebf-92b1-fe9619a1a05f] to complete...done.
Updating service [default]...done.
Deployed service [default] to [https://loonycorn-project00-187805.appspot.com]

You can stream logs from the command line by running:
  $ gcloud app logs tail -s default

To view your application in the web browser run:
  $ gcloud app browse
```

We have deployed our App Engine project to production.

Traffic splitting

Traffic splitting is useful when one or more URLs are referring to multiple versions of an application or a service. Traffic splitting can be used to accomplish pretty cool functionality such as A/B testing and green/blue deployments (more on these later).

It can be achieved through either the browser or the `gcloud` command line.

For example:

```
gcloud app services set-traffic [MY_SERVICE] --splits
[MY_VERSION1]=[VERSION1_WEIGHT],[MY_VERSION2]=[VERSION2_WEIGHT] --split-by
[IP_OR_COOKIE]
```

In the preceding command, the service name is the service you use. Version names can be of your choice, but the weight must be distributed in a way that the total of the weight becomes 1. For example, if you want to distribute traffic of my service evenly between two splits based on cookies, use the command in the following way:

```
gcloud app services set-traffic my-service --splits v1=0.5, v2=0.5 --split-
by cookie
```

Serverless compute with cloud functions

Google Cloud Functions allow developers to create standalone functions. It is a hassle-free lightweight solution for someone looking for implementing single-purpose functions in response to their public cloud (in this case, GCP) events.

Cloud Functions are to be written in JS (JavaScript) and are executed in Node.js environment on GCP. On the other hand we can use these cloud functions on any standard Node.js runtime as well which makes them a lot portable.

> **What are Cloud Functions?**
>
> On Google Cloud, compute choices are five,
> Five different ways to make your app live
>
> Cloud Functions are last, fired on the fly
> Rival AWS Lambda functions, or at least try
>
> Serverless lambdas, cloud functions are new
> Right now their triggers are relatively few
>
> HTTP webhooks, bucket changes and Pub/Sub
> And only Node.js, that's another rub
>
> But even if the product has to evolve yet
> Low cost and free tier - make it not a bad bet

Cloud Functions triggered by HTTP

HTTP cloud functions are used to invoke your functions through HTTP requests. In an HTTP function, the *request* parameter represents any call action sent to functions, while *response* represents return values:

1. Write the Cloud Function and save it as `index.js`:

```
/**
 * Responds to any HTTP request that can provide a "message" field
in the body.
 */
exports.helloWorld = function helloHttp  (req, res) {
 if (req.body.message === undefined) {
 // An error case because a "message" is missing
 res.status(400).send('No message defined!');
 } else {
 // Everything is ok
 console.log(req.body.message);
 res.status(200).end();
 }
};
```

2. Deploy the Cloud Function:

```
gcloud beta functions deploy helloHttp --trigger-http
```

3. Invoke the Cloud Function using **Client URL (curl)**. The `curl` command can be used to call the function and pass a simple message. Curl is a command-line utility that allows us to send or receive HTTP requests:

```
curl -X POST -H "Content-Type:application/json" -d
'{"message":"hello world!"}' YOUR_HTTP_TRIGGER_ENDPOINT
```

Your HTTP endpoint is typically the json schema that you wrote to invoke your functions via HTTP. In other words, YOUR_HTTP_TRIGGER_ENDPOINT reported by the previous command is used to create the function.

Cloud Functions triggered by Pub/Sub

The most common way to trigger a Cloud Function is with an HTTP request, as seen previously. In contrast, background functions are used to invoke Cloud Functions indirectly through a message, a Pub/Sub topic, or an object change notification from a Google Cloud Storage bucket. Such cloud functions take in an event as a parameter and, optionally, a callback as another. The event parameter has various properties that we can make use of within our function:

Parameter Property	Description	Type
eventId	Unique event ID	String
timestamp	Date and time of event creation	String (ISO 8601)
eventType	Type of event	String
resource	Resources emitted to event	String
data	Event data	Object

Now, we will invoke cloud functions via pub/sub notifications (event or object change)

1. Write the Cloud Function and save it as `index.js` (it will be stored under the VM of the Cloud Shell you have been provided with):

```
/**
 * Background Cloud Function to be triggered by Pub/Sub.
 */
exports.helloPubSub = function (event, callback)
{
 const pubsubMessage = event.data;
 const name = pubsubMessage.data ?
Buffer.from(pubsubMessage.data, 'base64').toString() : 'World';

 console.log(`Hello, ${name}!`);

 callback();
};
```

2. To deploy the function, the `gcloud beta functions deploy` command can be used:

```
gcloud beta functions deploy helloPubSub --trigger-topic
hello_world
```

3. Invoke (trigger) the Cloud Function.

4. Now, the deployed function can be called directly, or by publishing a message to the trigger topic. To test the direct invocation, use the following command:

```
gcloud beta functions call helloPubSub --data
'{"data":"dGVzdCB1c2Vy"}'
```

Here, *test user* is encoded in base64, thus you can see dGVzdCB1c2Vy. As a result, the function logs should show `Hello test user!`.

Cloud functions triggered by GCS object notifications

Similarly, Cloud Functions can also be triggered by changes in Cloud Storage buckets:

1. Write the Cloud Function and save it as `index.js`:

```
/**
 * Background Cloud Function to be triggered by Cloud Storage..
 */
exports.helloGCS = function (event, callback)
{
 const file = event.data;

 if (file.resourceState === 'not_exists')
{
 console.log(`File ${file.name} deleted.`);
 }
else if (file.metageneration === '1')
{
 // metageneration attribute is updated on metadata changes.
 // on create value is 1
 console.log(`File ${file.name} uploaded.`);
 }
 else
```

```
    {
    console.log(`File ${file.name} metadata updated.`);
    }

    callback();
    };
```

2. Deploy the Cloud Function:

   ```
   gcloud beta functions deploy helloGCS --trigger-bucket
   <BUCKET_NAME>
   ```

3. Trigger (invoke) the Cloud Function
4. As before, we can invoke this function either by uploading a file (say test.txt) to the bucket, or through an equivalent direct invocation:

   ```
   gcloud beta functions call helloGCS --data
   '{"name":"test.txt"}'
   ```

Once invoked, the logs should contain the log entry stating that test.txt file was uploaded to the GCS bucket.

Summary

Having read this chapter, you should now be familiar with the concept of containers and how they compare to VMs. You will have some clarity concerning how Kubernetes can be used to orchestrate containers in general and the use of GKE to deploy containers within GCP. We have also examined some of the features available in GKE, such as load balancing and autoscaling. And finally, we have seen how Google App Engine and Cloud Functions can be used to manage your apps and how they compare with GKE.

5
Google Cloud Storage – Fishing in a Bucket

Google Cloud Storage (GCS) is what you ought to use to store unstructured data such as images, videos, or other static content, as well as for backups, disaster recovery, and other cool or cold data. GCS stores data in the form of objects on an underlying distributed filesystem, called **Colossus**. Colossus is Google-proprietary and a very high-performance filesystem.

You can transfer data in or out of GCS using a command-line tool called `gsutil` (different from gcloud, which we've used for compute-related operations so far). Under the hood, `gsutil` makes RESTful API calls to the GCS service, so we can do the same and interact with GCS via the web console or client apps.

This chapter is meant to get you familiar with GCS and to give you an idea of where it would fit within with your overall infrastructure. We will be exploring the following:

- When it is appropriate to use GCS
- Fundamental concepts related to GCS
- Creating and managing GCS buckets
- The features available to manage data in GCS buckets

Knowing when (and when not) to use GCS

```
┌─────────────────────────────────────────┐
│   When would you use buckets?            │
├─────────────────────────────────────────┤
│                                          │
│   Like S3 on AWS, or Azure's blobs       │
│   Data unstructured, but data in gobs     │
│                                          │
│   Objects - accessed from anywhere       │
│   Hot or cold - but not a $ to spare     │
└─────────────────────────────────────────┘
```

Static data such as YouTube videos, thumbnails on Instagram, or the high-quality product images you find on Amazon (the ones that you zoom into while hovering) are perfect for use in buckets.

Like AWS and Microsoft Azure, GCP has a pretty wide range of storage options and knowing when to use which is important; both from the point of view of actual practical use, and if you'd like to clear the GCP certifications. So do pay attention to this table:

Use Case	GCP's Offering	Approximate Non-GCP Equivalents
Block storage	GCE Persistent Disks	NAS (Network attached storage), AWS Elastic Block Storage
Blob/object storage	Cloud Storage	AWS S3 buckets (and Glacier), HDFS
Relational data–small, regional payloads	Cloud SQL	MySQL, PostgreSQL; AWS RDS
Relational data–large, global payloads	Cloud Spanner	Oracle, AWS RDS
NoSQL document database	Datastore	MongoDB, Redis, AWS DynamoDB, AWS SimpleDB
NoSQL columnar	BigTable	Cassandra, HBase
Analytics/Data warehouse with SQL interface	BigQuery	Teradata, Hive, AWS Redshift, Data Lake

> **When would you _not_ use buckets?**
>
> *VMs prefer storage in blocks, i.e. disks*
> *But instance-level access carries its own risks*
>
> *And for structured data, please fly a different banner*
> *BigQuery, BigTable, Cloud SQL or Spanner*

We saw that persistent disks can be far more economical, easy to scale, and manageable than local SSDs for web hosting. But, what if you are running a photography blog or an online video archive? These use cases require the storage of vast amounts of static **Binary Large Objects** (**BLOBs**). Crucially, these are unstructured data, and in vast sizes, potentially far exceeding the limits of persistent disks.

This is where GCP's cloud storage comes in. Cloud storage can be considered as GCP's equivalent of AWS S3 or Azure's Blob storage:

- Cloud storage is simple and user-friendly; think of Google Drive. In addition to the web console, GCS has a command-line tool all of its own called `gsutil`
- You don't need to allocate capacity or create a storage server of any sort
- It scales, basically till infinity; unlike persistent disks that max out at 64 TB, or local SSD that max out at 3 TB, GCS supports datasets of any sizes
- The largest file size limit is 5 TB, so even for archival storage, it works great
- It supports 5,000 writes and 1,000 reads per second, so accessibility is rarely a bottleneck
- It has a **Graphical User Interface** (**GUI**) similar to other features of GCP

 In addition to the web console, GCS has a command-line tool all of its own–called `gsutil`. This is different from `gcloud`, which we use for most other GCP commands.

The way cloud storage works is simple. Google has its data center deployed in multiple regions worldwide. By creating cloud storage bucket instances under our GCP projects, we can ask for a scalable amount of storage in a particular region (there are variations, but more on that later). Unlike compute engine instances, we are not charged for a minimum of certain amount of storage.

Serving Static Content with GCS Buckets

How do GCP buckets compare with S3 buckets or Azure blob storage?

Like S3 on AWS, like Azure's blobs
So GCS buckets - unstructured data in gobs

That's the headline, never mind the fine print
Oh, and folks disagree on who will win in a sprint

The following diagram illustrates something interesting: just as we can place a backend service (for example, a group of VMs) behind a load balancer for dynamic content, we can also place backend buckets behind a load balancer. It would also make sense to use Google's **Content Delivery Network (CDN)** to cache the content in those buckets in front of the load balancer, but that is not actually shown in this diagram:

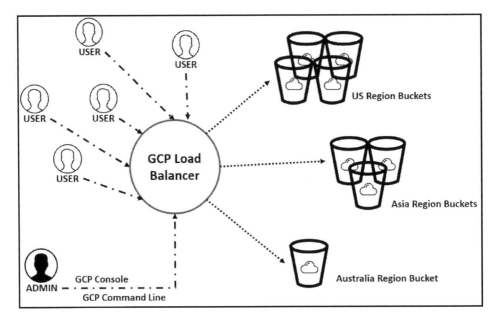

GCP also features content-based load balancing, where an HTTP(S) load balancer can be set up to distribute traffic to different backends depending on the URL path. For instance, if the video content for your website is stored in a bucket, you could configure your load balancer to direct all requests to URL paths that begin with `/video` to your bucket. All other requests can be served by your VM instances:

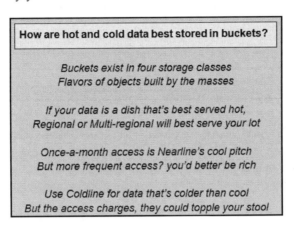

How are hot and cold data best stored in buckets?

*Buckets exist in four storage classes
Flavors of objects built by the masses*

*If your data is a dish that's best served hot,
Regional or Multi-regional will best serve your lot*

*Once-a-month access is Nearline's cool pitch
But more frequent access? you'd better be rich*

*Use Coldline for data that's colder than cool
But the access charges, they could topple your stool*

Storage classes–Regional, multi-regional, nearline, and coldline

Buckets are units of data storage in cloud storage. In terms of underlying storage, they can be considered as repositories linked to your project in Google's managed data centers. Buckets are mainly divided into four classes based on their availability, demographic relevance, and frequency of access:

Storage Class	Remember As	Use Case
Multi-regional	Hot and available	Globally accessed static content
Regional	Hot and local	Input into Dataproc or compute processing
Nearline	Cool, not cold	Backups (access ~ once a month)
Coldline	Cold and rich	DR (access ~ once a year)

- **Hot and available - Multi-Regional**: These buckets can be accessed from any region across the world, making them highly available.

  They are also Geo-Redundant, which means that data coming from any region will be stored in two separate copies at least 100 miles away (that is, in two distant data centers) to avoid data loss if any one center goes down. This is the most expensive class of Buckets and should only be used when you are certain that your traffic is global (we wouldn't opt for Multi-Regional storage if we are hosting images of the food in a restaurant in Pune, India, since most of my web visitors would presumably be local).

- **Hot and local–Regional**: These are best suited to high-access traffic from a certain region requiring high availability. In addition to web applications with highly concentrated traffic patterns, VM instances on cloud running Hadoop Dataproc clusters would also benefit from Regional Buckets as they provide lower latency and cost than multi-regional buckets.

  If you're using a staging bucket with a Cloud ML engine, prefer regional to multi-regional (the replication lag can sometimes trip up the training process).

  Regional buckets also make sense for use in backend buckets behind an HTTP load balancer with CDN caching turned on. The CDN service will replicate to each region, so you don't need multi-regional buckets here. Don't worry if this does not make sense yet.

- **Cool, not cold–Nearline**: Use these for data you'll expect to access about once a month, that is, cool data. Regional and multi-regional buckets charge you only for storage, not for access. In contrast, nearline and coldline buckets have a much lower charge for storage, but they have significant access charges, as well as minimum storage period commitments that you need to make (for instance, nearline storage will charge for 30 days of storage even if you pull your data out early).

- **Cold and rich–Coldline**: This is a cold storage facility for data that you would expect to access less than once a year. Suitable applications would be disaster data recovery or long-term archival storage, such as government records.

- **Coldline/Nearline v AWS Glacier**: Coldline and Nearline uses fundamentally the same technology as the buckets for hot data. This is a difference between GCP and AWS, where Glacier is a fundamentally different, and slower, technology. So, retrieval of cold data, for example during disaster recovery, will tend to be as fast as regular storage (but far costlier, of course). This could be an important advantage for you, so do keep this in mind.

   Choosing between the hot and cold storage classes comes down to a trade-off between storage costs and access costs. The hot bucket types do not charge at all for individual access, but their storage costs are quite high.

Consider this:

- Storing 10 TB of data for a year would cost ~$3,000 in multi-regional, but only ~$800 in coldline:
   - **Multi-regional storage**: 2.6 cents/GB/Month x 10,000 GB x 12 months = $3,120
   - **Coldline storage**: 0.7 cents/GB/Month x 10,000 GB x 12 months = $840
- Accessing that same 10 TB once each day of the year would cost nothing in multi-regional, but a whopping $180,000 in coldline!
   - **Multi-regional access**: Free
   - **Coldline access**: 5 cents/GB/retrieval x 10,000 GB x 365 = $182,500

Obviously, nobody in their right mind would use coldline for hot data. Also, note that the preceding calculations do not count the costs of network egress and other non-GCS costs.

This preceding comparison also tells us why traditional storage and data warehousing companies have seen the cloud disrupt their business models. If you think the preceding data storage costs are steep, consider this: How much would 10 TB of data take, to store, for a year in a Teradata system, or in Oracle? (BigQuery, which is the direct competitor to those products, costs roughly as much as nearline storage, so not that different from the preceding numbers).

Searching online will likely tell you, and in the answer to that question lies the tale of Teradata's stock price, which is down by more than half since 2012 (in the same time period, the US market as a whole has almost doubled).

Working with GCS buckets

Once you have figured out what class of bucket is best suited for your needs and how you plan to use it, the obvious next step is to get hands-on with GCP buckets. Let's try the usual stuff:

- Create a bucket
- Delete a bucket
- Access a bucket
- Manage other users' permissions on buckets
- Add/remove data from buckets
- Import data from other cloud resources to your bucket

Creating buckets

In GCP, there are multiple ways of interacting with objects. In case of Cloud Storage buckets, we can use the GUI console, `gsutil` command line, or REST (JSON or XML) API. Creating a bucket in GCP Cloud storage requires three fields:

- Region
- Storage class
- Universally unique name

> **When you create a regional bucket**, you are prompted for the region in which that bucket will be housed; you are not prompted for the specific zones though. The system decides that.

> **When you create a multi-regional bucket**, you are prompted to pick from one of three *multi-region locations*–Asia, the EU, and the US. Again, you can't pick which specific regions within that house your data; the system decides that too. This could be a significant issue if you have a statutory requirement to meet (for example, the data should never leave Country X within APAC).

We have already discussed the regions and storage classes and the naming, too, has its own set of rules to be followed. The name should be universally unique (that is, not just unique within your project or organization but within all of the GCP buckets worldwide) and end with an alphabet or a number.

Cloud Storage has a provision to affiliate your domain name to the bucket name as well, but the only difference is that you need to follow a domain verification process in order to do so. On a related note, GCP prohibits us from using dots in the bucket names if we are not linking it to our domain.

Creating buckets using the web console

The quickest way to get started with using Cloud Storage buckets is to create one from the console:

1. Click on the hamburger (the three horizontal lines in the upper-left corner) and select **Storage**| **Browser.**
2. If your project does not have any buckets yet, you will see a dialog box **Create Bucket** with a blue rectangle button; click on it.
3. If the project already has one or more buckets created, you will see them listed. Click on **Create Bucket** above them:

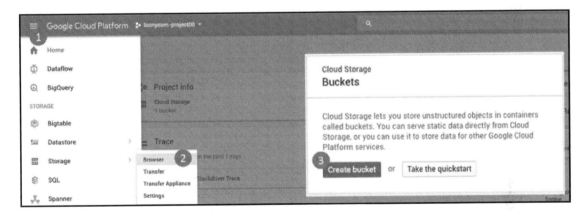

4. A new page will appear and it will ask you to name your bucket. Bucket names are universally unique. You can add letters, numbers, or underscores to keep your name unique. The **Help** tab suggest using dots to form a proper domain name as a bucket name. Let's say we name it **loonycorn-bucket-00**.

5. If your bucket name is a domain name, to verify your ownership, you will be asked to visit the verification console. In the console, you can verify your ownership by using one of the following methods:
   - Adding a special Meta tag to the site's home page.
   - Uploading a special HTML file to the site.
   - Verifying ownership directly from Search Console.
   - Adding a DNS TXT or CNAME record to the domain's DNS configuration.

6. After naming your bucket, pick the storage class. We will select the **Multi-Regional** storage class and **United States** region.
7. Optionally, you can also add label (key-value pairs, that is metadata) to your bucket by clicking on **+Add Labels.**
8. Finally, click on the **Create** button and, within a few seconds, your bucket will be ready, where you should be able to see a screen as shown in the following screenshot. We can add/remove files from buckets:

Creating buckets using gsutil

If you prefer to use the command line to provision a bucket, the `gsutil` tool is what you will use:

1. Use the `gsutil mb` command as follows to create the bucket. `-c`, `-l` and `-p` respectively stand for class (storage class), location (region), and project ID. If the project ID field is skipped, it opts for a default project ID and the URL is used for naming the bucket:

   ```
   gsutil mb -c nearline -l asia gs://loonycorn-bucket-00
   ```

2. Click on the **Refresh** button or use the `gsutil ls` command to verify your bucket creation.

It is possible to change the storage class of a bucket according to will, although regional and multi-regional classes are not interchangeable.

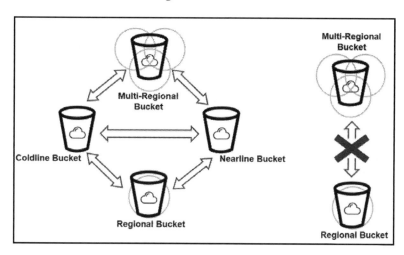

Notice how conversions from regional to multi-regional, or vice versa, are not directly allowed. That's because of some underlying implementation detail, so be sure to plan ahead regarding your choice of storage location.

One feature that might work a bit differently than you expect is the following: if we change the storage class of a bucket, that change will only affect new objects added to the bucket. The existing content will retain its old storage class. This is pretty important to keep in mind, and hints at the fact that GCS is not exactly traditional file storage. If it were, we'd expect the storage class to be a directory-level property that flows down to each file within the directory. That gets us to our next bit of doggerel:

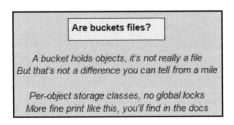

Changing the storage class of bucket and objects

You can modify the storage class for a bucket either from the console or with `gsutil` on the command line:

1. Go to the **Options** menu and select **Edit default storage class** and change it to your desired one by clicking on the radio button again:

2. Use the `gsutil rewrite` command and provide an object address depending on whose storage class you want to change:

```
gsutil rewrite -s coldline gs://loonycorn-bucket-00/image1.jpg
```

Transferring data in and out of buckets

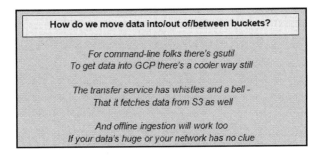

A bucket can contain any amount (petabytes) of data and data transfer with buckets can be done in multiple ways, such as:

- Uploading data to buckets
- Copying data between GCP buckets
- Moving data between GCP buckets
- Transferring data from other cloud storage (AWS S3) to GCP buckets
- Importing or exporting data offline

Uploading data to buckets using the web console

The console can be used to selectively upload individual files or entire folders to the bucket:

1. Click on the **Upload Files** button and you will find an explorer/finder window to find your desired file(s). It is likely that GCP will recognize your file format (even if it doesn't, you can find it by choosing the ***all files** option in explorer):

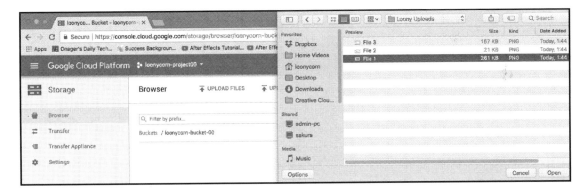

2. Optionally, you can also upload folders by clicking on the **Upload Folders** button and following a similar procedure to that of files.

Uploading data to buckets using gsutil

When using gsutil from the command line, you can treat the bucket as just another directory on the filesystem and specify that as the destination while copying files:

1. Use the gsutil cp command as follows to upload file(s) in the bucket. The command is followed by the source and destination URLs:

```
gsutil cp Desktop/image1.png gs://loonycorn-bucket-00
```

2. Do not forget to add a file extension properly or the file shall not upload.
3. Use the gsutil ls command to verify your upload.

Copying data between buckets using the web console

The console permits the copying (and moving) of files from one bucket to another. The steps are similar, but let us look at how the copy will work:

1. Navigate to the object you want to copy.
2. Click the more options button (three vertical dots) associated with the object. Click **Copy**:

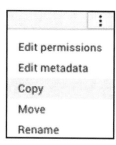

3. Select the destination for the copied object and the name for the copied object. Click and then click **Copy**. Note that we can use permissions from either the source or the destination:

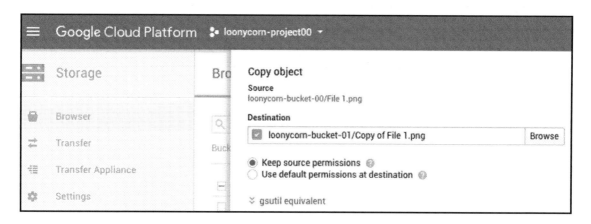

Copying data between buckets using the gsutil command line

When `gsutil`, we once again treat the buckets as source and destination directories:

1. Use the `gsutil cp` command as follows to upload file(s) to the bucket. Note that the command needs both source and destination URLs:

```
gsutil cp <Source> <Destination>
```

For instance:

```
gsutil cp gs://loonycorn-bucket-00/image1.png  gs://loonycorn-
bucket-01
```

2. Do not forget to add a file extension or the file shall not upload
3. Later, you can use the `ls` command to verify your upload
4. Similarly, the `gsutil mv` command can be used to move data from one bucket to another:

```
gsutil mv gs://loonycorn-bucket-00/image1.png gs://loonycorn-
bucket-01
```

5. While moving data from one bucket to another, the permission of the buckets may be different. We can make a choice between whether we want the moved objects to maintain their previous bucket's permission or whether we want them to inherit the new bucket's permission. Providing –p as the argument allows us to maintain the permissions from a previous bucket and the same logic applies to copying data as well:

```
gsutil mv -p gs://loonycorn-bucket-00/image1.png gs://loonycorn-bucket-01
```

Using the Transfer Service (instead of gsutil or the web console)

The Transfer Service is a more refined way of adding data to Google Cloud Storage buckets without having to manually upload it. We can ingest data from existing GCS buckets, Amazon's S3 buckets, or any HTTP(S) server. We can also schedule the import of data and filter the data that will be imported.

Transfer Service or gsutil?

There are no extra costs to using the Transfer Service; billing is the same as with gsutil or the web console. Google's docs recommend that we prefer gustil if we are copying files over from on-premise. If we are ingesting data from AWS or Azure, or from an external HTTP location, then transfer service is preferable.

Transfer service will only help get data into GCP, not out of it (this is important – do remember it):

1. Click on Hamburger (the three horizontal lines in the upper-left corner) on the GCP console.
2. Find **Storage** and click on the **Transfer** option.
3. When you get the dialog box, click on the **Create Transfer** button.
4. You will land on a transfer job creation page. Here, you will have to first select the source of your data. We will select **Google Cloud Storage bucket**.
5. Select the bucket that you want to use to get the data from. Remember that you need to have write permission on that bucket. Viewers cannot use this feature. We will select **loonycorn-bucket-00**. We can also add filters on data such as prefixes, postfixes, or its age.

6. After hitting **Continue**, we land on a destination selection that works in the same manner (the destination can only be a GCP location though – transfer service is for ingress only, not egress).

7. You can set additional transfer rules, such as overwriting in case of duplication, or removing objects from the source after transfer by checking them.

8. And finally, after deciding whether you want it as a one-time transfer or you want it daily (and clicking the appropriate radio button), click **Create**.

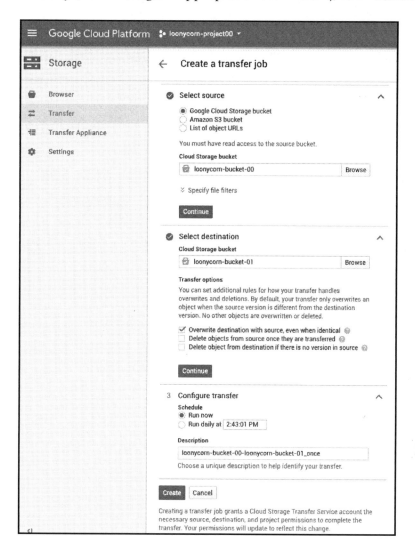

Importing or exporting data offline is a third-party solution provisioned by Google that allows us to send our storage units to these service providers and make them upload our data. It becomes useful when we have a slow or expensive internet connection and a huge amount of data. More details can be found in the following offline ingestion section.

Use case – Object Versioning

Object Versioning is the GCP's way of automatic archival. Once object versioning is enabled for a bucket, every version of the object (resulting from multiple writes) will be given an identification tag, which will be called *generation number* and all of the versions will be archived automatically.

Object versioning in the Cloud Storage bucket

This is an API and command-line exclusive (at the time of writing), so console will not provide any hints. Versioning can be set using `gsutil` with the following steps:

1. Apply the `gsutil versioning set on` command, with the appropriate values. This will enable object versioning for all objects in the bucket. The **Set off** argument will turn it off:

   ```
   gsutil versioning set on gs://loonycorn-bucket-00
   ```

2. Similarly, the get argument will check whether versioning is enabled or not:

   ```
   gsutil versioning get gs://loonycorn-bucket-00
   ```

3. The versions of an object are identified by their generation number. So, in order to list all of the objects in the bucket, including archived ones, use `ls` with `-a`.

4. To copy an archived version of an object, use the `cp` command as usual, but mention the object name URL with its generation number:

   ```
   gsutil cp gs://loonycorn-bucket-00/image1.png[GENERATION NUMBER]
   gs://loonycorn-bucket-01
   ```

Use case – object life cycle policies

It is pretty common that we'd want to automatically change storage classes of an object, so that it stays in a hot bucket for say a month, then gets relegated to a colder bucket, and finally is deleted altogether. This is what object life cycle management policies are meant for.

They allow you to specify how long the objects should exist under the same settings in your bucket before a specific action is triggered. For example, when we realize that there is archived data that has not been modified for over six months and is not likely to be accessed or modified any time soon, you can convert their class to nearline storage to save on cost.

You should note, however, that object life cycle actions are classified as *Class A operations*, which means that they can be expensive if you don't use them right. Do check out the fine print on pricing in the docs if you plan to do so.

Managing bucket life cycle using the web console

The conditions under which the bucket's objects will be transitioned, along with the available options for the transition, can be viewed when setting the life cycle from the console:

1. In GCP Cloud Storage browser, when you see a list of buckets, you will notice that the **Life cycle** column has entries written **None**. Click on it.
2. On the next page, you will be asked to click on **Add Rule** to create life cycle management rules and, after clicking on it, you will see a screen as follows:

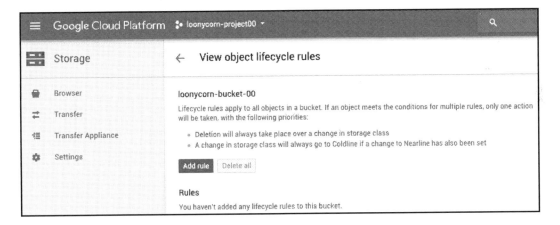

3. Under the **Select Object Condition** tab, you will encounter different options for your objects for sorting them, such as age, state (live or archived), storage class, and so on. We will select **Age** and set our object **Age** to 90 days.

4. Under the **Select Action** tab, you will have three options: converting their storage class to Nearline or Coldline or deletion. Click on **Delete**. Finally, click **Save**. This will mean that every object older than 90 days will automatically be deleted:

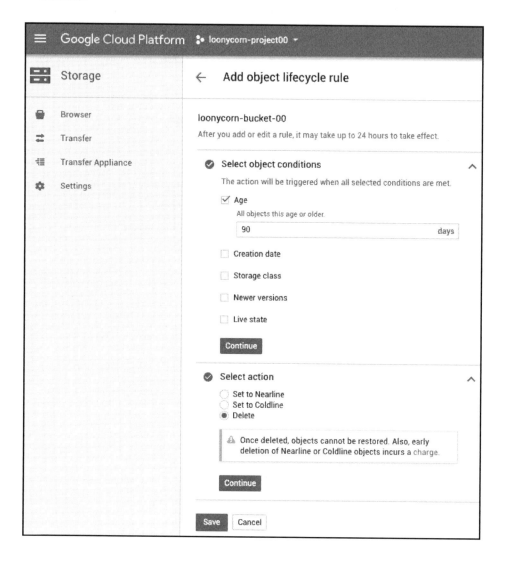

Manipulating object life-cycle via JSON file

For those who do not intend to use Web Console. Life-cycle management can also be handled by gsutil command line using a JSON file to pass life-cycle configurations.

1. Write your lifecycle configurations for GCS bucket in a JSON file as following:

```
{
"lifecycle": {
 "rule": [
 {
 "action": {
 "type": "SetStorageClass",
 "storageClass": "NEARLINE"
 },
 "condition": {
 "age": 365,
 "matchesStorageClass": ["MULTI_REGIONAL", "STANDARD",
"DURABLE_REDUCED_AVAILABILITY"]
 }
 },
 {
 "action": {
 "type": "SetStorageClass",
 "storageClass": "COLDLINE"
 },
 "condition": {
 "age": 1095,
 "matchesStorageClass": ["NEARLINE"]
 }
 }
 ]
 }
}
```

2. Run the `gsutil lifecycle set` command as following.

```
gsutil lifecycle set [JSON file] gs://[YOUR CLOUD STORAGE
BUCKET NAME]
```

Deleting objects permanently using the web console

Please know, firstly, that deletion is permanent—there is no way to undo bucket deletion, no grace period when you can change your mind. Deletion is final:

1. Click on the checkbox on the left-hand side of the file (for one or more files) and the **DELETE** button will become active. Click it.
2. A pop-up box will ask for your confirmation and, once confirmed, the file will be removed and billing will be adjusted accordingly:

Delete file

Are you sure you want to delete "File 3.png"? You can't undo this action.

CANCEL   DELETE

---

3. Optionally, you can also delete folders, or the bucket itself, exactly as you would delete files.

Deleting objects permanently using gsutil

Just as you would use the `rm` command to delete a file on your own system, the `gsutil rm` command can be used to remove files and directories within a bucket:

1. Use the `gsutil rm` command as follows to delete file(s) from the bucket. The command is followed by the source URL of the file and an optional `-r` to indicate removal of internal subdirectories along with files in a folder:

```
gsutil rm gs://loonycorn-bucket-00/image1.png
```

2. Do not forget to add a file extension properly or the file shall not be deleted. Later, you can use the `ls` command to verify your deletion.
3. Similarly, the `rb` command deletes the whole bucket, along with the files inside it.

Use case – restricting access with both ACLs and IAM

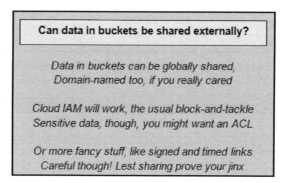

Can data in buckets be shared externally?

Data in buckets can be globally shared,
Domain-named too, if you really cared

Cloud IAM will work, the usual block-and-tackle
Sensitive data, though, you might want an ACL

Or more fancy stuff, like signed and timed links
Careful though! Lest sharing prove your jinx

IAM is an acronym for **Identity and Access Management**, and, as you'd imagine, it has to do with who can do what. More on this in the chapter on IAM, but for now, just know that:

- All GCP services have both identities (who is this?) and roles (what can they do?)
- Cloud storage is an exception because we can also use Access Control Lists (ACLs, pronounced *ackles*) to directly specify who can do what:

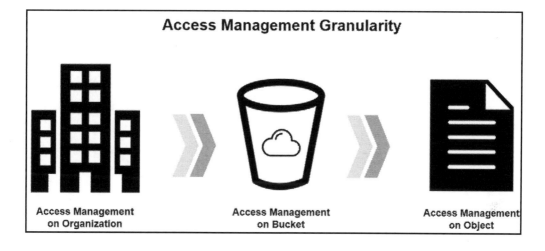

Access Management Granularity

Access Management on Organization   Access Management on Bucket   Access Management on Object

As the figure suggests, roles and permissions can be given at an organizational level (the organization that you have registered for your GCP project), storage bucket level, or at an individual object level. Of course, public access options will remain everywhere.

First of all, let's clear out the most obvious option, Public Access. The public URL for any object can be generated from the options menu and it will consist of strings such as `storage.googleapis.com` and our bucket name as well. Apart from that, in GCP, we can now provide roles to users at bucket level as well as object level. These roles determine the permissions of users:

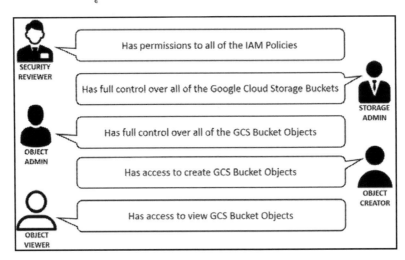

All the files in a folder or bucket will attain the same permission as its parent object. For this case, we have three images uploaded in our previously created bucket and now we will play with permission. Since, in this case, command line provides no advantage over console, we will explore the console part.

Managing permissions in bucket using the GCP console

It is possible to assign multiple roles to a set of users. However, for the sake of simplicity here, we will see how a single role can be assigned to a single user:

1. Click on the three vertically arranged dots next to your bucket and select the **Edit Permissions** option. This will bring up a dialogue that will allow you to give granular permissions to those users who should be able to access that object:

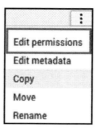

2. By selecting the desired user or group and selecting permission, we can control what every user in the organization can access. We will select `janani@loonycorn.com` and give her the role of **Storage Admin**.

3. You can also specify permissions on a file using object roles in the same manner as previously:

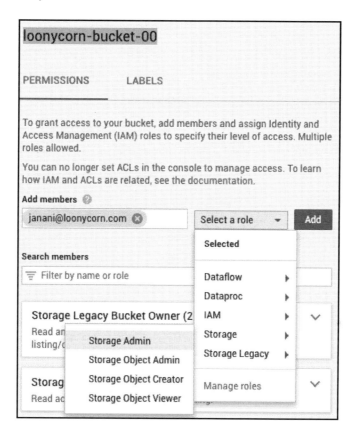

4. A similar approach is taken with each object in the bucket. Just click on the options menu and click **Edit Permissions** and you can see a dialog box as shown in the following screenshot. This is called the **Access Control List** (**ACL**) of the object. Even if you migrated your data from one service provider (say GCP) to another (say AWS), you can maintain these object-specific permissions through ACL:

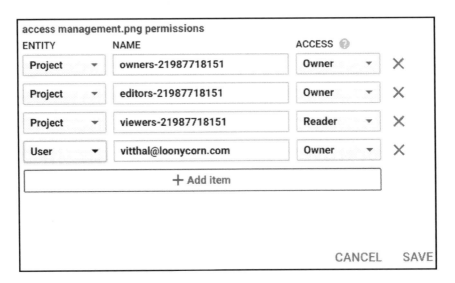

Use case – signed and timed URLs

In many applications, users within the organization will not be the only ones to need access to the objects. Third-party applicants or end users themselves may need to access a bucket or an object within it. Keeping track of all of them and giving them a viewer's role would be theoretically painstaking and practically erroneous to the extent of being impossible.

A simple solution to this problem is to give them public URLs, but that would only give them read access to the object. If we want to provide read, write, and even delete access for a certain length of time, the solution is to use signed URLs. These are time-limited; we have to specify a period of validity while creating them. The details are as follows.

Setting up signed URLs for cloud storage

These steps can be used to generate a private key and that can then be used it to sign a file in your bucket:

1. Generate a new private key, or use an existing private key. The key can be in either JSON or PKCS12 format:
    1. Click on the hamburger in the top left of the console and navigate to **API & Services** and then click on **Credentials**
    2. Click on **Create Credentials** and select **Service account key**
    3. In the drop down for Service Account, select **New service account**
    4. Give a name for the service account under **Service account name**
    5. Use the default Service account ID or specify one
    6. Choose JSON or P12 as your Key type and click **Create**
    7. A dialog will confirm the creation of your service account and the private key is downloaded automatically

2. Use the `gsutil signurl` command, passing in the path to the private key (stored on your computer) and the URL of the bucket or object you want to generate a signed URL for:
    - **Specifying Time-Validity**: In this command, the -d argument stands for duration, which is 10 minutes in our case. It means that after 10 minutes, the link will show the 404 error from any region:

    ```
    gsutil signurl -d 10m Desktop/private-key.json
    gs://loonycorn-bucket-00/image1.jpg
    ```

3. To remove the signed URL, simply go back to credentials and remove the signature!

Use case – reacting to object changes

When we use our GCP buckets for web applications, the objects in the bucket will be rewritten many times over. Clearly, we might need to detect specific object changes and react to them, for which we'd need to be notified when an object changes. This functionality is invoked using the watchbucket clause in `gsutil`.

Please know that these notifications are different from Pub/Sub notifications (Pub/Sub is the reliable messaging system for streaming data in GCP). Object change notifications happen using something called a **Channel**. This is a GCS-specific term used to describe the link between a bucket and all apps listening for changes on that bucket.

You should also be aware that object change notifications can be used to trigger cloud functions.

Setting up object change notifications with the gsutil notification watchbucket

The `gsutil` tool can be used to create a channel and also remove it once it is no longer required:

1. Once we run the command, as follows, it initiates a channel with the Channel ID we provide. It reports the notifications to whichever application (even if it is third party) we decide by providing the application's URL. Also, we can deploy watch on one or more buckets simualtaneously:

    ```
    gsutil notification watchbucket -i loony-channel -t my-client [App
    URL] gs://loonycorn-bucket-00
    ```

2. To stop notifications, we need to stop the channel itself, which is done with the following command:

```
gsutil notification stopchannel ChannelId ResourceId
```

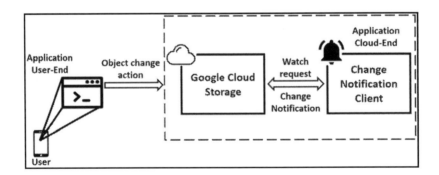

Use case – using customer supplied encryption keys

Data in GCS buckets is always encrypted, in-flight and at-rest. If we do nothing at all, the encryption occurs using Google-supplied keys. These keys are created, managed, and rotated by Google, and we need not bother with data encryption at all. This is the first option, called **Google Supplied Encryption Key (GSEK)**, which is the one most likely to work right out of the box. The keys are those associated with the respective users and governed by IAM:

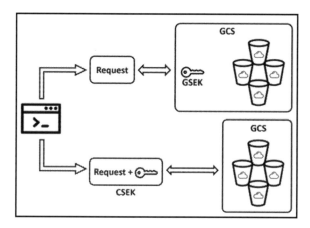

Alternatively, a customer might want more control, and insist on **Customer Supplied Encryption Key (CSEK)**. Here, the key resides on the customer's premise, but is sent across in raw form as part of the API calls. All GCP references to the key are in-memory only, the key actually never gets stored on the cloud.

A third option is **Customer Managed Encryption Keys (CMEK)**, where the customer uses a specific GCP service called the **Google Key Management Service (Google KMS)** to store keys on the cloud.

Notice that in CMEK, unlike in CSEK, the keys are indeed persisted on the cloud, and key protection is performed by the KMS. In CSEK, to download or modify the encrypted data, you always need to provide the user supplied key to perform the action. Finally, CSEK is only currently available in a small list of countries.

To implement CSEK using `gsutil`, use the following command:

```
gsutil cp Desktop/image1.png gs://loonycorn-bucket-00 encryption_key [KEY]
```

Without the key, GCS shows a permission denied error for modifications and a 404 error for downloading.

Use case – auto-syncing folders

A really common use case is keeping data in sync between the persistent disk of a VM and a specific GCS location, or two GCS locations. The `gsutil rsync` function is what we need here.

The source and destination URLs can either be a cloud storage bucket or a local directory. So, for example, if you want to sync data between two buckets, you can simply use the following:

```
gsutil rsync gs://loonycorn-bucket-00 loonycorn-bucket-01
```

Careful on the order of the arguments! If you reverse source and destination with a -d argument, all of your updates will be deleted forever unless you have an archival enabled. The `rsync` command makes the destination match the source. So rsyncing with an empty source directory makes the destination directory also empty.

It is also possible to specify various additional optional arguments, as follows:

```
gsutil rsync [-VARIABLE ARGUMENT] src_url dst_url
VARIABLE ARGUMENTS (OPTIONAL):
-a = also copies ACL channel
-c = computes checksum
-C = copies other files if some incur errors
-d = deletes data from destination which is not present in source
-n = "dry run" only lists the files to be copied. Doesn't copy them
-U = skips unsupported storage class objects
```

Use case – mounting GCS using gcsfuse

Filesystem in Userspace (FUSE), cloud storage is an open source FUSE adoption functionality provided by GCS. It allows users to access and operate GCS buckets from their Linux or OS X machines. It translates object storage names into a file and directory system and interprets the / character in object names as a directory separator.

Thus, objects with the same common prefix are treated as files in the same directory. Applications can interact with objects like files in filesystems. We now no longer need to recode our shell scripts to work with `gustil` commands and `gs://...` paths. This can be a significant win if our shell scripts are too complex or too important to rewrite. But on the other hand the filesystems mounted via `gcsfuse` are much slower than persistent disks.

Cloud storage FUSE itself is free. But charges for bucket storage, network access, and transfer instances are applicable, as usual.

Mounting GCS buckets

The following steps describe how you would mount a Cloud Storage bucket on a host running a Debian OS:

1. Add the `gcsfuse` distribution URL as a package source and import its public key:

   ```
   export GCSFUSE_REPO=gcsfuse-`lsb_release -c -s`
       echo "deb http://packages.cloud.google.com/apt $GCSFUSE_REPO
   main" | sudo tee /etc/apt/sources.list.d/gcsfuse.list
       curl https://packages.cloud.google.com/apt/doc/apt-key.gpg |
   sudo apt-key add -
   ```

2. Update the list of packages available and install `gcsfuse`:

   ```
   sudo apt-get update
   sudo apt-get install gcsfuse
   ```

3. Create a directory:

   ```
   mkdir newfuse
   ```

4. Create the bucket you wish to mount, if it doesn't already exist, using the Google Cloud Platform Console.

5. Use Cloud Storage FUSE to mount the bucket (for example, example-bucket):

   ```
   gcsfuse example-bucket /home/newfuse
   ```

6. Start working with the mounted bucket:

   ```
   ls /home/newfuse
   ```

Use case – offline ingestion options

Say you have a few hundred TB of on-premise data and a really slow network connection. Getting the data onto the cloud is a formidable task—particularly if you are using a VPN to connect on-premise to the cloud, further slowing your connectivity. To make things easier in such situations, Google offers offline ingestion options that roughly correspond to Snowball and Snowmobile from AWS.

It may be sufficient for you to merely know that such options exist, if you care about the fine print, please read on, otherwise feel free to skip to the end of the chapter:

- **Data Preparation**: Store and/or prepare your data. This can mean arranging it in servers, creating backup images, network settings, or even databases for machine learning:
    - The data should be arranged in the form of non-nested directories (in case of GCS), which then would turn into buckets. In other words, it should be less than 5 TB for each bucket.
    - The directory names should also follow the bucket naming guidelines.
    - Transfer appliance does not support NAT or PAT, but it does support SSH, FTP, and HTTP(S). So, networks should be configured accordingly.
    - Just to prevent last minute errors and delays, make sure your firewall rules are disabled or at least an exception is added for GCS.
- **Book Storage**: Once the data is prepared, you need to initiate the capture job. For this, you need to fulfill the given hardware requirements, which include at least 1 GBPS internet. If such requirements are not met, you can opt for Google verified third-party uploaders, but that option is only available in North America at the time of writing. In the capture job, Google Cloud Storage suggests how many buckets you require, and you get to decide accordingly.
- **Check Billing**: For 100 TB of storage usage, GCS charges $30 for migration per day and shipping charges are $250 per day (in two-day intervals). Thus, you will be billed accordingly and if it matches your budget, you can initiate the transfer.

- **Transfer**: After filling the transfer request and required storage size, it takes around 40-45 days for 100 TB of data to be migrated to GCS. If capture job is not possible due to hardware unavailability, you can also ship the data to a relevant zone (data center). The class of storage can be changed even after migration and rules for it remain the same. Mostly, this is done with Nearline and Coldline storage for large-scale archival purposes.
- **Operate**: Once the transfer is complete and data is stored into the buckets, you can access and manipulate it using the console.

Summary

In this chapter, we have seen how Google Cloud Storage can be used to store your static, unstructured data, and how it compares with other forms of data storage. You should now be familiar with how to create buckets, populate them with data, and then manage them using versioning and life cycle policies.We have touched upon securing data in the buckets using encryption, as well as restricting access using ACLs and IAM. We have also looked into how to integrate your GCS buckets with your existing infrastructure by mounting it to your hosts.

Now that we have seen how to manage unstructured data, we can move along and explore the various options supplied by Google Cloud to manage structured information.

6
Relational Databases

Relational databases are pretty familiar technology these days, so we won't spend a whole lot of time discussing exactly what they are. We will introduce them really quickly though, just in case you've never heard the term **Structured Query Language (SQL)** or **Relational Database Management System (RDBMS)**. Then we will jump to the couple of RDBMS options available under GCP, which are Cloud SQL and Cloud Spanner. We will explore both of them in detail and also make comparisons that would give you enough insight for determining the optimum option for your application.

We will go through the following topics in the chapter:

- Relational Databases, SQL and Schemas
- GCP Cloud SQL
- Automatic Backup and Restore
- Cloud Spanner

What is a relational database?

When would you use a relational database?
Three factors on which that decision you can base

One, relational data that lives in columns and rows
With a well-defined strong schema that everybody knows

Two, atomic support - that's pretty strong ACID
Transactional consistency that isn't for the flaccid

Three, queries you can write in plain old SQL
A language seen by more than the Star Wars prequel

Relational databases, SQL, and schemas

The heart of the RDBMS is the relational data model; data is expressed in rows and columns within tables. The names and types of the columns are defined up-front and are collectively called the schema. The rows represent the data stored in the RDBMS and can be accessed using a very popular language called SQL.

Current Accounts			Savings Accounts		
Acc_ID	**Holder_Name**	**Balance_$**	**Acc_ID**	**Holder_Name**	**Balance_$**
X2135	Tom Huddleston	6476	2239	Tom Huddleston	2344
X5658	Jerry Renner	6677	5546	Jerry Renner	90000
X7070	Popeye Sailor	56	0707	Popeye Sailor	0278
X0009	Tony Stark	5465464846	0001	Tony Stark	4912847192087
X6546	Thor Odinson	0000	9999	Thor Odinson	0000

In the preceding tables, each account holder has two accounts, one savings account and one current account, and each has different balances. This can be expressed in RDBMS like in the example given below. Here you can see that each account holder is given a unique key (**Customer_ID**), which makes querying for savings or current account balance a lot easier and faster:

Customer_ID	Holder_Name	Acc_ID	Balance_$
1	Tom Huddleston	X2135	6476
2	Jerry Renner	X5658	6677
3	Popeye Sailor	X7070	56
4	Tony Stark	X0009	5465464846
5	Thor Odinson	X6546	0000
1	Tom Huddleston	2239	2344
2	Jerry Renner	5546	90000
3	Popeye Sailor	0707	0278
4	Tony Stark	0001	4912847192087
5	Thor Odinson	9999	0000

In these tables, the column definitions are the schemas: for instance, the schemas of both relations **Current Accounts** and **Savings Accounts** have three columns named **Acc_ID**, **Holder_Name**, and **Balance_$**.

When data is inserted into these relations, or tables, the RDBMS will check and ensure that the rows being inserted match the schema and also satisfy constraints that might have been specified by users.

SQL is a common syntax that works with pretty much all RDBMS and is known and used by millions of individuals, including many non-technical folks. Business analysts, sales teams, even a few CFOs know how to write SQL queries. A typical SQL query that would pull all data from a relation might look as follows:

```
SELECT Customer_ID, Holder_Name from 'Savings Accounts'
```

SQL queries can get pretty complex, but they are a great abstraction that allows pretty much anyone in an organization to access the data they need from an RDBMS. In the days before the term *big data* caught on, SQL queries were the way to work with big data.

OLTP and the ACID properties

The great appeal of RDBMS lies in their support for **Online Transaction Processing (OLTP)**. The term transaction has a special meaning in the world of RDBMS, a transaction is a set of operations that constitute a unit of work. Transactions must be all-or-nothing; the most popular example is that of transferring money from one bank account to another. It would be a disaster if an RDBMS were to fail midway through such a transaction, such that the money vanished from one account and did not appear in the other.

This intuition is formalized in a set of properties called the ACID properties, and the most basic functionality of a conventional relational database is support for these ACID properties:

- **Atomicity**: Each transaction is all-or-nothing; partial execution of a transaction can never occur.
- **Consistency**: The state of the system should always be *correct* at the end of a transaction. In our bank transfer example, for instance, a transfer should never create or destroy money.
- **Durability**: Changes in system state wrought by a transaction must be permanent and survive power outages, crashes, and all such system issues.
- **Isolation**: Each transaction ought to execute as if it were the only transaction in the world—this way transactions will not interfere with each other's operations.

Building a robust RDBMS that actually works and delivers on these properties is difficult. Consider isolation for instance—a database server might need to deal with millions of simultaneous transactions (think ATM withdrawals, for instance), and yet the architecture must ensure that each transaction operates under the illusion that it is the only one executing in the system. So, relational databases are big, big business—several corporations makes tens of billions of dollars in annual revenues—Oracle, for instance, is a leader in the database business.

Scaling up versus scaling out

The business models of several leaders in the relational database world have been fundamentally threatened by the rise of cloud computing. Why? Because traditional RDBMS *scale up*, they rely on a single extremely powerful server, and that server often runs proprietary and non-standard hardware and software, and so is very expensive. The cloud, on the other hand, is all about *scaling out*, that is, assembling arrays of generic hardware running distributed software. At the time of writing, the cloud model of scaling out seems to be winning. Check out the sluggish stock performance of Teradata or Oracle, both leaders in the traditional data solutions world between 2012 and 2017. Now contrast those with the meteoric increases in Amazon or Google's stock over the same period; these stock prices tell a tale.

Each of the leading public cloud platforms AWS, Azure, and GCP offer their own cloud-based relational database solutions. On the GCP, there are two: Cloud SQL and Cloud Spanner.

Cloud SQL competes squarely with RDS on AWS and in many ways has fewer options currently. For instance, Cloud SQL lets users run MySQL or PostgreSQL, while RDS has several additional options. Cloud SQL is similar to traditional RDBMS, it scales up, not out. This implies that there is an upper limit on the data size, as well as latency for users from different regions.

Cloud Spanner is Google-proprietary, and unlike Cloud SQL, it offers horizontal scaling as well as multi-region replication. Google is very proud of Spanner's technology, which is really quite incredible. Cloud Spanner can scale to handle just about any dataset size; this does require us to increase the number of nodes, and consequently the cost. In some respects, Spanner resembles Redshift on Amazon (Redshift is a data warehousing/OLAP product, not an RDBMS, but like Spanner it scales linearly with the number of nodes).

GCP Cloud SQL

As the name suggests, Cloud SQL is an RDBMS offering on GCP.

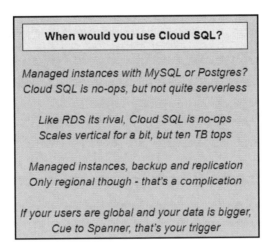

But with several advantages that arise from its cloud-based nature, which are as follows:

- It is implemented on cloud, so we do not need to physically set up systems and VMs. This makes it far more attractive than running an RDBMS on a VM (that would be the IaaS approach, Cloud SQL is a PaaS approach).
- It is mostly managed by Google, so we do not have to bother about common database management tasks such as backups and archival.
- Even if we are already using another form of RDBMS, migrating to Cloud SQL is relatively simple and reliable.
- Like all the other services on the GCP, Cloud SQL instances are scalable and customizable.

- Cloud SQL currently supports two open source RDBMS: MySQL and PostgreSQL where the choice depends on our structure of data.
- It provides strong ACID support.

As we mentioned earlier, the choice between MySQL and PostgreSQL depends on us. But, which one to pick? There is one more choice to make.

First Generation MySQL	Second Generation MySQL	PostgreSQL
•Compatible with most of the older versions of MySQL •Stores up to 500GB per instance. •Old password structure still acceptable •Tested default policies •Abundant information and resources available in community.	•Faster, cheaper, more scalable and more configurable •Stores up to 10TB per instance •Due to strict defaults, may face compatibility issues. •Old password structure completely removed. •Default and custom policies to be tested.	•Still in beta mode so may be rolled back to previous stable version. •Stores up to 3TB per instance. •Works well with complex queries •Provides better NoSQL support for OLAP than MySQL (for this, other GCP options are available)

Creating a Cloud SQL instance

Cloud SQL requires an instance to be set up before you can start using it. Which means it is not serverless.

> **What engines does Cloud SQL support?**
>
> *Compared to RDS, flavours supported are few*
> *MySQL is one, Postgres is two*
>
> *No Oracle, MS SQL Server or Maria*
> *Goes without saying, also no Aurora*
>
> *Don't despair if those engines are your choice*
> *Your own image on a VM still help you find your voice*

Now we will create a Cloud SQL instance called `bank-balance`:

1. Click on the **Menu** option (three horizontal lines on upper-left corner) on the GCP console.

2. Click on the **SQL** tab:

3. If your project does not have any Cloud SQL instances yet, you will see a dialog box suggesting to **Create Instance** with a blue rectangle button. Click on it. If you already have one or more SQL instances created (by you or by someone else from your organization) you will see them listed. **Create instance** will be above them under the search panel. As you may have figured, click on it:

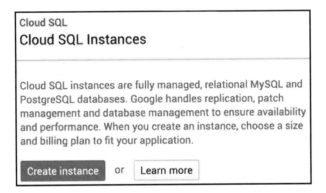

4. Cloud SQL supports MySQL, which is open source popular RDBMS, and PostgreSQL, which is open source RDBMS with features of an object-oriented database. For this demonstration, click on the **MySQL** radio button if it is not already clicked. Click **Next**:

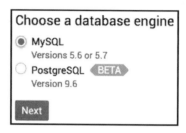

5. The next dialog box asks you to select between legacy and current version of MySQL with their consequences listed. In this case we click on **Choose Second Generation**:

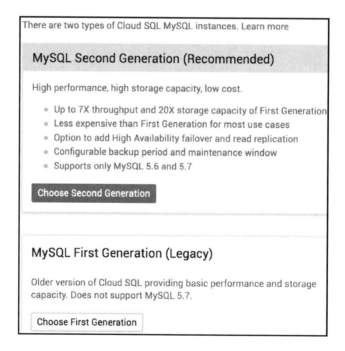

6. Set up your instance ID (bank-balance), root password, and location (region and zone). If you click on configuration options you will notice that you can add labels, flags, and networks. More importantly, you can also configure the underlying hardware where size and type of hard disk play an important part. Defaults are SSD with 10 GB, but if you can, customize them. We will stick to the defaults:

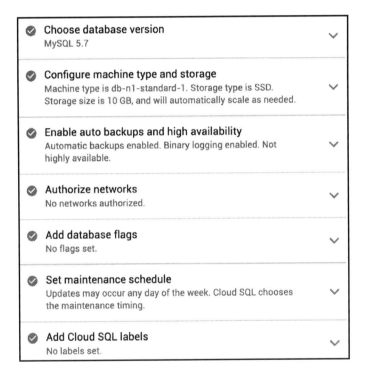

Once we have determined our database configurations, let's decide on the underlying hardware.

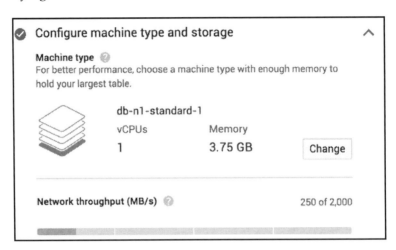

7. Click on **Create**:

Once you navigate into your created SQL instance, you will see a bunch of options that you can explore. We will skip the obvious ones and get to the important ones. In the case of SQL instances, the command line is much more comfortable and fast than a UI. You can simply treat it as your Linux command line. As with all command line operations using Google Cloud, we will use the `gcloud` utility. We have seen earlier that we can access this Cloud SQL instance from the Google Cloud Platform console. You also have the option to access Cloud SQL using Python and Java APIs if you want to do it programmatically.

Creating a database in a Cloud SQL instance

Time to get hands on with Cloud SQL. Let's start with creating a database:

1. On the command line simply type gcloud beta sql connect, specify the name of your Cloud SQL instance, and specify the user you want to connect as.

2. Here we just have one user, the root user. You will be asked for your root user password before the connection is successful. You will see the MySQL prompt when you log into your MySQL instance. In order to allow Cloud Shell to connect to your MySQL instance, MySQL whitelists the IP address of your Cloud Shell instance temporarily. Cloud Shell instances are ephemeral (destroyed once we close them), so when you reconnect your session changes and your IP address might change as well. This whitelist is temporary for that reason. Once you are in MySQL, run your MySQL commands exactly like you would in a local instance:

```
vitthal@loonycorn-project00-187805:~$ gcloud beta sql connect bank-balance
Whitelisting your IP for incoming connection for 5 minutes...done.
Connecting to database with SQL user [root].Enter password:
```

3. Create a database named accounts using the CREATE DATABASE command. Move into this database by using the USE accounts command:

```
mysql> CREATE DATABASE accounts
mysql> USE accounts
Database changed
mysql>
```

4. Create a table named Holders using the CREATE TABLE command. Specify the names and the data types of the columns, that is, ID and name and specify the primary key. Which in this case is customer_id:

```
mysql> CREATE TABLE Holders(
    -> customer_id INT64 NOT NULL AUTO_INCREMENT,
    -> holder_name VARCHAR(100) NOT NULL,
    -> acc_id INT64 NOT NULL,
    -> balance INT64 NOT NULL,
    -> PRIMARY KEY (customer_id)
    -> );
```

5. Show tables will show you the tables that have been created within this database just as one table here now, the students table.

6. As account holders I have added details from our previous explanation. You can run simple `SELECT` queries on these tables. And if you want to get out of your MySQL instance, type `exit`:

```
mysql> INSERT INTO Holders VALUES (1, "Tom Huddleston", 2239, 2344);
Query OK, 1 row affected (0.20 sec)

mysql> INSERT INTO Holders VALUES (2, "Jerry Renner", 5546, 90000);
Query OK, 1 row affected (0.20 sec)

mysql> INSERT INTO Holders VALUES (3, "Popeye Sailor", 0707, 0278);
Query OK, 1 row affected (0.20 sec)

mysql>

mysql> SELECT * FROM Holders;
+-------------+----------------+--------+---------+
| customer_id | holder_name    | acc_id | balance |
+-------------+----------------+--------+---------+
|           1 | Tom Huddleston |   2239 |    2344 |
|           2 | Jerry Renner   |   5546 |   90000 |
|           3 | Popeye Sailor  |    707 |     278 |
+-------------+----------------+--------+---------+
3 rows in set (0.20 sec)

mysql> exit
```

Another way to connect to Cloud SQL is to use the Cloud SQL proxy. It means connecting to it via mysql client using the IP of the Cloud SQL instance. Also, using Cloud SQL proxy enables facilities like using instance names for logging in instead of IP etc. To set it up, follow the procedure below:

1. Navigate to your dashboard and search for `Google Cloud SQL API` in the search bar. This will lead you to **Services and API** sections'. Click on **Enable**, also, make sure your service account is set-up.

2. Install the proxy by downloading it and making it executable with following commands:

```
wget https://dl.google.com/cloudsql/cloud_sql_proxy.linux.amd64
-O cloud_sql_proxy
chmod +x cloud_sql_proxy
```

3. Navigate to your instance and copy its name from it since it will be used in further steps. Start the proxy with Cloud SDK authentication:

```
/cloud_sql_proxy –instances=<COPIED INSTANCE NAME>=tcp:3306
```

4. Now you can access it from anywhere, start your MySQL client and connect it using TCP socket through 127.0.0.1 IP:

```
mysql -u <USERNAME> -p --host 127.0.0.1
```

Importing a database

Apart from the databases we create on Cloud SQL instances, we can also import other databases from other sources (otherwise nobody would ever switch to Cloud SQL in the first place!):

1. We can download one of the sample databases from the official MySQL website using the wget command:

```
wget https://codeload.github.com/datacharmer/test_db/zip/master
-O sampledb.zip
```

2. After downloading you will have a sampledb.zip file. Unzip it. This will create a test-db-master directory in your current working directory.

3. Navigate there using the cd command and find employees.sql using the ls command.

4. After examining this file you will find that it contains a number of SQL statements to drop existing databases and recreate the database and tables within them.

5. Using the gcloud command line you can connect your SQL instance and run all the commands that are present in the employees.sql file. This will create an employees database and create all the tables mentioned in it:

```
gcloud beta sql connect bank-balance --user=root< employees.sql
```

Now we have two databases; Accounts and Employees. Before making a shift from our dominant RDBMS to Cloud SQL, we also need to test whether it delivers what it promises!

Testing Cloud SQL instances

Time to test the databases that we created. Let's try a few queries on them:

1. Run the `describe` command to check the consistency of database fields. (Remember? ACID!):

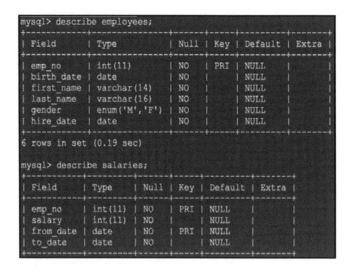

```
mysql> describe employees;
+------------+---------------+------+-----+---------+-------+
| Field      | Type          | Null | Key | Default | Extra |
+------------+---------------+------+-----+---------+-------+
| emp_no     | int(11)       | NO   | PRI | NULL    |       |
| birth_date | date          | NO   |     | NULL    |       |
| first_name | varchar(14)   | NO   |     | NULL    |       |
| last_name  | varchar(16)   | NO   |     | NULL    |       |
| gender     | enum('M','F') | NO   |     | NULL    |       |
| hire_date  | date          | NO   |     | NULL    |       |
+------------+---------------+------+-----+---------+-------+
6 rows in set (0.19 sec)

mysql> describe salaries;
+-----------+---------+------+-----+---------+-------+
| Field     | Type    | Null | Key | Default | Extra |
+-----------+---------+------+-----+---------+-------+
| emp_no    | int(11) | NO   | PRI | NULL    |       |
| salary    | int(11) | NO   |     | NULL    |       |
| from_date | date    | NO   | PRI | NULL    |       |
| to_date   | date    | NO   |     | NULL    |       |
+-----------+---------+------+-----+---------+-------+
```

2. In the `Employees` database we have employees and salaries tables. We will run a joint query on both of these to calculate the average salary for all employees who joined in a particular year.

```
mysql> SELECT avg(s.salary) avg_salary_by_hire_year, YEAR(e.hire_date)
    -> FROM employees e, salaries s
    -> WHERE e.emp_no = s.emp_no
    -> GROUP BY YEAR (e.hire_date);
+-------------------------+-------------------+
| avg_salary_by_hire_year | YEAR(e.hire_date) |
+-------------------------+-------------------+
|               66966.7550 |              1985 |
|               66187.3453 |              1986 |
|               65199.4887 |              1987 |
|               64205.4734 |              1988 |
|               63658.8510 |              1989 |
|               62736.4975 |              1990 |
|               61765.4281 |              1991 |
|               60962.9784 |              1992 |
|               60393.9920 |              1993 |
|               59372.7106 |              1994 |
|               58369.3347 |              1995 |
|               57724.8363 |              1996 |
|               56797.7335 |              1997 |
|               56390.4280 |              1998 |
```

3. Looks good! Since we are done with this instance, we will delete it to avoid heartbreaking bills. This task is simple and familiar. Navigate to the instance, find our three friendly vertical dots, press **Delete**, and voila!

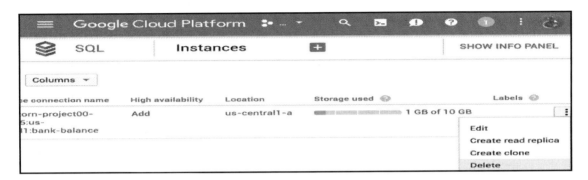

[DIY] Since the data is stored in the Cloud storage we can again access to it by **IMPORTING** it (get the hint, genius!) using another ephemeral Cloud SQL instance. This time, it is best to locate the instance in the same region as Cloud Storage Bucket for least latencies.

Use case – managing replicas

Our database would not be considered *managed* unless we have figured out how to get replicas created and managed. Cloud SQL by default does not provide replicas, but we can create them. There are four types of replicas to choose from. Despite of all of this, the reason behind creating such replicas is to increase query capacity for read intensive databases:

Type 1: Read Replicas:

These are low cost low availability replicas of the master instance, which contains root password and changes made to the master. The changes are least likely to be real time. The replicas can also face disruptions due to server outage or sudden upgrade:

- The configuration of the replica instance may be different from the master instance based on the choices we make and it is viable to make read replicas that have lower configurations if the application is not mission critical.
- They cannot be backed up or restored.
- They need to be promoted as master before we delete the master instance.

- Master needs to have binary logging enabled in order to have a replica.
- Replica cannot have replicas (What would be the point anyway!).
- Steps to create a read replica:

    1. Check the status of the instance for binary logging:

       ```
       gcloud sql instances describe bank-balance
       ```

    2. If `binaryLogEnabled` is false, enable it using the following command:

       ```
       gcloud sql instances patch --enable-bin-log bank-
       balance
       ```

    3. Create the replica:

       ```
       gcloud sql instances create bank-balance-replica-0 --
       master-instance-name=bank-balance
       ```

Type 2: Failover Replicas:

A second generation replica within a different zone is called a **Failover Replica**. This allows us the flexibility to treat production level instances and not-so-mission-critical instances differently:

- In case of outage in master instance, Cloud SQL promptly directs to a failover replica, which would be safe since it would be in another region. The Cloud SQL proxy is failover aware so the application using it doesn't need to update its configurations. We only need to restart the session.
- The update window is smaller and having more than one failover replica set up with different update windows can provide complete failover immunity theoretically.
- To set up failover replica:
    - We can create a master instance along with its failover replica:

      ```
      gcloud sql instances create bank-balance --backup-
      start-time 00:00 --failover-replica-name bank-balance-
      fo --enable-bin-log
      ```

    - We can also master a failover separately since the only variations are different arguments of the `gcloud` command:

      ```
      gcloud sql instances create bank-balance-fo --master-
      instance-name=bank-balance--replica-type=FAILOVER
      ```

Type 3: External Replicas:

These are external MySQL Read replica instances replicated from Cloud SQL instances. There are a few rules to be followed for external replicas:

- Binary logging for master
- Same or higher MySQL version of replica compared to master
- Replicating to another Cloud platform's MySQL instance is not possible
- To create an external replica:
    - Connect to your Cloud SQL instance using the Command Prompt:

        ```
        gcloud sql connect bank-balance --user=root
        ```

    - Create a special user for replica:

        ```
        CREATE USER 'bank-balance-replica-user'@'%' IDENTIFIED
        BY '********';
        ```

    - Provide replication privileges to the user:

        ```
        GRANT REPLICATION SLAVE ON *.* TO 'bank-balance-
        replication-user'@'%';
        ```

    - Create an export dump file from the master instance for the replica. For this, we will create a Cloud Storage Bucket for the export and add replica's service account in the access control list of the bucket with `Writer` permission and finally we will export it:

        ```
        gsutil mb -p loonycorn-project-01 -l asia
        gs://loonycorn-bucket-00
        gcloud sql instances describe bank-balance
        gsutil acl ch -u yourserviceacc@yourdomain.com:W
        gs://loonycorn-bucket-00
        gcloud sql instances export bank-balance
        gs://loonycorn-bucket-00/sqldumpfile.gz --database
        holdersdump.sql
        ```

    - Go to the machine where you want to host the replica. It can even be a compute engine instance. Seed the export file we created earlier:

        ```
        mysql --user=root --password < holdersdump.sql
        ```

- Open the MySQL settings file typically named `my.cnf`:
  `nano /etc/my.cnf`
- Add the following fields to it. Among these fields, server ID is a unique numeric value across all of the servers and replicas, which means no two replicas can have the same server ID:

```
[mysqld]
server-id=[SERVER_ID]
gtid_mode=ON
enforce_gtid_consistency=ON
log_slave_updates=ON
replicate-ignore-db=mysql
binlog-format=ROW
log_bin=mysql-bin
expire_logs_days=1
read_only=ON
Exit and re-enter the mysql process to make sure
configurations are updated.
Enter the following command:
CHANGE MASTER TO MASTER_HOST='[IP ADDRESS OF MASTER]',
MASTER_USER='bank-balance-replication-user',
MASTER_PASSWORD='********', MASTER_AUTO_POSITION=1;
```

- Start the replication process with the following command:

  START SLAVE;

- You can also check the state of replica by entering the following command. Make sure it gives a result as **Waiting for master to send event**:

  SHOW SLAVE STATUSG;

- **Replica Management**: As handy as replicas may be, they need to be managed. Sometimes we need to enable/disable them as per our requirements or we need to change their role as well!
  - **Enabling Replicas**: If a replication instance is disabled for a longer time interval, replicating updated master may take significant time. In which case, it makes sense to enable a new replication instance:

    gcloud sql instances patch <<YOUR REPLICA>> --enable-database-replication

- **Disabling Replicas**: This does NOT mean deletion of a replica instance. In other words, even if you don't replicate anything from master, the instance will contribute to the billing. This is only advisable for temporary use such as debugging:

  ```
  gcloud sql instances patch  <<YOUR REPLICA>> --no-
  enable-database-replication
  ```

- **Promoting Replicas**: A replica can be turned into a standalone instance, which means it will stop replicating the master, but the action is irreversible. Thus if you do it by mistake, you will have to delete it and create a new replica:

  ```
  gcloud sql instances promote-replica <<YOUR REPLICA>>
  ```

- **Maintaining Replicas**: Finally, you can check the status of a replica or delete it altogether, which of course would be an irreversible action. For doing so, treat a replica instance just as any other one and use the following command:

  ```
  gcloud instance delete <<YOUR INSTANCE>>
  gcloud instance describe <<YOUR REPLICA>>
  ```

Type 4: External Masters:

External master is a MySQL master instance, which is not a part of Cloud SQL. This arrangement has multiple uses such as increasing the reliability of your database and thus increasing ACID parameters as well. On another note, sometimes the network is not strong enough to keep updating CLoud SQL, in which case having a local master is helpful. It is important to remember that external masters are only supported by 1st generation of MySQL instances which is not the preferred choice in the most cases:

- **Prerequisites**: Before setting up an external master, you must have a working service account, billing, a cloud storage bucket, at least one replica of master instance, and binary logging set up:
- **Procedure**: First of all, create a `mysqldump` file with GTID permissions and triggers turned off:

  ```
  mysqldump --databases <<DATABASE>> -h <<INSTANCE IP>> -u
  <<USERNAME>> -p --skip-triggers --set-gtid-purged=OFF
  --default-character-set=utf8 > [SQL_FILE].sql
  ```

- Now create a CSV file from your local Cloud SQL server (external) with the following command:

```
mysql --host=<<IP>> --user=<<USER NAME>> --password <<DATABASE
NAME>> -e " SELECT * FROM <<TABLE NAME>> INTO OUTFILE
'<<FILENAME>>' CHARACTER SET 'utf8' FIELDS TERMINATED BY ','
OPTIONALLY ENCLOSED BY '"' ESCAPED BY '"' "
```

- Now, provided that you already have an external SQL server running, create a CLoud SQL internal master with the credentials to be external master. Run the following command on the Cloud Shell command line:

```
ACCESS_TOKEN="$(gcloud auth application-default print-access-
token)"
curl --header "Authorization: Bearer ${ACCESS_TOKEN}"
--header 'Content-Type: application/json'
--data '{"name": "<<CLOUD SQL MASTER INSTANCE>>",
"region": "<<REGION>>",
"databaseVersion": "DATABASE VERSION OF EXTERNAL MASTER",
"onPremisesConfiguration": {"hostPort": "<<IP>>"}}' -X POST
https://www.googleapis.com/sql/v1beta4/projects/<<PROJECT ID>
/instances
```

- Now, the internal master is created and has also been provided the credentials of external master. Once it is fully initialized, create a replica with the user account information of external master and storage details of the dump you created with cloud storage bucket:

```
curl --header "Authorization: Bearer ${ACCESS_TOKEN}"
--header 'Content-Type: application/json'
--data '{"replicaConfiguration":
{"mysqlReplicaConfiguration":
{"username": "[REPLICATION_USER]", "password": "<<REPLICA
PASSWORD>>","dumpFilePath": "[BUCKET_LOCATION]" }},
"settings": {"tier": "[TIER]","activationPolicy": "ALWAYS"},
"databaseVersion": "[EXTERNAL_MASTER_DATABASE_VERSION]",
"masterInstanceName": "[INTERNAL_MASTER_INSTANCE_NAME]",
"name": "[REPLICA_NAME]", "region": "[REGION_NAME]"}' -X POST
https://www.googleapis.com/sql/v1beta4/projects/[PROJECT-ID]/in
stancesas
```

- **High availability**: Highly available instances are the ones created under second generation configuration and a failover replica in a different zone. A new instance can be created with high availability and existing instances can be converted:

  - **New Instance**: While creating the master instance make sure to also set up the failover replica and configure the root user for the master:

    ```
    gcloud sql instances create <<MASTER INSTANCE>>
      --backup-start-time 00:00
      --failover-replica-name <<REPLICA INSTANCE>>
      --tier <<TIER TYPE>> --enable-bin-log
    ```

  - For root user configuration:

    ```
    gcloud sql users set-password root %
    --instance <<MASTER>> --password *******
    ```

  - **Existing Instance**: High availability is an option only for master instances, so in case of a replica it wouldn't work. After determining your master instance, enable automatic backup and binary logging on it:

    ```
    gcloud sql instances patch <<MASTER>> --backup-start-
    time 00:00
    gcloud sql instances patch --enable-bin-log <<MASTER
    INSTANCE>>
    ```

  - Finally, create a failover replica to turn your existing instance into a high availability instance:

    ```
    gcloud sql instances create <<REPLICA INSTANCE>>
    --master-instance-name=<<MASTER INSTANCE>>
    --replica-type=FAILOVER
    ```

Use case – managing certificates

We can connect to a Cloud SQL instance using SSL. This comes in handy when we don't want to manually access it, but want our application to access the SQL automatically. Cloud SQL uses two certificates; self-signed on server side and public/private key pair on client side for authentication. This enables encryption on the communication between Server and Client. You must have both a valid server certificate and a valid client certificate (key pair) to support encrypted communication. Use the following steps to interact with certificates:

1. Configure the instance to mandate SSL connection:

   ```
   gcloud sql instances patch bank-balance --require-ssl
   ```

2. Create an SSL certificate and store the key securely on your system or bucket if you trust the role owners:

   ```
   gcloud sql ssl-certs create bank-balance-cert client-key.pem --instance bank-balance
   ```

3. To retrieve the public key of your certificate:

   ```
   gcloud sql ssl-certs describe bank-balance-cert --instance bank-balance --format='value(cert)'
   ```

4. Create a file named `client-cert.pem` and copy the certificate completely (then paste it on it). This will be your public key:

5. To get the server certificate:

   ```
   gcloud sql instances describe bank-balance --format='value(serverCaCert.cert)'
   ```

6. Again, copy the certificate in a file named `server-ca.pem`.

7. To make these configurations active, restart the instance.

8. Now, to retrieve the client certificate:

   ```
   gcloud sql ssl-certs describe bank-balance-cert --instance bank-balance --format='value(cert)'
   ```

9. And finally, to delete the certificate:

   ```
   gcloud sql ssl-certs delete bank-balance-cert --instance bank-balance
   ```

10. Restart the instance for changes to take place.

Use case – operating Cloud SQL through VM instances

On your local machine or VM, you can connect to Cloud SQL using your local MySQL client as well. We will take Debian flavor for this use case. The following are the steps for this:

1. Install the `mysql-client`:

   ```
   sudo apt-get update
   sudo apt-get install mysql-client
   ```

2. Note your Cloud SQL instance IP and connect to your instance from your VM or local machine:

   ```
   mysql --host=[INSTANCE_IP] --user=root --password
   ```

3. The MySQL prompt will now be visible. From the steps of the previous section, we have our CA certificate, public key, as well as private key. Exit the prompt and start it again using these SSL credentials:

   ```
   mysql --ssl-ca=server-ca.pem --ssl-cert=client-cert.pem --ssl-
   key=client-key.pem
   --host=[INSTANCE_IP] --user=root --password
   ```

4. Once the MySQL prompt appears again, hit the `/s` command to verify that the connection is using SSL.

Automatic backup and restore

Automated backups are a service provided by Cloud SQL where it stores at least seven backups of the instance at any point of time. At the time of writing this book, the charges were $0.17/GB/month for SSD and $0.08 for HDD. Network egress is free if backups are stored in the same region (which is advisable if the application is not mission critical). The size of backups varies depending on changes in the SQL instance between the window of the current backup and the previous one. This means only changes are stored in the subsequent backups.

Although the default time window for backups is four hours you can ask for backups anytime on-demand. The command for it is as follows:

```
gcloud sql backups create --async --instance <<YOUR INSTANCE>>
```

For disabling automated backups of a certain instance:

```
gcloud sql instances patch [INSTANCE_NAME] --no-backup
```

For scheduling automatic backups:

```
gcloud sql instances patch [INSTANCE_NAME] --backup-start-time [HH:MM]
```

For deleting backup instance:

1. Navigate to the Cloud SQL instances page in the console and click on the **Backups** tab
2. Choose the backup that you want to remove and click on the **Options** button (three vertical lines)
3. From the drop-down menu, select the **Delete** option

For restoring backed-up data, list the available backups and select the backup that you need to restore. It is important to keep in mind that the restore process overwrites all of the current data, so if there is any progress that has not been backed-up or if the backup is too old you may lose a significant amount of data:

```
gcloud sql backups list --instance <<YOUR INSTANCE>>
gcloud sql backups restore <<INSTANCE ID>> --restore-instance=<<YOUR
INSTANCE>>
```

Cloud Spanner

Cloud Spanner is another Relational Database management service provided by GCP. This is different from Cloud SQL in many aspects, such as:

- It is a Google Proprietary technology (no open source)
- Costlier
- Stronger ACID values (ACID++)
- More reliable
- More relational
- More transaction specific
- Fully managed

You ought to pick Spanner over Cloud SQL in use cases involving the following:

- Data sizes exceeding 10 TB
- Heavy usage, with QPS (queries per second) exceeding 5K
- Users in multiple regions (spanner has replication across regions, Cloud SQL is regional)

The technology behind Cloud Spanner is cutting edge. Unlike traditional RDBMS, here rows with the same primary key (which are the most related ones in most cases of transactional applications) are brought together and converted into a new entity called a split. Each split is replicated multiple times over failure independent zones, which mostly removes the probability of data loss and also achieves geo-redundancy by default. This also reduces latency regardless of the regions. Here is an example of such a representation. All of this does make Cloud Spanner a costlier option compared to Cloud SQL but we are spared from manual scaling and managing the instance so users have to make the trade-off:

Customer_ID	Holder_Name	Acc_ID	Balance_$
1	Tom Huddleston		
Customer_ID	Holder_Name	Acc_ID	Balance_$
1	Tom Huddleston	X2135	6476
1	Tom Huddleston	2239	2344
2	Jerry Renner		
Customer_ID	Holder_Name	Acc_ID	Balance_$
2	Jerry Renner	X5658	6677
2	Jerry Renner	5546	90000
3	Popeye Sailor		
Customer_ID	Holder_Name	Acc_ID	Balance_$
3	Popeye Sailor	X7070	56
3	Popeye Sailor	0707	0278
4	Tony Stark		
Customer_ID	Holder_Name	Acc_ID	Balance_$
4	Tony Stark	X0009	5465464846
4	Tony Stark	0001	4912847192087

Split

Concept of splits can be understood more accurately with the following figure:

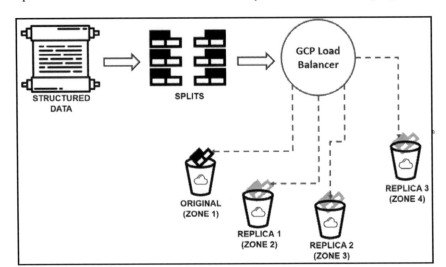

As we can see in the table, a unique customer ID is provided to each user, which acts as their primary key. User rows are arranged based on their primary key, which grants Cloud Spanner faster access to all of the fields of a single user. This also creates a parent-child relationship between rows. Each row with one field holding the primary key value is considered the parent and the other rows with the same primary key are arranged below it, which are called Child rows. The combination of parent and child rows is what exactly a split is.

Each query is attempted using a primary key, which makes the atomicity as good as absolute. These primary key based arranged rows create a split. In our case, Tony Stark or Jerry Renner are individual splits in the same schema. Coming to the next figure, each of these splits are stored individually in Cloud Storage buckets with optimum configuration (scalable SSDs forever) and is also replicated a minimum of two times.

Google assures us that each replica is stored beyond regional point of failures. So if your original split is in US, the replica may reside in Mumbai (for multi-regional nodes, more on that later). And they also assure us that there are enough replicas to avoid potential data loss. And all of this is managed by Google itself. Although generally the split shown in the figure is ideal, practically, parent-child combinations with identical primary keys (sequential mostly) end up in the same split and while making write requests and multiple writes may end up on the machine handling the same split while other zones or nodes remain idle.

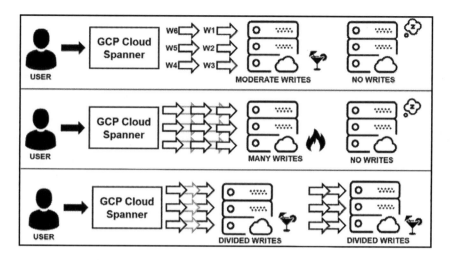

The preceding figure gives a conceptual representation of divided writes, let's look at them with the same data example.

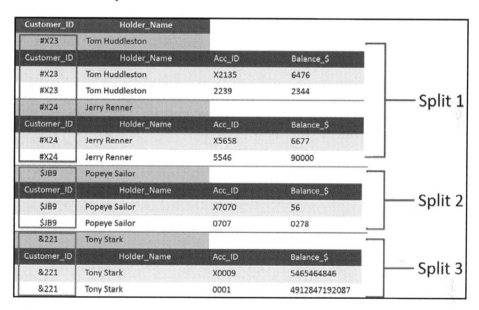

As shown in the preceding diagram and table, to avoid hotspotting on a single node or server, it is advisable to hash our primary keys in a way that they turn into different splits. This way Cloud Spanner can have proper splits due to which the operational load of write cycles can be divided equally.

Apart from this, Spanner also saves logs of each query and its outcome with precise timestamps. This is one of the aspects of Cloud Spanner that helps it in increasing the ACID values. In case of Atomicity, sometimes we do know that serialized queries are atomic, but we are not sure about their exact order of execution. In case of Cloud spanner, splits keep the queries atomic, while timestamp logs assure that they were performed in the correct order. All of this needs heavy processing and scheduling. And so, Cloud Spanner queries (or calls as they name them) are divided into three categories:

- **Locking Read-Write transactions**: These are the slowest ones. But this is the only mode that supports writing of data, so in many cases its use is inevitable. But it does not become much bothersome since in the case of OLTP, writing of data is not as latency sensitive as reading (you would gladly spend a couple more seconds in setting up your payment details for the first time, speed would be demanded while making payments where we only read credentials. Even in the case of modifying the remaining balance after a transaction, people normally wait without complaint for a few more seconds).

- **Read-only transactions**: These transactions are consistent for several reads, but do not allow to commit writes. Rather they do not commit at all! They are faster than R/W transactions and we can also read stale data (data from a timestamp in the past).

- **Single Read Calls**: While Google docs only list two types and consider this one as a special case, it is safe to list single read calls as the fastest reads among three. These calls are not treated as transactions. They only apply to single rows or splits (single or hotspotted primary key holding rows) and reads are performed in a single process. This does not count as transaction in Google's backend, so obviously no commits are made and here too, we can demand a stale read.

Now, let's play with Cloud Spanner a bit.

Creating a Cloud Spanner instance

In order to create a new instance of Cloud Spanner, follow these steps:

1. Click on the **Navigation** sidebar and choose spanner and then you will see the button to create a new instance.

2. I am going to call the instance `bank-details` and it generates an instance ID for me automatically. The instance ID is the same as my instance name. The instance ID is permanent and it will be used to identify your spanner instance. As you can see in the following screenshot, every region offers a slightly different set of features, but the consistency and throughput remains almost the same. One way to get the best of Spanner is to have multiregional nodes. Each option is also priced differently:

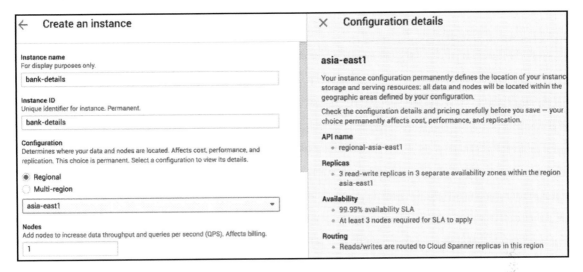

3. I am going to locate my Cloud Spanner instance in Asia. Collocating your Cloud Spanner instance to where your traffic is going to come from will make it fast.

4. Cloud Spanner is a scalable database used for mission critical applications (heavy words!). This means it has multiple nodes on which it needs to run. Typically, you will specify at least three nodes for your cloud Spanner production environment. But since we are doing it for learning purposes, I have limited the number of nodes to one.

5. Click **Create** and wait for Google to provision your Cloud Spanner instance.

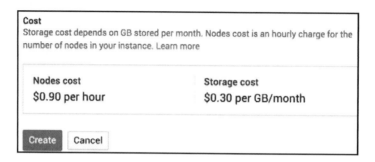

Creating a database in Cloud Spanner instances

With the following steps, we can create a database in Cloud Spanner from the GCP console itself:

1. Click the **Create Database** button.
2. We will create a database called `holder_details` and add its schema. Like previous examples, here too we have customer ID, name, account, and balance columns. We have also defined their datatypes. As you may have already noticed, all of this is happening without creating any instance.

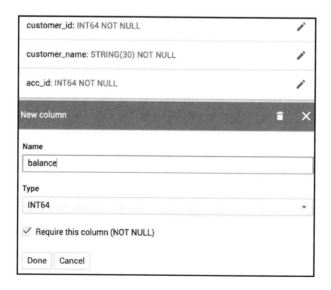

3. Once you have defined all of your columns, click on the **Create Table** button and it will lead you to the screen where you can verify your table and start adding data. There is another way of editing the schema as text where you need to set up your schema in Data Definition Language, which is pretty similar to MySQL, but is not mySQL (one of the downsides of making things proprietary you know!). You can check out the documentation for it:

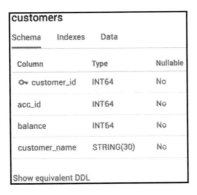

4. Notice that the customer_id as the primary key for this table is indicated by a little key icon in that particular row. We can add data in this table from the **Data** tab. Here you will find fields for all the columns and due to obvious reasons, the primary key column field cannot be left empty in any entry. In a similar way, we can enter all the data we want.

5. Another variation that you can bring to your table is to customize its key to avoid hotspotting. In this small table hotspotting should not be an issue, but for larger databases, as we discussed earlier, consecutive keys can create larger splits that create hotspotting. To avoid this, we can have a primary key and a secondary key and change their datatypes to strings.

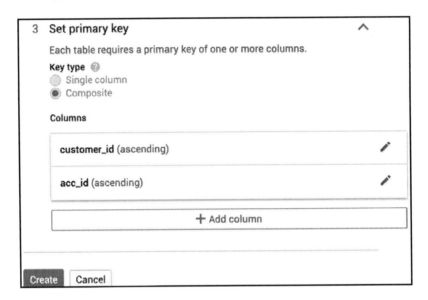

We have created the format of the composite keys, let's take a look at the outcome.

acc_id	customer_id	balance	holder_name
2239	#X23	2344	Tom Huddleston
X2135	#X23	6476	Tom Huddleston
5546	#X24	90000	Jerry Renner
X5658	#X24	6677	Jerry Renner
0707	$JB9	278	Popeye Sailor
X7070	$JB9	56	Popeye Sailor
0001	&221	4912847192087	Tony Stark
X0009	&221	5465464846	Tony Stark

Querying a database in a Cloud Spanner instance

Just like Cloud SQL, Cloud Spanner also supports standard queries. Here is an example of a standard query that will only give us Customer IDs:

1. To do it, just find a **Query** tab on the **Navigation** pane and click on it.
2. Write your query in the textbox and tap **Run** to execute it.

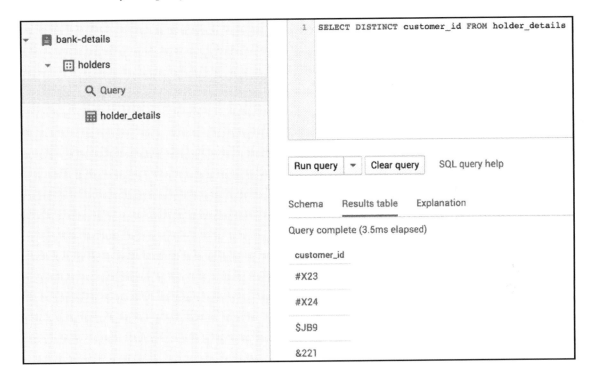

Interleaving tables in Cloud Spanner

Interleaving means creating a parent child relationship between two tables. This is done by sharing primary and/or secondary keys. The child table inherits parent's keys:

1. To do so, while creating another table, select the **Interleave in another table** option. This option will be available if you have created at least one table in the same database before. You also need to specify which table you want as the **Parent table**. Here, you can select to delete child rows with the same primary key as the parent's row. The table_2 is about whether all of the accounts have credit cards allotted to them or not, so the fields in the credit card column are Boolean.

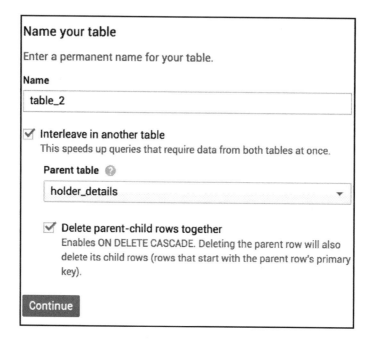

2. Once you have created the table and added data in it, you can test the parent child relationship, we will delete one row from the holders table and see whether it exists on the child table (`table_2`) or not.

We have deleted row 2239, let's see the impact on the other table.

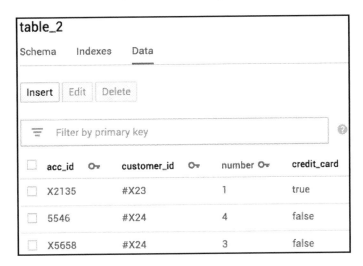

3. The row with account ID 2239, which we deleted from the parent table, is not seen in the child table either. Thus the interleaving is successful!

Summary

Having read this chapter, you should now be familiar with the concept of relational databases on the cloud, transactions, and ACID-support. You will have some clarity around how Cloud SQL can be used to set up MySQL or PostgreSQL databases on the GCP and some of the considerations in choosing between Cloud SQL and Cloud Spanner. You will also be familiar with the intricacies of replicas and backups on Cloud SQL. Finally, we have also discussed how Cloud Spanner represents a cutting-edge, Google-proprietary RDBMS that can scale horizontally to support pretty much any dataset size and level of QPS (queries-per-second).

7
NoSQL Databases

In the previous chapter, we took a closer look at the RDBMS services of GCP, Cloud SQL, and Cloud Spanner. These are great for many use cases, but there are also several situations in which they are not quite the right tool. The NoSQL offerings on the GCP, Bigtable, and Datastore might come in handy here. Bigtable is similar in many ways to Apache's HBase, while Datastore is a document database that competes with alternatives such as MongoDB.

Now, one little bit of fine print: in this chapter, we will use the terms NoSQL and RDBMS as if they are perfect alternatives; that is, it might seem like any storage solution that is not an RDBMS is a NoSQL database. That's not quite strictly true. BigQuery, for instance, is a SQL-compliant data warehouse, which is certainly not an RDBMS. So, the term NoSQL really only means that the data is not accessed via SQL; the alternative could be either:

- Product-specific syntax (such as the scan syntax in HBase)
- Programmatic access (from a programming language such as Java or Python)

Relational databases use tables, columns, rows, or schemas to store and retrieve data. NoSQL databases do not use these structures since they opt for more flexible data models, such as documents or rows of key/value pairs (for example graph stores which store social connections as key-value pairs). Popular expansions of NoSQL include *not SQL* or *not only SQL*. Relational databases have important limitations that make them unsuitable for semi-structured data. Common types of semi-structured data include user and session data; chat, messaging, and log data; time series data such as IoT and device data; and large objects such as video and images.

Let's start with an understanding of the internal data representation in a couple of important types of NoSQL databases—but first, a small digression!

A Random Childhood Reminiscence

When I was a little child, I'd have chores assigned to me, and one of them was to wake up bright and early each morning and buy a dozen eggs from a mom-and-pop store nearby.

That mom-and-pop store was a very small one, run by a couple who knew exactly where everything was in their little store. No matter what you wanted, they'd reach an arm out and get it in a moment. But because they were rather set in their ways of doing things, if you tried to return something to a shelf because you didn't want it, they'd take a while to figure out where it went.

As you'd expect, the Mom and Pop who ran the store were not very tech-savvy. They'd enter each item you bought into a document in a big old-fashioned notebook.

Mom and Pop were very nice people - if a loyal customer was running low on cash, they'd sell stuff on credit. But they were very intelligent, and you'd underestimate them at your peril. If the situation demanded it, they could be very tough and transaction too.

We loved the store for a few other reasons as well - stuff was cheap there, and the old couple would never hassle you to set up a membership card or anything like that. You just walked in, bought what you wanted, and left.

A few months each year, Mom and Pop would shut the store down and head out to spend some time with their children who were settled abroad. The store was very easy to shut down.

This digression above is meant to help us remember all that we really need to know about Datastore. Here is the same text, now annotated to make it relevant to NoSQL databases!

Mom-and-Pop _Store_ ~ Data_store_

When I was a little child, I'd have chores assigned to me, and one of them was to wake up bright and early each morning and buy a dozen eggs from a mom-and-pop store nearby.

That mom-and-pop store was a very small one (Datastore is great for the small end of big data - data order of TB, not PB), run by a couple who knew exactly where everything was in their little store. No matter what you wanted, they'd reach an arm out and get it in a moment. (Datastore's big attraction is fast lookup achieved by indexing basically along every column. So query time is pretty much independent of dataset size) But because they were rather set in their ways of doing things, if you tried to return something to a shelf because you didn't want it, they'd take a while to figure out where it went. (Fast lookup is achieved via hash indices, and these have the trade-off that insertion becomes slow)

As you'd expect, the Mom and Pop who ran the store were not very tech-savvy. They'd enter each item you bought into a document in a big old-fashioned notebook (Datastore is a document database, suitable for XML-like hierarchical data).

Mom and Pop were very nice people - if a loyal customer was running low on cash, they'd sell stuff on credit. But they were very intelligent, and you'd underestimate them at your peril. If the situation demanded it, they could be very tough and transaction too. (Datastore supports transactions, but you can also use it in a non-transactional manner)

We loved the store for a few other reasons as well - stuff was cheap there (Datastore is a lot more economical than BigTable, the other NoSQL option on the GCP), and the old couple would never hassle you to set up a membership card or anything like that. You just walked in, bought what you wanted, and left. (Datastore is serverless - you never need to provision a server or specify a number of nodes)

A few months each year, Mom and Pop would shut the store down and head out to spend some time with their children who were settled abroad. The store was very easy to shut down. (Scaling down to zero is easy thanks to the serverless nature of the technology)

Now, once we've gotten the essential attributes of Datastore into our heads, remembering the essential characteristics of Bigtable is a lot easier; check out this table given below:

Datastore	Bigtable
Datastore is great for the small end of big data; data order of TB, not PB.	Bigtable is definitely meant for the big end of Big Data; order of several TB or PB. If the data size < 10 TB, performance is not great.
Datastore's big attraction is fast lookup...	Bigtable is best for high-speed scans (all rows, or all rows satisfying a condition) along a single column.

...achieved by indexing basically along every column.	Bigtable effectively only indexes along the row key; what is more, it also sorts data by the row key.
Fast lookup is achieved via hash indices, and these have the trade-off that insertion becomes slow.	Bigtable is the best game in town if you need fast and frequent writes; insertion is very fast (updates along row key are slow though).
Query time is pretty much independent of dataset size.	Both queries and updates specified using the row key are super-fast (order of milliseconds!), while operations on other columns are slow.
Datastore is a document database, suitable for XML-like hierarchical data.	Bigtable has a data model similar to columnar databases like HBase and works best for very large data with a clear sort order.
Datastore supports transactions, but you can also use it in a non-transactional manner.	Bigtable is ACID at the row-level, and only supports eventual consistency.
Datastore is a lot more economical than BigTable, the other NoSQL option on the GCP.	Bigtable can get costly as the cluster size grows.
Datastore is serverless; you never need to provision a server or specify a number of nodes.	Bigtable requires explicit provisioning of a cluster, and choices about the kind of disks in VMs in that cluster.
Scaling down to zero is easy thanks to the serverless nature of the technology.	Scaling down to zero is hard, as with any service that involves a cluster.

NoSQL databases

Now that we have gotten right to the essential attributes of the two main NoSQL services on the GCP, let's understand how their internal data models differ from traditional RDBMS. As an example, consider the relational representation of simple data about individuals in this relational table called **Persons**:

Persons			
PersonID	Name	Age	Salary
P1	John	32	$400000
P2	Johnny	33	$410000
P3	Janet	31	$400000
P4	Jeremy	32	$450000
P5	Justin	33	$600000
P6	Jazmyn	35	$250000
P7	Judy	30	$900000
P8	Jolly	33	$100000
P9	Jack	31	$120000

If we had additional information about the children and pets of these individuals, we would have additional tables and each of those tables would reference the `PersonID` field of the `Persons` table as the foreign key. That would lead to a fairly typical star-schema:

Children			
PersonID	Name	Birthday	Height
P1	Susan	01-01-2006	4'1"

Pets			
PersonID	Name	Age	Breed
P1	Tom	6	Siberian Husky

Here is how the same data would be represented in a few different types of NoSQL databases:

- **Key-value data stores**: Each individual column and the associated value would be stored as a key-value pair. Redis, for instance, is a key-value store, and so is Memcache on the Google Cloud Platform. Key-value stores are optimized for queries of the form *please give me the value corresponding to this particular key.*

Unstructured Data: Key-value	
Kid_Name	Suzan
Kid_Birthday	01-01-2006
Kid_Height	4.1
Person 1_Name	John
Person 1_Age	32
Person 1_Salary	400000
Dog_Name	Tommy
Dog_Age	6
Dog_Breed	Siberian_Husky

- **Document stores**: This time, rather than storing individual key-value pairs for each column, the entire document is stored in the database. The whole point of document stores is that they are able to perform extremely fast hierarchical queries; document stores are optimized for queries of the form *please give me the value at this particular path from the root node of the document.* Such hierarchical queries are common in JavaScript, for instance, where the programmer uses the **document object model (DOM)** to parse elements in the HTML:

Unstructured Data: Document Store	
Parameters	file
Subject, Names, age, salaries, Birthday, Pet Height, Pet Age, Pet Breed, Kid Age...	Unstructured_data.csv

- **Wide-column stores**: These are an entirely different beast from the two other categories we discussed. The emphasis here is on flexible schemas and data sorted on a particular key, called the row key:

Columnar Data Representation: Persons, Pets, Children			
Row Key	Column Family	Column Name	Value
Person1	PersonalInfo	Age	John
Person1	PersonalInfo	Salary	32
Person1	PersonalInfo	Name	$400,000
Person1	ChildInfo	Name	Susan
Person1	ChildInfo	Birthday	01-01-2006
Person1	ChildInfo	Height	4'1"
Person1	PetInfo	Name	Tommy
Person1	PetInfo	Age	6
Person1	PetInfo	Breed	Siberian Husky
Person2	PersonalInfo	Age	John
Person2	PersonalInfo	Salary	32
Person3	PersonalInfo	Age	John
Person3	PersonalInfo	Salary	32

This table is key to understanding the differences between relational and columnar databases, so let's pay some more attention to it:

- In the columnar world, column family ~ table/relation
- Dynamic schemas: Columns can be added on the fly without expensive DDL operations such as `ALTER TABLE`
- Less redundancy: Default values or NULLs need not be in the data at all
- No normalization: The previous format has no foreign keys, and violates just about every normal form (Boyce and Codd would be turning in their graves looking at this)
- In reality, each value is timestamped, so it is also possible to retrieve specific versions of a particular data item.

- For this reason, this data model is said to be four-dimensional; any data item can be accessed if we have four pieces of information: row key, column family, column name and timestamp
- Data is stored in sorted order of row key; this is a very important point to keep in mind

The Google Cloud Platform offers two options for those of us who'd like to store their data in non-relational, distributed, and horizontally scalable structures:

- Cloud Bigtable
- Datastore

In this chapter, we will explore the implementation, features, and functionalities of both of these NoSQL storage options, starting with Bigtable, Google's alternative to HBase.

Cloud Bigtable

Cloud Bigtable is Google's NoSQL wide-column database service similar in use case to Hadoop's HBase. It serves as the database that powers many core Google services such as Search, Analytics, Maps, and Gmail. It is a compressed, high performance, and proprietary data storage system built on top of a few Google technologies such as the Google File System, Chubby Lock Service, and SSTable.

Google describes Bigtable as a *sparsely populated table that can scale to billions of rows and thousands of columns*. Bigtable was designed to support applications requiring massive scalability and was intended to be used with petabytes of data. The database was designed to be deployed on clustered systems and uses a simple data model, which is the wide column store.

Data is assembled in order by row key, which is a single value in each row, and indexing of the map is arranged according to row, column keys, and timestamps. It is also sensitive to hot spotting and hence the key structure design has to be done carefully. According to Google, Cloud Bigtable is ideal as a data source for MapReduce operations and a storage for very large amounts of single-keyed data with very low latency, as it supports high read and write throughput at low latency. BigTable is exposed to applications via a gRPC API and an HBase-compatible API in Java.

There are several key advantages of BigTable over a self-managed HBase installation:

- **Scalability**: You can scale your cluster up to handle more queries by increasing your machine count, as opposed to a self-managed HBase installation which has a design bottleneck that limits performance after a certain QPS is reached.
- **Simple administration**: Cloud Bigtable handles upgrades and restarts transparently, as well as automatically maintaining high data durability, unlike HBase which requires managing masters, regions, clusters, or nodes.
- **Cluster resizing without downtime**: The size of your Cloud Bigtable cluster can be increased for a few hours to handle a large load, then reduced again, all without any downtime. It typically takes just a few minutes under load for Cloud Bigtable to balance performance across all of the nodes in your cluster, after you change a cluster's size.

Fundamental properties of Bigtable

Following are the fundamental properties of Bigtable:

- HBase is a wide-column data store (similar conceptually to the columnar data stores described before)
- Data is stored in sorted order of row key; this is equivalent to indexing along a single column (the row key)
- It supports denormalized storage
- Focuses on CRUD operations
- The only operations where ACID properties (that is, Atomicity, Consistency, Isolation, and Durability) are guaranteed are row level operations

Let's understand each of these properties in detail.

Columnar datastore

A columnar database is a **database management system (DBMS)** that stores data in columns instead of rows. Here, all the column one values are physically together, followed by all the column two values, and so on. The data is stored in record order, so the 100th entry for column one and the 100th entry for column two belong to the same input record. This allows individual data elements, such as customer name for instance, to be accessed in columns as a group, rather than individually row by row.

Say you have the data from a notification service in an e-commerce website. Notifications will have properties like ID, recipient, the notification type (an offer or a sale notification), and the message content. In a traditional relational database, we would store this data in the form of a table with four rows and a number of columns.

In a columnar data store, there would only be three columns and these three columns would map to the columns of our relational data as illustrated in the following figure. The first would be an ID column, which would be common between the columnar data store and the relational database representation. The second column in the columnar data store is a column identifier, which will contain the values that correspond to the columns from the relational database. Effectively, what we have done is we have encoded the columns from the RDBMS as the fields in the columnar data store. To complete the representation of any one row of data, we are going to need to add columns corresponding to each of the cell values from the RDBMS tuple. Every row from the relational database now has multiple rows in the columnar store. In fact, it has one row for each column from the RDBMS.

In addition, the columnar data store is also not normalized. To make up for this, the columnar data store has a couple of powerful advantages.

The first has to do with the ease with which it handles sparse data. If you have data with lots of null values, you wouldn't be wasting much space. Having an extremely large dataset with lots of empty values in each row becomes a real problem as the datasets explode in size. This is where columnar stores come in handy as we simply do not have rows corresponding to null values. The other has to do with the dynamic nature of attributes or columns. In a columnar datastore, columns can be added dynamically without changing the schema, unlike RDBMS where the alter table operation—with a significant penalty—would be required for the same.

Denormalization

We have already discussed how storage in columnar datastores doesn't fit into the traditional definitions of normalization. In traditional RDBMSs, minimizing redundancy is an important objective, which gave rise to the different normal forms. Normalization in traditional database design was largely driven by the need to save space, which in turn was driven by the monolithic nature of database servers. As distributed databases came along, the bandwidth became the bottleneck. Your normalized data could end up storing related data items in distant nodes. Even if you saved a few bytes, if you had to access the network three times instead of once, that would give terrible performance. Consequently, in the distributed world, disk seeks are expensive rather than storage, as we have a large number of generic machines, each with a lot of attached storage. What is really costly in a distributed filesystem is making lots of disk seeks to servers or to data that resides on different machines. This is why columnar data stores do away with the idea of normalization. Data is stored such that all the data for one entity resides together.

Support for ACID properties

BigTable only supports ACID properties at the raw level. Recall that ACID stands for Atomicity, Consistency, Isolation, and Durability, which is transaction support as provided by a traditional RDBMS. Any operations you carry out that affect a particular row ID will either affect all of the columns corresponding to that column or none. But, this only extends as far as a single row is concerned. Updates to multiple rows are not atomic as the worldview of the columnar data store is restricted to groups of data with the same row ID:

Traditional RDBMS	Bigtable
Data arranged in rows and columns	Data arranged in columns
Supports SQL	NoSQL database with its own syntax
Complex queries such as grouping, aggregates, and joins	Only basic operations such as create, read, update, and delete
Table schemas are static and hard to change	Schemas are dynamic and easy to change
Keys and foreign key constraints are enforced during writes	No foreign key constraints; key constraint only on row key
Normalized storage to minimize redundancy and optimize space	Denormalized storage to minimize disk seeks
ACID compliant	ACID compliant at the row level

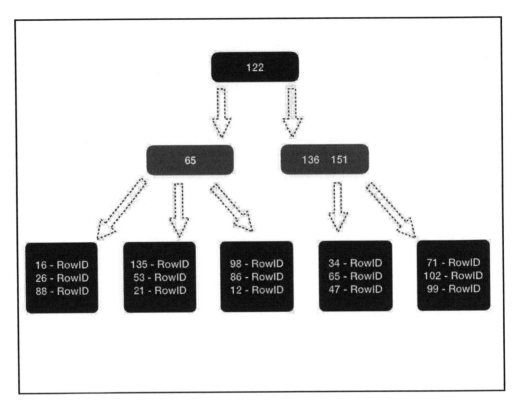

Now contrast this architecture with that of a B-tree index. The similarities are unmistakable:

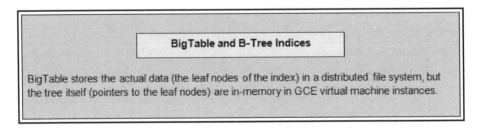

BigTable and B-Tree Indices

BigTable stores the actual data (the leaf nodes of the index) in a distributed file system, but the tree itself (pointers to the leaf nodes) are in-memory in GCE virtual machine instances.

While working with Bigtable, I find it really helps to keep in mind the architectural representation. Going back to our story about the mom-and-pop store, we mentioned that Datastore can be thought of as a set of hash indices (fast lookup) along every column. In contrast, Bigtable can be thought of as a single giant B-tree index along just one column.

Now, as the previous diagram shows, they store the actual data in the leaf nodes (and that data is in sorted order). The non-leaf nodes that constitute the tree help find the data to pull:

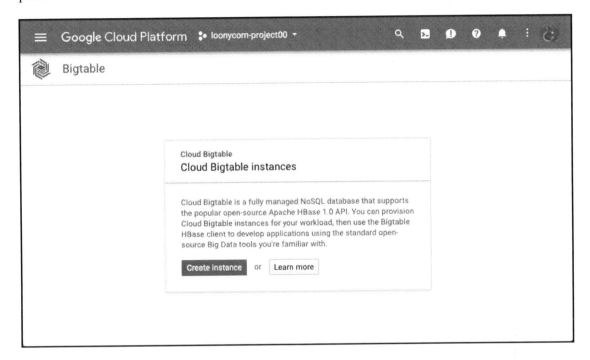

This really is a key insight, and once we get this, a bunch of little details start to make sense:

- **Auto-tuning**: Bigtable uses some ML-like algorithms internally and moves around the pointers from the different VMs in response to traffic patterns. This reduces hot-spotting and is only possible because the pointers are being moved around, not the data itself.
- **Cluster Nodes**: When we create a Bigtable cluster we have to specify how many nodes we'd like. Those nodes effectively are the GCE VMs from the previous diagram.
- **SSD or HDD**: While provisioning a Bigtable cluster, the choice of SSD versus HDD makes a big difference. That's because the pointers are retrieved from these disks on the GCE VMs. Clearly SSD disks are way faster for random access, and that's why this choice matters.

Working with Bigtable

In this section, we will discuss the advantages and implementation details of Bigtable. We will also take a look at what it is good for and when to use it.

When to use Bigtable

Avoid Bigtable under the following set of circumstances:

- Do not use Bigtable if you require transaction support because, as we have already discussed, Bigtable will only offer row-level ACID guarantees and that is just not enough. Use Cloud SQL or Cloud Spanner if you need to carry out OLTP.

- Do not use Bigtable if your data size is going to be less than 1 TB. That's because Bigtable needs to do a set of smart optimizations related to sharding and distributed storage, and you just won't be able to do that if your dataset is too small.

- Do not use Bigtable if you plan to use Analytics, Business Intelligence, or data warehousing use cases. BigQuery is a better option as BigQuery supports an SQL-like interface that many data analysts are familiar with, as well as complex types of queries such as partitioning and windowing operators. All of these are really important in OLAP (Online Analytics processing) which is used for Business Intelligent operations. OLAP involves complex calculation and multidimensional analysis of statistical and business data.

- Do not use Bigtable for very highly structured or hierarchical data. That is more in the realm of document-oriented databases such as Datastore on GCP, or MongoDB or CouchDB if you are not on GCP. Bigtable requires a key value relationship at least around the row ID. Hence, using it for immutable data like blobs or media files does not make sense.

Let's now talk about the cases where Bigtable excels:

- The first and obvious one has to do with very fast scanning with low latency, high throughput applications where you would be scanning on sequential row IDs.

- Think of Bigtable any time you have non-structured but key/value data. Because it is non-structured, relational databases won't work and if there are multiple keys, think of a document-oriented database like Datastore.

- Here are some further guidelines on the types of data size. Use Bigtable when each data item is less than 10 MB and the total dataset size is greater than 1 TB.
- If you have write operations that are very infrequent or not important, and you don't care about ACID support but you care about fast scans, or if you are using time series data, use BigTable, as different timestamps can be used as a part of the row key.

Solving hot-spotting

Recall that while talking about the row key in the four-dimensional data model, we mentioned that data is stored in sorted lexicographic order of the row key. This is similar to Cloud Spanner. Data is sharded based on those key values, so that data that has the same key value will be grouped together. This implies that performance will be really poor if all of the reads and writes end up being concentrated in some particular shards or some ranges of the key values. A classic example is if sequential key values are used. There are some fairly typical techniques to solve hot-spotting, one of which is field promotion.

Here, the idea is that you use a structured key that is arranged in a reverse URL order, like a Java package name, for instance. Thus, keys will have similar prefixes but they will have different endings. If the sequential scan is based on some subset of the key prefix, all of the related values will be picked in one go. Reverse URL order is a pretty standard way of arranging keys in HBase.

The other common way of avoiding hotspots is salting, which is the descriptive term for the practice of hashing the key value. A surprising feature of Bigtable, colloquially known as warming the cache, is the fact that Bigtable will tend to improve in performance over time. The reason for this is that Bigtable observes the read and write patterns in your data and then redistributes the data in smart ways so that those reads and writes are evenly distributed over all of the shards of the distributed partitions. Bigtable is more proactive about moving data around in order to eliminate hotspots. An important implication of this is that if you are testing the performance of your Bigtable system, you need the test to last for several hours in order to get a true sense of the performance. If you run an inordinately short test of maybe half an hour or less, it wouldn't give Bigtable enough time to carry out all of the smart data movements to eliminate a hotspot and you will get a misleadingly poor indication of performance.

Choosing storage for Bigtable

Another decision to make while designing your Bigtable implementation is whether you want SSD or HDD disks. The simple rule of thumb is to use SSDs unless you are really operating on a shoestring budget. SSDs can be up to 20 times faster than ordinary hard disks on individual row reads, although that advantage is a lot less when you are considering batch reads and sequential scans. Another advantage of SSDs is that they are more predictable in terms of their throughput. This gives Bigtable room to learn and predict how it is going to operate. If the performance is very variable, that could throw Bigtable's calculations off. Consider using ordinary persistent disks only if your data size exceeds 10 TB and if your common usage pattern is only for batch queries. The greater the proportion of random access that you perform in your Bigtable, the stronger the case for SSD. If all of your data usage takes the form of random access, then Bigtable may not be the right tool for you. You should be looking at a document-oriented database such as Datastore instead.

Solving performance issues

Because Bigtable is rather complicated, reasons for its poor performance are often hard to find. Here are some pointers that might help you if you are suffering from a badly performing Bigtable:

- The first place to look would be at the schema design. Check if you have sequential keys causing hot-spotting, or causing the reads and writes to be concentrated in some specific shards. Some obvious keys to avoid are numeric sequences like 1011, 1012, 1013 and so on.
- The next set of possible causes has to do with inappropriate workloads. Maybe your dataset is too small, less than 300 GB. That is not enough for Bigtable to really show its talents. Bigtable is best used when there is more than 1 TB of data and it can be used up to petabytes in size.
- Another possible problem has to do with the usage pattern. Your queries may be running in short bursts. Bigtable performs best when it has hours of observations to tune performance internally.
- There are also some of the usual suspects, for instance maybe your cluster is just too small.
- Another possibility is that your cluster has just been fired up or just been scaled up. In either one of these cases, it is going to take some time for Bigtable to understand the patterns and allocate the newly added resources optimally.
- It might also be a case of you using HDDs instead of SSDs.

Ideal row key choices

Bigtable does a lot more in production than it does in development. Schema design is very important with Bigtable. Recall that each table has just the one index, the row key. Hence, you will need to choose that index well. Unlike in Datastore or Cloud Spanner, you don't have the luxury of picking multiple indices per table.

Next, recall that row keys are going to be sorted lexicographically and rows will be arranged in that order. Hence, you will need to be smart about your choice of row key. Do not use patterns like a sequentially increasing integer count.

All operations are atomic, that is, ACID properties are supported only at the row level. Multi-row operations are not ACID guaranteed. The beauty of the four dimensional data model means that related entities will be stored in adjacent rows and this can give rise to the really fast sequential scanning performance that we hope for from Bigtable.

Using reverse domain names is the first choice that should jump to mind. String identifiers are fine as well because they will typically hash evenly. And lastly, use timestamps but only as key suffixes. Do not include timestamps as the first or the prefix portion of your key. This is likely to be a sequentially increasing field in order of insertion and that will cause hot-spotting.

In the list of row keys to avoid, first is regular domain names rather than reverse domain names, as it will cause adjacent values to not be logically related. A similar problem is sequential numeric values that cause hot-spotting. It's usually a pretty bad idea to use timestamps alone as the row IDs and it's also a bad idea to use row keys that are prefixed by timestamps. As data storage is so tied to row key values, do not use as row keys fields that are likely to be changed repeatedly. A good example of row key can be something like `com.loonycorn.topics` which would not cause hot-spotting and is least likely to change as well. Plus the reverse domain order makes sure to avoid conflicts with organisation or domain names.

Ideally, your row key should be immutable. Bigtable also have some recommendations for different size limits. Your row keys should not exceed 4 KB per key value. You should not have more than a hundred column families. Individual column value should not exceed about 10 MB in size and the total row size should not exceed about 100 MB. All in all, Bigtable has a complicated set of performance considerations and these are complicated for a good reason. They are tied to the equally complicated underlying physical representation of the data store that Bigtable uses.

Performing operations on Bigtable

This section will walk you through creating a BigTable instance and leveraging it for storage:

1. Move to Bigtable in your side navigation menu and click on **Create instance**:

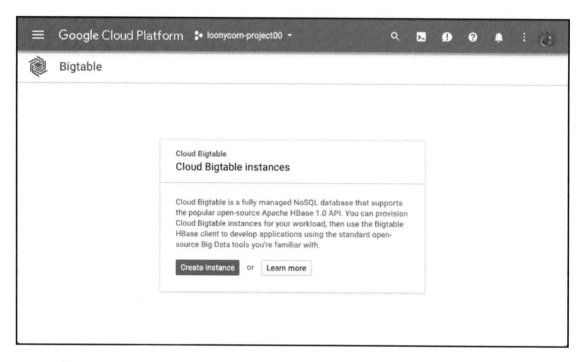

2. The web console will as usual make things very easy for you and walk you through creating a new Bigtable instance. Give the instance a name, which is just for display purposes. The instance ID is permanent and will be used to refer to the instance.

3. At this point, you have two choices. You can choose a production instance, which is what is recommended. We are setting up a real web app which is going to serve real traffic. This needs a minimum of three nodes and it's highly available. Once you set up this instance though, you cannot downgrade it later. You need to keep it or delete it if you no longer need it. If you are just playing around with Bigtable in order to understand it, you can choose the development instance. It has a lower cost and it is meant for development. It's not highly available, but you can upgrade it to a production instance later.

4. In addition to an instance ID, you need to specify a cluster ID as well for Bigtable. This too is permanent and there are some constraints on what characters a cluster ID can accept.

5. Specify the zone where you want your instance to be located.

6. Next, you have a choice here as to the kind of storage your Bigtable instance should use. You can choose the high performance, low latency SSD. That's what is recommended. Or if you have huge datasets, want to lower your storage cost, and don't care about latency, you can choose an HDD to store your data:

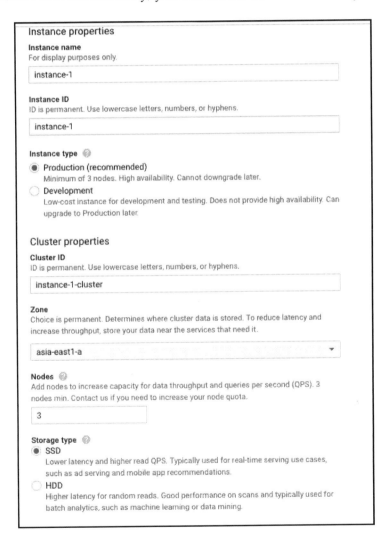

7. Click on **Create** and it will go ahead and create a Bigtable instance for you.

8. Google Cloud Platform provides you an HBase shell where you can use HBase commands to connect and work with Bigtable. In order to use the HBase shell, you need to download the Google Cloud Bigtable quick start from this URL: `https://storage.googleapis.com/cloud-bigtable/quickstart/GoogleCloudBi gtable-Quickstart-1.0.0-pre4.zip`.

9. Unzip the file. This zip file has a script that can quickly set you up with the HBase shell then allow you to connect to your Bigtable instance. Of course performing all of this on cloud shell will spare you a lot of file-moving-around.

10. Note that there is a quickstart folder that has been created in your current working directory. In that folder, we will run the script to connect to Bigtable using the HBase Shell. This script will work only if we have a Bigtable instance set up. You can run 'gcloud beta bigtable instances list' and see the list of Bigtable instances that you have.

11. This script works under three conditions:
    - You are authenticated and logged in using Google oauth login
    - You have a default project set up
    - You have a Bigtable instance set up

12. Simply run *quickstart* using the `./quickstart.sh` command and it will take you to the HBase Shell. If you are familiar with the HBase Shell, what you are going to see will be very straightforward for you. You can run the `list` command to see what tables you have set up within Bigtable.

Creating and operating an HBase table using Cloud Bigtable

You can use the create command to create an employee table, and within it we will add a column family: personal. As Bigtable is a columnar store where all columns are logically grouped into column families, a table should have at least one column family.

Running the list command now should confirm that exactly one table, the employee, table has been set up, as shown here:

```
hbase(main):002:0> create 'employee', 'personal'
0 row(s) in 0.7850 seconds

=> Hbase::Table - employee
hbase(main):003:0> list
TABLE
employee
1 row(s) in 0.2490 seconds

=> ["employee"]
```

1. To insert our first row into this table, we will need to specify a row key, the column family, and the name of the column where this insert should occur. The row key uniquely identifies a row and is used to index all the columns and column values that are present in one row. It is this index row key that allows very fast lookup operations and quick scan operations in HBase and Bigtable. When we insert a value in a particular row we need to specify. Say, the row key is 12345, *Personal* is the column family that we set up, name is the column name and Jane is the value. The command would then be

    ```
    put 'employee', '12345', 'personal:name', 'Jane'.
    ```

2. We can add the other values for the same row as well using `put` statements, within employee, with the same row key 12345. Let us say Jane lives in the state of Texas and add that information to the table, using this command:

    ```
    put 'employee', '12345', 'personal:state', 'Texas'
    ```

3. Let's add another employee, Dana, with a different row key, repeating this set of commands.

4. Running the command `scan 'employee'` in this HBase Shell will list all the information in the employee table, as shown here:

```
hbase(main):008:0> scan 'employee'
ROW                          COLUMN+CELL
 12345                       column=personal:name, timestamp=1512623595860, value=Jane
 12345                       column=personal:state, timestamp=1512623532601, value=Texas
 12346                       column=personal:name, timestamp=1512623571336, value=Dana
 12346                       column=personal:state, timestamp=1512623585555, value=LA
2 row(s) in 0.5920 seconds
```

This table has just two rows of information, which we added in this session. The row keys are repeated because there are two columns' worth of data. On the right-hand side for every row key we can see the name of the column family and the name of the column. Each of these values is associated with the timestamps. This forms the versioning information for these Bigtable values. We have the value for each of these columns, name, and state. If you want to delete this table, you simply run the `drop 'employee'` command, after disabling it.

Exporting/Importing a table from Cloud Bigtable

Execute the following steps to export or import a table from Cloud Bigtable:

1. To export a table from Cloud Bigtable, first we need to identify its column families. To do so, first install the `cbt` utility:

   ```
   gcloud components update
   gcloud components install cbt
   ```

2. Use the `cbt` tool to list out the column families and determine which column families you want to export:

   ```
   cbt -instance <<INSTANCE_ID>> ls <<TABLE_NAME>>
   ```

3. Create a Cloud Storage Bucket using the `gsutil mb` command.

4. Now, the table will be exported as sequence files. To export them, download and install import/export jar for Bigtable using this URL:

   ```
   curl -f -O
   http://repo1.maven.org/maven2/com/google/cloud/bigtable/bigtabl
   e-beam-import/1.1.2/bigtable-beam-import-1.1.2-shaded.jar
   ```

5. Run the following command and replace <<Export_path>> and <<Temp_Path>> as per your requirement:

   ```
   java -jar bigtable-beam-import-1.1.2-shaded.jar export
       --runner=dataflow
       --project=<<Project_ID>>
       --bigtableInstanceId=<<INSTANCE_ID>>
       --bigtableTableId=<<TABLE_ID>>
       --destinationPath=gs://<<BUCKET_NAME>>/<<EXPORT_PATH>>
       --tempLocation=gs://<<BUCKET_NAME>>/<<TEMP_PATH>>
       --maxNumWorkers=<<10x_NUMBER_OF_NODES>>
   ```

6. Similarly, to import a table into Cloud Bigtable, use the following command:

```
java -jar bigtable-beam-import-1.1.2-shaded.jar import
  --runner=dataflow
  --project=<<PROJECT_ID>>
  --bigtableInstanceId=<<INSTANCE_ID>>
  --bigtableTableId=<<TABLE_ID>>
  --sourcePattern='gs://<<BUCKET_NAME>>/<<EXPORT_PATH>>/part-*'
  --tempLocation=gs://<<BUCKET_NAME>>/<<TEMP_PATH>>
  --maxNumWorkers=<<5x_NUMBER_OF_NODES>>
```

Scaling GCP Cloud BigTable

There are times when we have to provision automatic scaling of our NoSQL database due to parameters like the following:

- The cluster's CPU load
- The number of nodes in the cluster
- The distribution of server request latencies for a table

To do this programmatically, we can use either Java or Python sample tools. We will see how to do it using Java sample tool. To use them, use the following procedures:

Java:

- This tool is built on Apache Maven. If it is not installed on your shell, download it from `https://maven.apache.org/download.cgi` and extract it.
- Run `mnv -v` in a new shell instance to confirm its installation.
- Now, to build the sample tool, run:

```
mvn clean compile mvn exec:java -
Dexec.mainClass="com.example.bigtable.scaler.MetricScaler" -
Dexec.args="<project-id> <bigtable-instance-id>"
```

The sample tool mentioned above adds or removes nodes when CPU load goes above or below a specified threshold. The `project-id` and `bigtable-instance-id` tags make sure that it is our very instance which will autoscale.

The Google Cloud Datastore

The Google Cloud Datastore is a fully managed NoSQL database service, built upon Google's Bigtable and Megastore technology, to support automatic scaling, high performance, and ease of application development.

Datastore is something that we turn to when we are looking for document-oriented storage in a NoSQL database. This is something that datastore offers in competition with other products such as MongoDB and CouchDB. Cloud Datastore features are best remembered via the story at the start of the chapter, so please do go back and read it if you skipped past it the first time.

Comparison with traditional databases

In a traditional RDBMS, you have atomic transactions, which is true for Datastore as well. Datastore does support atomic transactions and the ACID properties, mostly due to the need to keep all of the internal indices consistent. Both traditional RDBMS and Datastore make heavy use of indices for fast lookup. But in Datastore, every query makes use of indices, which is far beyond what traditional RDBMS do. Consequently, the query execution time in Datastore is basically independent of the size of the underlying dataset, which is certainly not the case with traditional RDBMSs.

Traditional RDBMS use relational data, that is, rows and columns, but without many hierarchical relationships within those entity relations. Datastore on the other hand is document-oriented, which implies it is optimized for hierarchically structured data such as XML or HTML. It has the form of a tree in its internal representation, like the **document object model (DOM)** in an HTML document.

There is also a slight change in terminology in terms of what rows, columns, and attributes are called. In a relational database, rows are stored in tables. In a document database, entities are of different kinds. The word *entity* corresponds to a row and *kind* corresponds to *table*. Note the absence of the word *stored*. Because entities are of different kinds, entities are not really stored in kinds. For example, consider HTML tags: a HEAD tag or a BODY tag would be an entity in a document data store. Rows consist of fields in a traditional RDBMS while entities consist of properties in a datastore. If you have a HEAD tag with some nested tags, those are the properties.

Traditional databases have primary keys as a unique ID. In Datastore, the word primary is not used, but you refer to them as keys.

In a traditional RDBMS, all rows of the same table need to have the same schema or the same properties. In other words, they will have the same number of columns and those columns will be all of the same type. In contrast, it's perfectly acceptable for different entities of the same kind to have different properties. For instance, you may have two HTML documents, with a `head` tag each. Inside one of the head tags is a body while the other does not have any body tags at all. This is accepted in a document-oriented store.

This applies to types as well. In a relational database, all of the values in a particular column must have the same type. On the contrary, Datastore types of different properties with the same name can be different. Say you have two XML documents with a `body` tag each and inside one of them, and the `body` tag has another property called ID, which is an integer. The other `body` tag also has a property called ID but it happens to be a string, which is absolutely acceptable in a document-oriented store.

Datastore also differs from traditional databases in which operations it will and will not support. For instance, unlike traditional relational databases, a data store does not support joins, filtering on subqueries, or more than one inequality filter in a query. This table summarizes the comparison between traditional DBMS and the Cloud Datastore concisely:

Traditional RDBMS	DataStore
Atomic transactions	Atomic transactions
Indices for fast lookup	Indices for fast lookup on every column
Some queries use indices	All queries use indices
Query time depend on both size of dataset and size of result set	Query time independent of dataset, depends on result set alone
Structured relational data	Structured hierarchical data (XML, HTML)
Rows stored in tables	Entities of different kinds
Rows consist of fields	Entities consist of properties
Primary keys for unique ID	Keys for unique ID
Rows of table have same properties (schema is strongly enforced)	Entities of a kind can have different properties
Types of all values in a column are the same	Types of different properties with same name in an entity can be different

Working with Datastore

In this section, we will understand the ideal set of circumstances that should warrant the use of Cloud Datastore, when not to use Datastore, and the ideal design choices to make when using Datastore.

When to use Datastore

Here is a list of scenarios where you probably shouldn't choose Datastore as your storage option:

- Don't use Datastore if you need very strong transaction support. If you are doing hardcore OLTP, you should use something like Cloud Spanner.
- If you want basic ACID support, Datastore is probably enough for you.
- Datastore works best when data is hierarchical and highly structured. If you have data which is non-hierarchical or unstructured, Bigtable is probably a better NoSQL technology.
- Do not use Datastore for analytics, OLAP, or Business Intelligence applications. BigQuery is a lot better because it has complex queries that are optimized for numerical calculations rather than documents.
- Datastore requires key values and a host of indices. If you are storing immutable blobs such as movies, which might be greater than 10 MB in size, Cloud Storage would be a better choice. The extremely heavily indexed nature of Datastore implies that you should not use it if your application is going to carry out a lot of writes and updates on your key columns.
- If you really want strong consistency guarantees, then of course you ought to use an RDBMS such as Cloud Spanner or Cloud SQL.

Turning to those situations where Datastore shines, the basic use case we discuss is, of course, the scaling of read performance. When you have hierarchical documents with key/value data, then obviously the document store is what you would want. There is also full indexing and its implications to consider when picking Cloud Datastore.

Full indexing and perfect index

Recall that there are built-in indices in Datastore on every property of every entity. This only applies to individual properties, but there are also composite indices. These allow the indexing of multiple property values all at once. If you are absolutely certain that a property will never be queried, you can explicitly exclude it from full indexing, which might give you some performance benefits, particularly in write operations where you don't want to be updating unnecessary indices.

The way Datastore works, every query will be evaluated using something known as its perfect index. The perfect index is an interesting concept. Given a query, the perfect index is that index which will most optimally return the query's results. The perfect index is evaluated based on the following conditions:

- If there is an equality filtering condition, that will be treated as the perfect index
- If there are inequality filters on columns, they will be used provided there is only one and no equality filter
- If there is neither an equality filter nor an inequality filter but a sort condition, the index on whatever property it is that is being sorted will be used for the perfect index.

Thus, the perfect index will be the equality filter, which means optimization of the needle-in-a-haystack type use cases. If there is no equality filter, then there can be at most one inequality filter which makes a range query. If neither inequality nor equality filters apply, then the sort order will be considered.

Full indexing is a wonderful feature of Datastore but it also has some important implications which we need to grasp. The first of these is that updates are really slow but lookups become blazingly fast. Another implication of full indexing is that joins are not supported. This is another similarity with Bigtable and another difference from relational databases. In addition, it is not possible to filter results based on subquery results and more than one inequality filter isn't acceptable.

Using Datastore

This section will walk you through working with Google Cloud Datastore:

1. On your Google Cloud Platform dashboard, go to the side *navigation bar*.
2. Click on **Data store** and choose **Entities**.

3. This is where we can create the entities that will live in our Datastore. Click on the create entity button to get started.

4. You need to specify the namespace where your entities will live. If you plan for your Datastore to be multi-tenanted, you should use different namespaces for your entities. This is how you separate entities for multiple clients. Note here that we are directly jumping into the creation of entities. This implies that Datastore is serverless. We don't create an instance of Datastore before we populate it. Create an entity within the default namespace, say, of the kind products. Recall that kind corresponds to table in a relational database.

5. Within this entity, set up a key identifier. It can be set to numeric, in which case it will be autogenerated. Entities stored in Cloud datastore have a hierarchical relationship, which means you can specify a parent entity for the entity that you are creating. Since this is our first entity, there is no parent here so the field is completely empty:

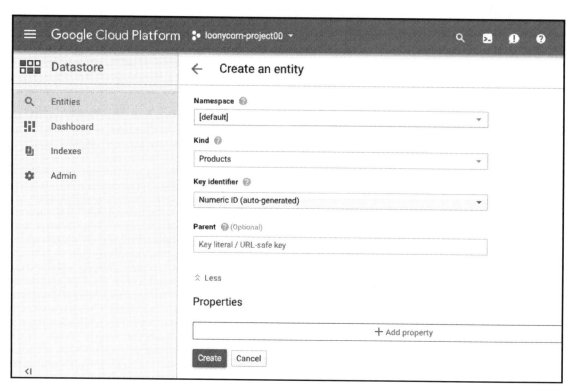

6. Click on **Add property** and specify the name for the property, a type, which in this case is string.

7. Since it's a products entity, let's add a value, `iphone6s`. Properties in an entity are essentially a key value pair. Specify the type for the value and click done. Repeat this to add other properties such as the cost, color, and availability of the product. The UI will update to accommodate these different data types:

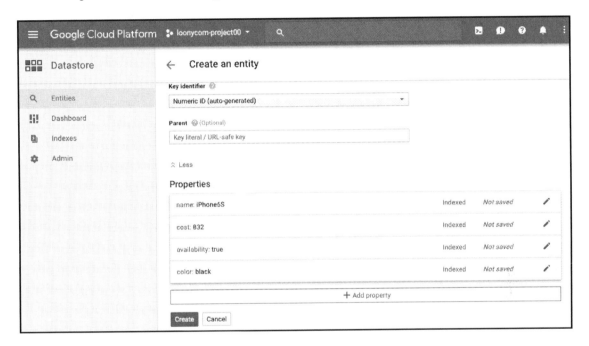

8. When you are done, hit the **Create** button and this entity will now be created. Note that all properties of an entity are indexed by default in Datastore. If you hit **Create** button once again, you will find that the web console will helpfully pre-populate the kind and the properties that we specified for our earlier entity.

9. Let's create a new entity of the kind products. Recall that in Datastore all entities in a kind need not have the same properties, or even the same datatype for properties that are the same across entities. The next product does not have a color property associated with the entity. You can also choose to change the datatype of any property within this entity. It's a Samsung Galaxy phone. The name specified is Samsung Galaxy and a new property called screen size is added:

10. Creating a new kind is simply a matter of creating an entity within that kind. Click on create entity and specify the kind as orders. Create some entities under this kind as well.

11. Using the filter at the very top, you can choose to view either the products or the orders kind and see all the entities that are within it. You can also filter entities further by using their properties. If you want to use Datastore as the backend for an e-commerce site, you would want to be able to filter your products by their availability. You can specify multiple filters as well by using the + icon on the right. All of this uses the web UI, which makes things very easy for you:

12. You can also query Datastore using **Google Query Language** (**GQL**). You can simply specify a SQL-like query in order to query Cloud datastore.

In this section, we discussed the concepts that power Cloud Datastore, its features and functionalities, the right design choices when using it, and the right circumstances for its use. We set up entities and populated them with properties and values. We have seen that entities of the same kind in Datastore can have different properties, and each of those properties can have different data types across entities as well.

In this chapter, we discussed the two NoSQL storage options that Google Cloud Platform provides: Cloud BigTable and Cloud Datastore. We started off by understanding the types and properties of NoSQL databases. We have seen how data is stored in both BigTable and Datastore. We have explored the common performance issues and fixes and the recommended design choices for both these storage options. We saw how to create BigTable instances and set up tables in it, as well as how to create entities in Datastore and populate them with kinds and properties.

Summary

This chapter explores the two main NoSQL database services from Google Cloud Platform:

- Bigtable
- Datastore

Bigtable is optimized for fast scans: range queries or select all queries along a single column, and with very large datasets, on the order of petabytes in size. Datastore, on the other hand, is meant for far smaller data, on the order of terabytes, where the use case involves fast lookups independent of dataset size.

8
BigQuery

BigQuery is probably the single most compelling reason to adopt the GCP right now. It is a data warehousing service that is really fast, really price-competitive, and incredibly easy to use. Unlike some other Google Cloud services, BigQuery is widely used and so has little unpredictability in its behavior. I like to joke that if you interact with a Google Cloud sales professional, no matter what your question, the answer that comes back is, just use BigQuery for that!

In this chapter, you will learn about the following:

- BigQuery as Google's fully managed petabyte scale serverless database
- Architecture of BigQuery
- Working with BigQuery using web console
- Working with BigQuery using CLI

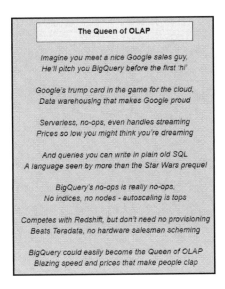

The Queen of OLAP

Imagine you meet a nice Google sales guy,
He'll pitch you BigQuery before the first 'hi'

Google's trump card in the game for the cloud,
Data warehousing that makes Google proud

Serverless, no-ops, even handles streaming
Prices so low you might think you're dreaming

And queries you can write in plain old SQL
A language seen by more than the Star Wars prequel

BigQuery's no-ops is really no-ops,
No indices, no nodes - autoscaling is tops

Competes with Redshift, but don't need no provisioning
Beats Teradata, no hardware salesman scheming

BigQuery could easily become the Queen of OLAP
Blazing speed and prices that make people clap

BigQuery competes with proprietary data warehousing solutions such as Teradata, but has obvious and major advantages over them, notably that it is cloud-based, serverless, and supports auto-scaling (so that you really pay only for what you need). There is no need for prohibitively expensive purchases of proprietary hardware.

Within the world of cloud providers, BigQuery probably most directly competes with Amazon's RedShift and the comparisons between these two technologies get folks quite riled up. In a nutshell, Redshift allows you to provision nodes (similar to Bigtable or Spanner in GCP), and the more you provision, the better the performance, but also the higher the cost. With BigQuery on the other hand, you don't provision a cluster or create indices, or really do any ops at all. The advantage of that is convenience, but the downside, is that you have less control over performance, and you have really no control at all over how your queries are executed. This can really take some getting used to for most folks. The idea that you don't create indices and you can't specify failover replicas or interface with the underlying hardware at all is quite different from the traditional way of doing either OLTP or OLAP.

In the previous chapters, we saw various storage options of GCP for various use cases. For blob storage, we have GCP Cloud Storage buckets, for creating VMs we have Compute Engine, which also provides persistent disks, for schema-strict relational databases we have Cloud SQL and Cloud Spanner, and for NoSQL databases we have seen Cloud Bigtable and Datastore. All of these options require more or less administration from the user's end. This requires time, skills, and expert administrators. Google's BigQuery is a step further. It is a large scale (typically, in petabytes) fully managed data warehouse. This frees admins from managing databases so they can focus more on analysis.

To explain this further, you do not need to deploy your resources and keep track of them, or even worry about scaling them. All of this is handled by Google so we can directly run our queries efficiently and save the ones we need to retrieve later. Just like other resources from GCP, BigQuery queries are directly managed and tracked under a project. It supports CSV, JSON, datastore backups, and Apache Avro input data formats.

Underlying data representation of BigQuery

When we load data into BigQuery, each column of that data is stored separately. The values in each column are compressed, run-length encoded, and encrypted, and the corresponding data file is replicated. Each of these replicas is then stored in the underlying distributed filesystem, known as **Colossus**.

This peculiar representation, columnar, compressed, and replicated, explains a couple of features of BigQuery that otherwise strike us as odd:

- **Does not support indices**: This makes it very different from traditional RDBMS. This makes sense, given that each column's data is effectively stored separately anyway, and uses a representation not that different from many indices
- **Cost more for each column they pull in**: This also makes sense if you consider that each additional column requires access to a different file in the underlying file system.

BigQuery public datasets

BigQuery has a number of publicly available datasets that you can use to play around with, or to build and train data models. The storage for these is free, that is, paid for by Google, so you only have to pay for queries that you run against these datasets. These queries are charged like all other queries.

In the following examples, we will make use of such public datasets, which can be accessed from within queries using notation such as `bigquery-public-data.samples.natality`.

Legacy versus standard SQL

BigQuery, like many other GCP services, has been widely used within Google for several years. That usage initially relied on a non-standard variant of SQL, which is now called **legacy SQL**. Legacy SQL is pretty powerful and pretty easy to use in some specific cases, but it has a big downside: it is not standard!

To remedy that, BigQuery has added support for standard SQL 2011, with some extensions that have to do with nested and repeated fields. The query examples shown next are in standard SQL.

How can you tell at a glance whether a query is written in legacy SQL or standard SQL? Just look at the syntax used to specify tables or project names.

- **In legacy SQL**: Use square brackets to start and end the table name, and use a colon (:) to delimit dataset and table names:

```
[bigquery-public-data:samples:natality]
```

- **In standard SQL**: Use the backtick character (`` ` ``) to start and end the table name, and use the period character (.) to delimit dataset and table names:

```
`bigquery-public-data.samples.natality`
```

Working with the BigQuery console

BigQuery can be accessed using both GUI and command line. To access BigQuery using a GUI console:

1. Click on the menu button on the top-left corner of the console and select **BigQuery** from the drop-down menu. You will encounter a new console looking something like this:

2. Click on the **COMPOSE QUERY** button to enable the text area where queries can be written:

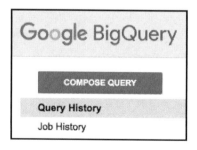

3. To query a public dataset, paste the following text into the text area:

```
#standardSQL
SELECT
  weight_pounds, state, year, gestation_weeks
FROM
  `bigquery-public-data.samples.natality`
ORDER BY weight_pounds DESC LIMIT 10;
```

4. Click the **RUN QUERY** button to run the query and observe the results, which will look like this:

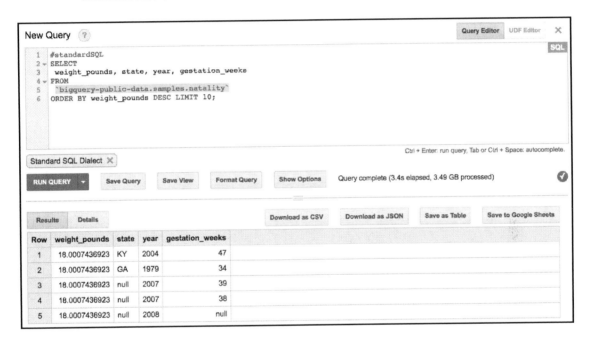

Here as we can see, a public dataset named `samples.natality` is queried and 3.49 GB of data takes as low as 3.4 seconds to be processed. This speed and simplicity makes BigQuery almost ideal for OLAP.

Loading data into a table using BigQuery

Using pre-created or custom datasets is also a very common practice in data analytics. Thus, to load data into a table:

1. Download or locate the data you intend to load. For example, we are using the `babynames` ZIP file, which is an open dataset. Download it using this URL: `http://www.ssa.gov/OACT/babynames/names.zip`.

2. Extract the file at your desired location and you will notice a `yob2014.txt` file, which is a CSV file.

3. Go to the console of BigQuery and locate a downward arrow near your project name. Then, click on the **Create new dataset** button:

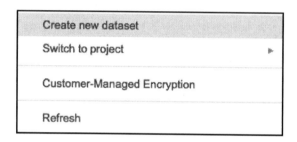

4. Give the dataset an ID of `babynames`:

5. Keep all of the other settings as default. Click the **OK** button

6. Find the drop-down icon near dataset ID and click on the **Create new table** option:

7. To upload the datafile, click on the **Choose file** button and enter the path of your datafile, which is `yob2014.txt` in our case:

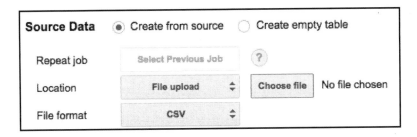

8. Enter any name as destination table. We are keeping `names_2014`:

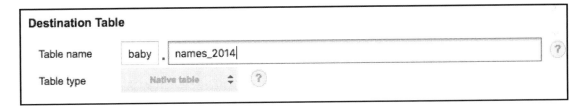

9. Now, let's edit the schema of the database. Click on the **Edit as Text** option, which can be found in the bottom-right corner of the database and input the following string as text:

```
Name:string,gender:string,count:integer
```

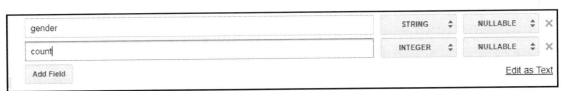

10. Finally, click on the **Create table** button and check out the preview. Now this table is ready to be queried:

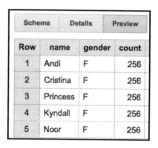

Deleting datasets

Once we are done with the dataset, we should remove it from storage to save on cost:

1. Hover over the dataset name, which is `babynames` in our case.

2. Again, click on the drop-down icon and select the **Delete dataset** option:

3. The console will ask you to confirm your action by typing the dataset name again. Do it and click **OK** to delete the dataset:

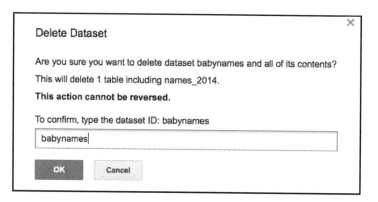

Working with BigQuery using CLI

BigQuery can also be accessed and operated using the `bq` command. Here are some of the operations using the `bq` command in Cloud Shell:

- To view a table in your database:

  ```
  bq show projectId:datasetId.tableId
  ```

- To run a certain query:

  ```
  bq query "<<<query text>>>"
  ```

- To create a new table:

  ```
  bq mk <<<dataset name>>>
  ```

- To list the tables:

  ```
  bq ls
  ```

- To load the dataset along with the schema:

  ```
  bq load <<<dataset_name.filename schema_text>>>
  ```

- For example, to load the same `babynames` dataset as the GUI example:

  ```
  bq load babynames.names2010 yob2010.txt
  name:string,gender:string,count:integer
  ```

- Finally, to remove a dataset, use:

  ```
  bq rm -r <<<datasetID>>>
  ```

BigQuery pricing

BigQuery is serverless and fully managed; it is also one of the most cost-effective offerings of GCP. This is probably also because BigQuery is often the first GCP service that prospective customers try out and getting the pricing on this right is very important to drive adoption.

Pricing details change pretty quickly, and the information here is current as of March 2018. Despite the ever-changing nature of cloud pricing, we have chosen to include this, because it shows, broadly, how BigQuery is priced and why it is such a cost-effective competitor in the data warehousing space.

Action	Cost
Storage	$0.02/GB/month (first 10 GB/month free)
Long-term storage (no edits for 90 days)	$0.01/GB/month (first 10 GB/month free)
Queries	$5/TB (first 1 TB/month is free)
Flat-rate for 2,000 slots	$40,000/month
Loading data	Free
Copying data	Free
Exporting data	Free
Streaming Inserts	$0.01 for 200 MB

A few points worth calling out on the pricing:

- Notice the very generous free tier on the important aspects of storage and querying
- There are also flat-rate pricing plans for heavy users, where you effectively pay $40,000 per month and that's it
- Storage works out similar in pricing to regional buckets (~2 cents/GB/month), but if you leave the data in there, it quickly gets considered as long-term storage, and the pricing becomes more like nearline storage (~1 cents/GB/month)
- BigQuery also supports streaming ingestion at a very fast throughput (you can stream data in at about 100,000 events/second), but streaming is relatively expensive.

Analyzing financial time series with BigQuery

Here we will run a time-series analysis on a public dataset called gbpusd which is a curated time series made publicly available with historical data on the exchange rate between the British Pound (GBP) and the US Dollar (USD).

1. Make a dataset called timeseries using following command on Cloud Shell。

   ```
   bq mk timeseries
   ```

2. Load gbpusd dataset with following command:

   ```
   bq load timeseries.gbpusd_0114 gs://solutions-public-assets/time-
   series-master/GBPUSD_2014_01.csv /
   venue:STRING,
   currencies:STRING,
   time:TIMESTAMP,
   bid:FLOAT,
   ask:FLOAT
   ```

3. Now, run following query:

   ```
   SELECT FORMAT_UTC_USEC(time) AS time, venue, currencies, time, bid,
   ask
   FROM  timeseries.gbpusd_0114
   ORDER BY time ASC
   LIMIT   1000;
   ```

5. Download the query results as CSV file
6. Open Google Sheets. Import the downloaded CSV file by clicking on **File |
   Import**
7. When prompted, select **Replace Current Sheet**

8. Select all of the cells and click on **Insert | Chart** and choose your appropriate chart type. You should get a result like following:

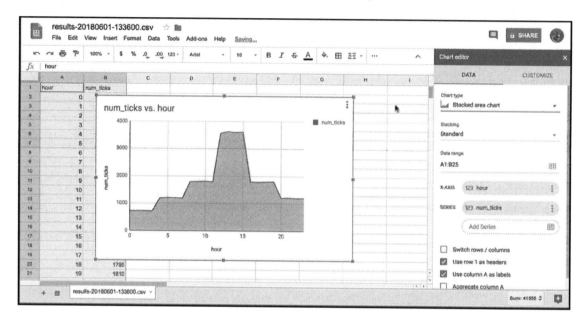

Summary

This chapter covered the basics of why BigQuery is important for users who do not want to dive deep into managing a database and directly want to query it (mostly for larger datasets). We saw how easy it is to operate BigQuery using both the GUI and the CLI.

We also saw how BigQuery's pricing model works, and why that pricing model is an important reason for its popularity.

9
Identity and Access Management

We have seen a lot of GCP's resource offerings in previous chapters, but all of them would crumble if their access is not managed properly. **IAM**, which stands for **Identity and Access Management**, lets you control access to all of the GCP resources in terms of roles and permissions. All of the services related to IAM are completely free of charge, so we do not need to bother about billing in this chapter. Let's take a look into how IAM lets you manage resource access.

You will learn about the following:

- IAM
- Roles and permissions
- Types of identities
- Working with IAM

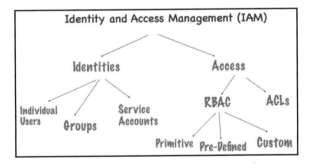

If you can keep this one diagram in mind, you're good. This is basically what you need to keep in mind about identity and access management on the GCP.

This diagram is quite involved though, so let's take it one step at a time:

Identity and Access Management = Identity + Access

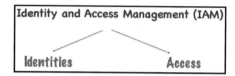

OK! So far, so good. Let's consider identities; common sense suggests that these could be:

- Humans
- Groups of humans
- Programs

Those categories map nicely to reality!

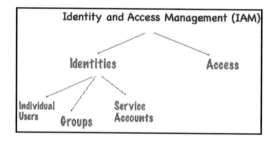

Previously, Identities (which are human identities as GCP users) could only come from Gsuite (not Active Directory or LDAP)! But now GCP has become more flexible and any user with a Gmail or Gsuite administered account can create his GCP identity.

Identities: GSuite and GCP

Identities of individuals, groups or domains must be created and managed in GSuite, which is a different offering, separate from GCP.

If your organization is not currently on GSuite - for instance if you use Microsoft's Active Directory, you will probably need to federate the two sets of identities using something GCDS (Google Cloud Directory Sync)

Service accounts, which are identities for one service trying to access another, are defined purely within GCP and do not interface with GSuite.

Cool, let's now turn our attention to the access side of the equation. Access can be managed in a couple of ways, and both are quite standard:

- **Access control lists (ACLs)**: Where permissions are directly granted to users
- **Role-based access control (RBAC)**: where permissions are assigned to roles, and users are then assigned to roles as well:

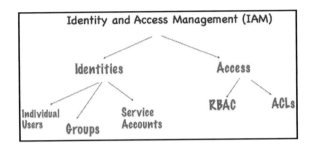

We discussed ACL-based access for some specific use cases involving cloud storage buckets, but barring that one specific circumstance, the preferable way is to use RBAC.

The two main advantages of RBAC are:

- Roles can be reused
- Roles are GCP resources themselves, and you can monitor them and assign roles for role management

The Google Cloud Platform has three types of role:

- Primitive project roles such as owner, editor, and viewer
- Predefined roles for each service, literally dozens of them, with names such as `storage.objectViewer`
- Custom roles, these are in beta, and allow the creation of new roles from a set of underlying permissions

Our tree is now complete, just remember this one mental representation and IAM will make a lot more sense.

Resource hierarchy of GCP

Google Cloud Platform follows a fixed hierarchy to organize and distribute resources:

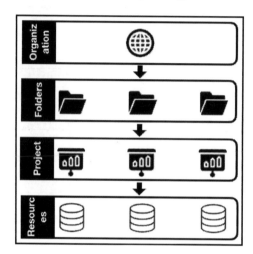

- **Organization**: The highest unit is an **Organization**. An **Organization** is set up (in GCP) using GSuite, which is the productivity toolkit by Google, and Cloud Identity, which is ID as a Service Enterprise Mobility management platform. It is a common practice to register your domain name as the organization name. All of the roles related to one domain go under the same organization in terms of IAM and billing.
- **Folders**: **Folders** fall one layer below **Organization**. An organization can have one or more folders affiliated to it and each folder can contain multiple projects or folders. As a common practice, folders represent departments in an organization. There are some limitations to folders, like having a maximum of 100 folders under one folder or to perform up to four levels of folder nesting.
- **Projects**: A **Project** is a unit of resource management below **Folders**. It contains a set of users, API permissions, billing information, and provisioned resources. They are identified by their project ID, which should be unique within the organization, although it is not something to worry about since Project IDs are auto-generated by GCP. Users and roles are specified per project.

- **Resources**: Resources are the offerings and services of GCP used by an organization. Every resource instance is provisioned under a certain project, which links it to an appropriate billing account. Roles are defined for these resources to manage their access.

Permissions and roles

The management of access to resources is handled by permissions. To make handling permissions easier, GCP IAM has roles that can be allotted to users, and the roles carry the necessary permissions:

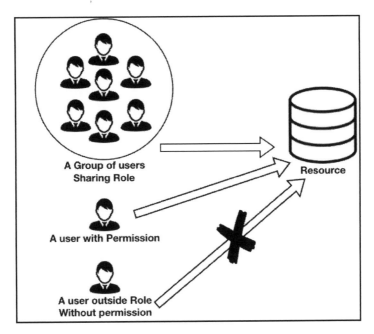

- **Permissions**: A permission can be defined as a token to allow access to a GCP API. Generally, permissions are assigned via roles and one role may contain one or more permissions.

- **Role**: A role is a collection of permissions and a convenient way to pass them to users. Some examples of roles are shown next. Custom roles can also be written by admins, but they are an alpha feature at the time the book is being written:

Role	Description
Organization role admin	Provides access to all custom roles within the organization.
Role admin	Provides access to all custom roles within a project.
Organization role viewer	Provides **read** access to all custom roles within an organization.
Role viewer	Provides **read** access to all custom roles within a project
Security reviewer	Provides permissions to list all resources and IAM policies on them.

To gain access to any of the resources under any project in an organization, users should have one of the following units of identity.

Units of identity in GCP

Cloud IAM can grant access to resources to members of an organization. The specifics of access are defined by roles and respective permissions. Being a member of the organization implies having one of the following Identities:

- **Google account**: This is, for most intents and purposes, an email address associated with gmail.com or any other domain managed by G Suite. The account can represent a developer, admin, or someone with access to GCP.
- **Service account**: This is pretty similar to a Google email account, apart from the fact that it belongs to an application instead of a user. Mostly these accounts are used for executing different logical components of the application (for example client, server, and so on).
- **Google groups**: This is a collection of various Google accounts, which may even include service accounts. They have a unique email address to identify them. These are convenient ways to pass similar roles to multiple users instead of passing them to each account individually. It is possible to add the members in the group. Their addition or removal from the group will also lead to their gaining access to permissions of the roles affiliated to the group. Similarly, being removed from the group means having the roles revoked.

- **G Suite domains**: This is a collection of all the accounts created under the organization's (domain's) G Suite account. G Suite domains do not contain the identity of each user, but they are useful for managing permissions and roles.
- **Cloud identity domain**: This is a lot like the G Suite domain in terms of IAM administration, but the users of the cloud identity domain do not have access to G Suite applications.
- **Other users**: Apart from all of these users, the ones approved by an admin or ones with access to GCP APIs under a certain project can also be managed by IAM.

Creating a Service Account

Service accounts in GCP are affiliated with application or resources (such as Compute Engine VM). One service account can link to multiple resources. It is created in order to avoid conflict with user account and to call the Google APIs of services. These accounts are then given permissions to access or edit resources or data. There are two types of service accounts:

- User managed service accounts
- Google managed service accounts

Service accounts are authenticated via GCP managed key-pairs. The keys are rotated almost every week. Optionally, we can also create external keys to be used as default application credentials and so on.

To create a service account, following are the steps:

1. From the dashboard of the console, navigate to **IAM & admin** | **Service accounts**

2. Click on **Create Service Account**

3. Name your service account. Make sure to name it in a way that the name itself describes the purpose of the account. The name will be structured as YOUR_NAME@projectID.iam.googleserviceaccount.com

4. For example, in a project named Cloudsql, you can create an account called sql_editor and the name will be sql_editor@cloudsql.iam.googleserviceaccount.com

5. Once the account is created, you can grant it an appropriate role. We will give it **Cloud SQL | Cloud SQL Editor role**.

6. Finally, click on the checkbox near **Furnish a new private key** to download your JSON key and use it.

More about granting roles is described in the section below.

Working with cloud IAM – grant a role

Working with IAM is fairly simple, as it mostly involves operating the console itself. Here are some of the tasks that can be performed with Cloud IAM. First of all, we will grant an IAM role to one of the project members:

1. Go to the GCP web console and navigate to the menu button, which is on the top-left corner with three lines.

2. Select **IAM & admin** and navigate to the **IAM** section:

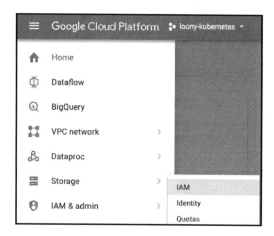

3. You will find a list of roles for the project that you were working on. Currently, I am on a project called **loony-kubernetes** so the roles for this are visible:

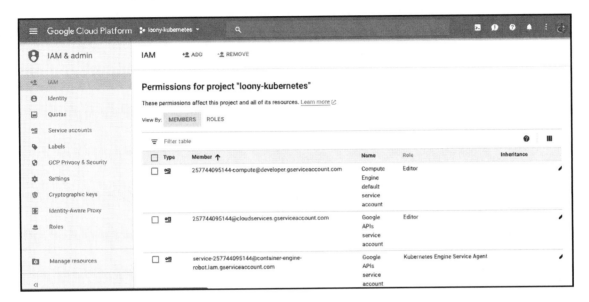

4. By clicking on the **ADD** button, you will find a popup to add new members to the project:

5. We will add `janani@loonycorn.com` to the project and shall give her the role of Project Billing Manager.

6. By clicking on add more roles, you can provide even more roles to the same user:

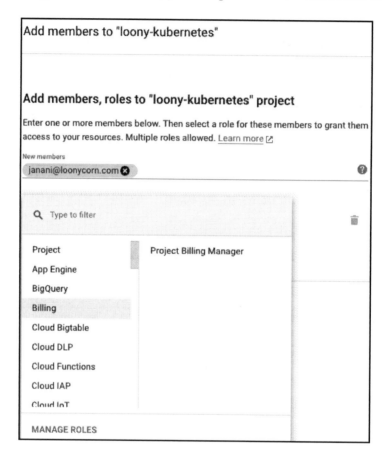

7. Confirm the action by clicking on **Add**.
8. Similarly, a role can be removed from a user using the **Manage Roles** option.

Working with IAM – creating a custom role

Although this is an alpha feature at the time of this book being written, it is expected to be stabilized soon. You can create custom roles with custom permissions as per your requirements using IAM roles:

1. Navigate to the **Roles** tab in the **IAM & admin** panel:

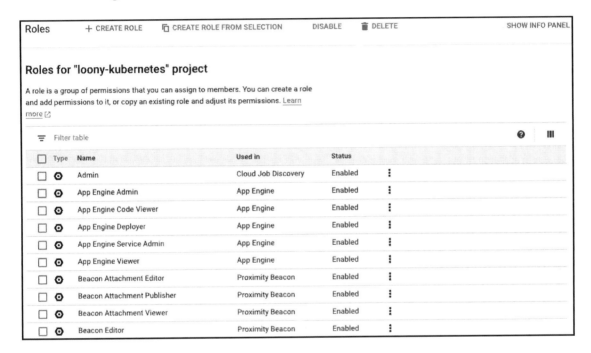

2. Click on the **Create Role** button to add the role you desire.
3. Name the role and enter a convenient **Role ID**.

4. Enter the desired permissions. While doing so, you will be prompted to enter the status of the permission so that you can avoid adding permissions that are not supported:

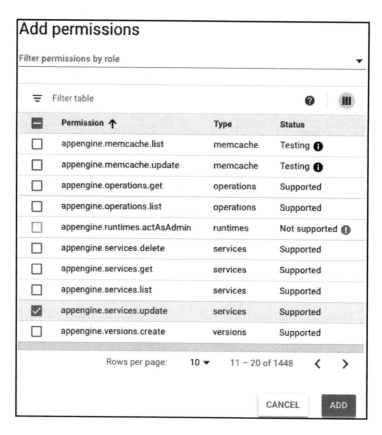

5. You can also choose the availability of the role; since the feature is in alpha stage, you can chose to activate it immediately or after it becomes GA.

6. Confirm your action by clicking create, and the role will be created and will be available to be assigned to any member of the organization:

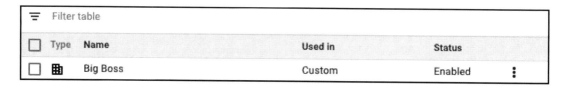

7. Similarly, a permission can be removed from a role using the **Manage Permissions** option.

8. We granted the Role to an individual Gmail user account, but the procedure remains the same for service account, group, or any other unit of identity supported by GCP.

Summary

In this chapter, you took a closer look at the access administration end of Google Cloud Platform, which is Identity and Access Management. You also learned about the hierarchy of resources and units of identities and administration. Finally, you learned about permissions and roles, and how to create and grant them.

10
Managing Hadoop with Dataproc

When you intend to expand your business, parallel processing becomes essential for streaming, querying large datasets, and so on, and machine learning becomes important for analytics. In the case of GCP, Dataproc is a managed and cost-effective solution for Apache Spark and Hadoop workloads.

In this chapter, you will learn about the following:

- Google Cloud Dataproc
- Dataproc cluster instances
- Running jobs on Dataproc clusters
- Scaling Dataproc clusters

- Deleting clusters

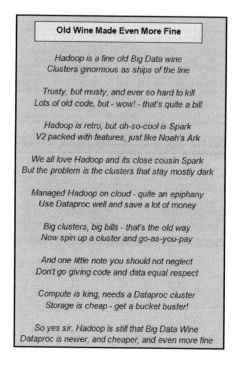

Hadoop and Spark

Hadoop is a venerable technology now; the *grand old man* of distributed computing technologies. We won't spend too much time dwelling on Hadoop's internals, but a brief introduction is required for this chapter for it to make sense to folks who are not from a big-data background:

The MapReduce programming paradigm is what really matters to a user. It defines a map and reduces tasks using the MapReduce API, and submits them to that part of the Hadoop ecosystem:

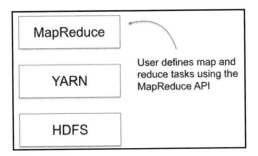

When a job gets triggered on the corresponding cluster, this brings YARN into play. This involves prioritizing among different jobs and sharing resources such as compute capacity:

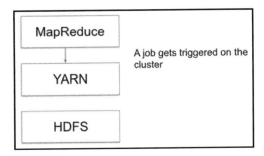

YARN is the acronym for **Yet Another Resource Negotiator**, and it plays the role of a scheduler and resource allocator on the Hadoop cluster. YARN will figure out where and how to run the job:

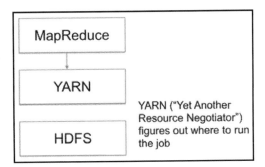

This process also involves copying over the JAR files (Java archives) to each of the nodes in the cluster; this is essentially moving compute to be where the storage is. This tight coupling between storage and compute is a key feature of Hadoop, and loosening this coupling is a key insight that major cloud services such as Dataproc exploit. Once the job is entirely run, the results are collected and stored back in HDFS:

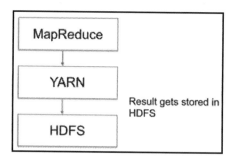

This also gives us an important insight that we should remember. Hadoop, at heart, is a batch processing system. The user interacts with MapReduce by defining MapReduce tasks. The results end up being on a distributed filesystem. It's not the most convenient way, or the most intuitive way, of interacting with parallel computing programs. Partly to compensate for this slightly abstract nature, and partly to compensate for the batch nature of Hadoop, a whole bunch of tools have sprung up around Hadoop:

- **Hive**: Hive serves as a SQL-like wrapper of top of the distributed file system HDFS
- **HBase**: HBase is a columnar data store that is created for Hadoop data
- **Pig**: Pig is a transformation tool that helps get data semi structured or unstructured data into HDFS
- **Kafka**: Kafka helps deal with streaming data
- **Spark**: Spark is a really powerful computing engine and represents possibly the hottest big-data technology today

There are several other elements in the Hadoop ecosystem, as it has come to be known, and, collectively, these constitute nothing less than an entire big data suite.

Perhaps the most important and noteworthy of these is Spark. Spark is a powerful big data and machine-learning engine, which can be used in a variety of programming languages such as Python, Scala, Java, and R. The most common technologies used to work with Spark are Python (Python on Spark is often just called **PySpark**) and Scala (in which Spark is actually written). Spark need not be run on Hadoop, but it is often used on top of Hadoop, making use of YARN and HDFS but not MapReduce:

```
Spark For Big Data and ML

Hadoop = YARN + HDFS + MapReduce
Spark ~ YARN + HDFS + Spark Engine
PySpark ~ Spark accessed via Python
```

Hadoop on the cloud

Hadoop and MapReduce are standard, cookie-cutter ways of taking complicated jobs that parallelize the jobs that run on a number of machines and get the results back for your convenience. The power and versatility of the MapReduce programming paradigm and the great design underlying Hadoop have spawned an entire ecosystem of its own. One side effect of this Hadoop ecosystem and popularity is the rise of clustered or distributed computing. But it is a simple fact that configuring a cluster of distributed machines is quite complicated and expensive. Ask yourself how many companies or organizations do you know that run Hadoop in a fully distributed mode with raw Hadoop, without making use of nice company versions such as Cloudera. The answer is probably none. That's because it takes a lot of work to get Hadoop and MapReduce going in fully distributed mode, and this really is where cloud computing helps and comes into its own.

Managed Hadoop services are now offered by all of the major cloud providers. Dataproc is Google's offering and Amazon's version is called **Elastic MapReduce**. The basic idea of these managed Hadoop offerings is simple and very clever: the storage component of a traditional Hadoop cluster is now separated from compute by moving the data from HDFS to buckets (GCS or S3); the compute can simply be performed on cloud VMs, and those VMs can be done away with when the job is completed.

This is a brilliant insight because the main drawback of gigantic Hadoop/Spark clusters is their fixed costs and low utilization. Far too many companies have made the mistake of investing in enormous Hadoop clusters with hundreds or even thousands of nodes, and then found that the cluster is rarely used. Measuring the utilization of a Hadoop cluster is not all that straightforward, but it is fairly common for this to be in the sub-20% utilization range. When you consider the amount of fixed-asset investment and depreciation expenses that such a cluster entails, you can get a sense of why finance professionals tend to like cloud-based solutions: there is no depreciation, no fixed assets, and no politically charged conversations around utilization (albeit at the cost of potentially higher operating expenses).

This rise of Hadoop on the cloud has had serious negative implications for Hadoop providers such as Cloudera and Hortonworks. The complexity of Hadoop was key to their business model, and, now that complexity has been stripped away by the cloud providers, they could face challenging times ahead.

It is worth mentioning, in the context of Dataproc, Google's managed Hadoop offering, that Google initially had an arrangement with Hortonworks (with a nice press release dated January 2015). That arrangement basically centered around a utility called bdutil, which was a command-line tool that ran HDP on the GCP. Then, a year later, Google launched Dataproc, which made bdutil obsolete and there's been not a peep about a special relationship with Hortonworks after that. Dataproc runs Apache Hadoop; if you really need to run HDP or Cloudera, your best bet is to use virtual machines and run the third-party orchestrator (something like Cloudera director) from those VMs. So, in a nutshell, Dataproc is the recommended, Google-approved way to run Hadoop on the GCP. If you decide to try a third-party distro, you are largely on your own.

Google Cloud Dataproc

Dataproc As Managed Hadoop

Hadoop = YARN + HDFS + MapReduce
Dataproc = YARN + GCS + MapReduce

Dataproc clusters still have an internal HDFS area, but this is on the persistent disks of the Dataproc VMs, and will not exist beyond the life of the cluster

So - don't use HDFS, use GCS instead

As mentioned earlier, Google Cloud Dataproc is a managed Spark and Hadoop solution from Google. Its nature of being managed and of being on the cloud gives users the ability to turn the clusters off when they are not required, which saves a lot of cost. So, Dataproc is not only simple and time saving, but it is also cost effective.

Just like other managed services from Google, we can use GCP APIs to interact with Dataproc. We will get into the details later in this chapter. While the initial vision of Dataproc was to provide managed Hadoop and Spark, the current state boasts managed support for open source Apache Hive, Pig, Hadoop, and Spark, and integration with Cloud Storage and BigQuery through connectors, on top of being monitored by Stackdriver. Just like Hadoop, Dataproc also has Master, Client and Worker nodes configurations where Master nodes manage storing data into HDFS and running parallel operations using MapReduce. While worker nodes store the data and run computations.

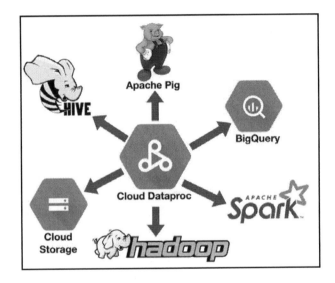

Apart from these, resource management facilities such as YARN, HDFS, and MapReduce can also be leveraged from the web interface of Hadoop. These web interfaces can be accessed by SSH or SOCKS proxy.

Compute options for Dataproc

Dataproc cluster instances are built on Google Compute Engine instances, which means we have a wide variety of machines to choose from, according to our use and budget. Just like Compute Engine instances, Dataproc instances can also use both predefined and custom machine types. In the beta update of Dataproc, we can also use f1-micro CPU to decrease the cost even further, whereas for performance-heavy applications we can choose persistent SSD over persistent disks. Apart from these basic configurations, the following are optional customizations possible with Dataproc instances:

- GPUs
- Automatic zone selection
- Optional preemptibility for lower cost
- High availability
- Scheduled deletion of clusters
- Live scaling (without bringing apps down)
- Single-node sandbox clusters

Working with Dataproc

In this section, we will learn how to set up a Dataproc cluster, submit a job to the cluster, and do some interesting things with Dataproc.

1. Navigate to the project where you wish to set up the cluster.
2. Click on the menu button in the top-left corner with three horizontal lines and choose **Dataproc** from the drop-down menu:

3. Click on the **Create Cluster** button and fill in the required information for the cluster, which is cluster name, memory and CPU configurations, region, GPU, and disk configurations. We will name our cluster `my-cluster` and choose single node globally:

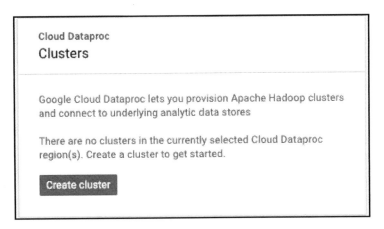

4. To configure the cluster further, you can visit the staging bucket for the cluster, which is used to store configurations and control files. The staging buckets are separate for each region, so make sure your staging bucket is in the same region as your cluster. To view it, use the following command:

```
gcloud dataproc clusters describe <cluster-name>
```

The output should look something like this:

```
clusterName: your-cluster-name
clusterUuid: <<Cluster_ID_Generated_by_Dataproc>>
configuration:
  configurationBucket: <<Bucket_Name>>
```

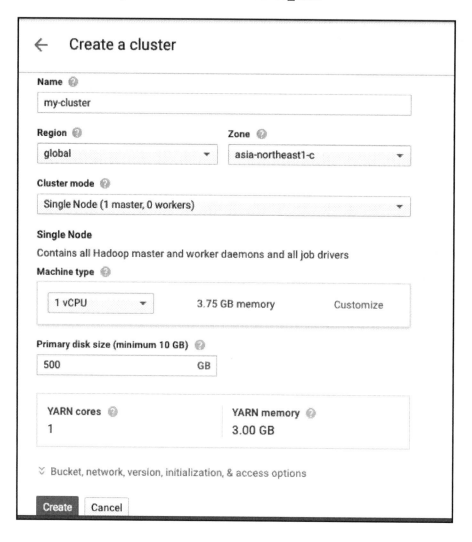

5. Now, our cluster is ready to use. To submit a job to the cluster, use the following command:

```
gcloud dataproc jobs submit <<<job-command>>> --cluster
<<<cluster-name>>>
job-specific flags and args
```

6. Let's understand this using the example of a classic PySpark hello world. The following program submits a spark job to the GCP Dataproc cluster. While the job may be defined individually for each example, in this case it means that the `hello-world` program will be divided into pieces to be executed by different nodes. But since we have specified only one node to make sure that the running cost of the examples remains within the free credit boundry, it will be executed via single node itself:

```
$gcloud dataproc jobs submit pyspark --cluster <<<cluster-name
>>> gs://dataproc-
examples-2f10d78d114f6aaec76462e3c310f31f/src/pyspark/hello-
world/hello-world.py
```

The output should be something like the following:

```
Job [58e753abd7e6465bb9072125d47f0cb5] submitted.
Waiting for job output...
18/04/18 10:32:52 INFO org.spark_project.jetty.util.log: Logging initialized @5684ms
18/04/18 10:32:52 INFO org.spark_project.jetty.server.Server: jetty-9.3.z-SNAPSHOT
18/04/18 10:32:52 INFO org.spark_project.jetty.server.Server: Started @5857ms
18/04/18 10:32:52 INFO org.spark_project.jetty.server.AbstractConnector: Started ServerConnector@78485c51
{HTTP/1.1,[http/1.1]}{0.0.0.0:4040}
18/04/18 10:32:53 INFO com.google.cloud.hadoop.fs.gcs.GoogleHadoopFileSystemBase: GHFS version: 1.6.4-had
oop2
18/04/18 10:32:54 INFO org.apache.hadoop.yarn.client.RMProxy: Connecting to ResourceManager at my-cluster
-m/10.146.0.2:8032
18/04/18 10:32:58 INFO org.apache.hadoop.yarn.client.api.impl.YarnClientImpl: Submitted application appli
cation_1524047190416_0001
['Hello,', 'world!']
```

The status of the job would be displayed as follows:

```
reference:
  jobId: 58e753abd7e6465bb9072125d47f0cb5
  projectId: loony-kubernetes
status:
  state: DONE
  stateStartTime: '2018-04-18T10:33:25.431Z'
statusHistory:
- state: PENDING
  stateStartTime: '2018-04-18T10:32:34.219Z'
- state: SETUP_DONE
  stateStartTime: '2018-04-18T10:32:38.789Z'
- details: Agent reported job success
  state: RUNNING
  stateStartTime: '2018-04-18T10:32:41.240Z'
yarnApplications:
- name: hello-world.py
  progress: 1.0
  state: FINISHED
```

7. To move further, you can scale the cluster with the following command:

```
gcloud dataproc clusters update <<<cluster-name>>>
<<<--num-workers>>> <<<new-number-of-workers>>>
```

8. To make sure that downscaling happens after the currently running task is completed, you can use graceful decommissioning with the following command. Note that the maximum possible delay is 24 hours:

```
gcloud dataproc clusters update
 --graceful-decommission-timeout="timeout-value"
other args ...
```

9. To access the Hadoop web UI using SSH, use the following command. In that command, -N instructs gcloud not to open a remote shell and -n to avoid reading stdin:

```
gcloud compute ssh --zone=master-host-zone <<master-host-name>> --
-D <<Dynamic application forwarding port>> -N -n
```

10. Now we have the SSH tunnel set-up. To use Hadoop web UI from Cloud Shell use following command:

```
gcloud compute ssh <<master-host-name>> \
--project=<<project-id>> --zone=<<master-host-zone>>  -- \
-D 1080 -N
```

11. The tunnel supports traffic proxying with SOCKS protocol which stands for Socket Secure protocol. If you are using Google Chrome, use following command. This would be a better option since it opens Hadoop UI in a new window:

```
Google Chrome executable path
 --proxy-server="socks5://localhost:1080"
 --host-resolver-rules="MAP * 0.0.0.0 , EXCLUDE localhost"
 --user-data-dir=/tmp/master-host-name
```

12. The `user-data-dir` flag forces Chrome to open a new window that is free from the existing session, whereas the `MAP * 0.0.0.0` rule prevents it from sending any DNS requests. This is how it creates a proxy session.

13. To delete the cluster, you can either click on the **Delete cluster** button from the web console and provide confirmation, or use the following command:

```
gcloud dataproc clusters delete <<<cluster-name>>>
```

Summary

In this chapter, we looked into Google Cloud Dataproc and how to create a customized Dataproc cluster. We also learned how to submit jobs and how to manage a cluster, and, finally, the management part included scaling, graceful decommissioning, and deleting the cluster.

11
Load Balancing

We have seen the use of Compute Engine as IaaS, including Kubernetes clusters, which also rely on Compute Engine VM instances, and persistent disks. We don't have to worry about issues such as the proper distribution of internet traffic, requests, or processing when we use only one VM instance. Even in the case of overload, we can always scale our instances vertically and fulfill the processing requirements. But when we use more than one VM for a heavily accessed application or multi-tier application, load balancing becomes essential.

We may have to guide the traffic to the machines serving the corresponding tier, or we may have to guide it towards the same tier, while making sure that none of our machines get overloaded while other machines are chilling out. Fortunately, GCP provisions quite a sophisticated load balancer, which allows the routing of internet traffic based on the requested instance group (tier in practical application), available computing, and storage capacity, as well as distance from the region of the instance with respect to the user. In this chapter, we will go through HTTP, TCP, and network load balancing with reference to their concepts and implementation.

This chapter covers the following topics:

- The importance of load balancing
- HTTP(S) load balancing
- Other load-balancing rules

Why load balancers matter now

Load balancers are discussed a lot more often these days than they used to be, say, a decade or two ago. They used to be somewhat arcane tools that only some network planners or architects really had to worry about during edge-case planning; now, they are absolutely mainstream, and even developers and app architects need to understand what kind of load balancer to choose, and why.

Why have load balancers become such a conversation starter these days? The answer lies in two important features of compute on the cloud—ephemeral external IP addresses and autoscaling of backends:

O Brother, Where Art Thou?

Back in the days before the cloud
You knew every VM and that made you proud

You knew it by name and fame and IP address
The smallest scratch and you'd seek redress

Those were good times but they had a big failing
That, my friends, was before autoscaling

Well this cloud world is no more like that
Ephemeral IPs change at the drop of a hat

Now VMs come up and VMs go down
Big reason to smile and a small one to frown

How is a client to know whom to reach
When the backends keep changing like waves on a beach?

Ah! That's the cue for the load balancer crew
Static front-end that clients know too

Lots of cool options for all protocols - or most
And a hardened front-end called a bastion host

Either Content-based or cross-regional
HTTP loves you, the feeling is mutual

So that is the ballad of the LB gang
Fresh from the earth yesterday they sprang

In the cloud world, load-balancer devices are an essential static entry point for apps. They have a static IP address that clients can be sure will remain unchanged, and accept incoming client requests and distribute them to a variable set of backend instances. The size of that set of backend instances can keep changing—that's the whole point of autoscaling abstractions such as managed-instance groups.

Taxonomy of GCP load balancers

Each of the major cloud providers supports several different types of load balancer, and cloud architects can choose the type that best suits their use cases. Here is a taxonomy of load balancers that are available on the GCP:

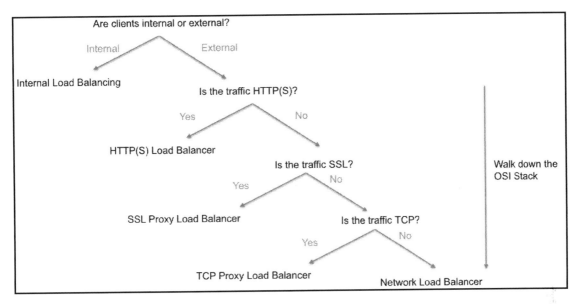

As this diagram illustrates, load balancers can operate at different layers of the OSI stack. HTTP(S) load balancers operate at the application layer, SSL is a session-layer protocol, TCP is a transport-layer protocol, and network load balancers operate at the level of IP, which, of course, is a network protocol.

The rule of thumb is this: *go with the highest layer of the OSI stack possible*. So, for instance, if your application is based on HTTP or HTTPS, use HTTP(S) load balancing. If not, try to work at the session layer, and so on. The reason for this is the higher in the stack you are, the more *real-world* the abstractions become.

HTTP(S) load balancing

HTTP(S) load balancers are the most popular and most widely used, simply because there is so much that can be done at this layer. It is possible to distribute traffic based on the type of incoming request; for instance, requests for static content go to one set of servers, while requests for video content go to another. This is called content-based load balancing.

It is, of course, most common to simply route requests to the nearest backend servers that can field a request; if those backend servers reside in different regions, then this is called cross-regional load balancing. This is something that can be used, for instance, to direct traffic originating in India to servers that are also located there.

HTTP/HTTPS (commonly written as HTTP(S)) load balancers deal with HTTP requests on the instances. They support both IPv6 and IPv4 traffic from clients. The following is the architecture of a GCP HTTP load balancer.

- The request first passes through global forwarding rules and is guided to a target proxy. The rules use tags to identify the appropriate target proxy.
- Each request is checked against a URL map, which determines the appropriate backend service for it.
- The requests are passed through backend services. Each backend instance's health is determined by a HTTP(s) health check.
- Finally, the request is guided to the desired backend instance.
- The process is similar for both HTTP and HTTPS. The only difference is that, in the case of HTTPS, the target proxy must have/provide an SSL certificate for verification.
- If the data of the request is to be stored, backend services store it in backend buckets, which are Google Cloud Storage buckets in this case.

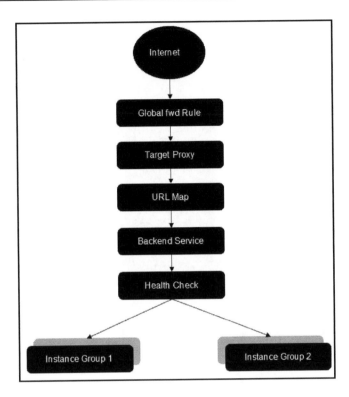

In case things do not go as planned, HTTP(S) load balancing has two different types of timeout:

- **Response timeout**: This is a configurable timeout where the load balancer will wait for the backend process to return the completion flag. The default waiting duration is 30 seconds. If it takes longer than that, then the counter will reset and the request will be skipped.
- **Session timeout**: This is also called an Idle timeout. It is fixed, so the value cannot be configured. In this case, the value is fixed at 10 mins (600 seconds). The only exception to session timeouts are WebSockets.

On the other hand, the logging and monitoring of a load balancer works the same as any other component and is served by Stackdriver.

Configuring HTTP(S) load balancing

Let's take an example where we create two VMs in different regions with the same tag, and test them for HTTP(S) load balancing:

1. Use the following command to create a VM and allow HTTP(S) traffic to it. Here, we are installing Debian on the VM and running commands such as updating it, installing Apache on it, and hosting a simple web page on it. You can name these instances sequentially for convenience, for example, www-1, www-2, and so on:

```
gcloud compute instances create <<<first-instance-name>>>  \
    --image-family debian-8 \
    --image-project debian-cloud \
    --zone us-central1-b \
    --tags https-tag \
    --metadata startup-script="#! /bin/bash /
sudo apt-get update /
sudo apt-get install apache2 -y /
sudo a2ensite default-ssl /
sudo a2enmod ssl /
sudo service apache2 restart /
echo '<!doctype  / /html><html><body><h1>instance-1-
name</h1></body></html>' | tee / var/www/html/index.html /
        EOF"
```

```
gcloud compute instances create <<<second-instance-name>>>  \
    --image-family debian-8 \
    --image-project debian-cloud \
    --zone us-central1-b \
    --tags https-tag \
    --metadata startup-script="#! /bin/bash /
sudo apt-get update /
sudo apt-get install apache2 -y /
sudo a2ensite default-ssl /
sudo a2enmod ssl /
sudo service apache2 restart /
echo '<!doctype  / /html><html><body><h1>instance-2-
name</h1></body></html>' | tee / var/www/html/index.html /
EOF"
```

```
gcloud compute instances create <<<third-instance-name>>>  \
    --image-family debian-8 \
    --image-project debian-cloud \
    --zone europe-west1-b \
    --tags https-tag \
    --metadata startup-script="#! /bin/bash /
```

```
sudo apt-get update /
sudo apt-get install apache2 -y /
sudo a2ensite default-ssl /
sudo a2enmod ssl /
sudo service apache2 restart /
echo '<!doctype  / /html><html><body><h1>instance-3-
name</h1></body></html>' | tee / var/www/html/index.html /
EOF"
```

2. Now, we will create a firewall rule which will allow external traffic to our instances. Notice the HTTPS tags, which specify it to allow HTTPS traffic and use port 443 for this:

```
gcloud compute firewall-rules create www-firewall
    --target-tags https-tag --allow tcp:443
```

3. Now, to verify that our instances are running smoothly, list them and note their external IP. We can try to access them with a curl command and notice their response:

```
gcloud compute instances list
curl -k https:<<<//IP_ADDRESS>>>
```

4. Since our instances are running well, let us configure load balancers for them. This starts with providing IPv4 and IPv6 global static external IP addresses:

```
gcloud compute addresses create lb-ip-cr
  --ip-version=IPV4
  --global
gcloud compute addresses create lb-ipv6-cr
  --ip-version=IPV6
  --global
```

5. Now, let's create an instance group for each zone. Repeat this command for the Europe zone as well:

```
gcloud compute instance-groups <<<group name>>> create
  us-resources-s --zone us-central1-b
```

6. Now let's add our instances to their respective instance groups according to their zones. Repeat the command for Europe zone:

```
gcloud compute instance-groups <<group_name>>> add-instances
  us-resources-s
    --instances wwws-1,wwws-2
    --zone us-central1-b
```

7. Let's get a health check:

```
gcloud compute health-checks create https https-basic-check
   --port 443
```

8. Now, let's create a backend service for each content provider. In this case, we will set the protocol as HTTPS and use the health check that we created earlier:

```
gcloud compute backend-services create <<<service name>>>
   --protocol HTTPS
   --health-checks <<<health-check-name>>>
   --global
```

9. Now, let's add the instance group that we created as the backend. As you may have guessed, repeat the command for europe's zone:

```
gcloud compute backend-services add-backend
   web-map-backend-service
   --balancing-mode UTILIZATION
   --max-utilization 0.8
   --capacity-scaler 1
   --instance-group us-resources-s
   --instance-group-zone us-central1-b
   --global
```

10. Now, let's create a URL map which directs all incoming requests to our instances:

```
gcloud compute url-maps create <<<map name>>>
   --default-service  <<<service name>>>
```

11. To manage HTTPS requirements, let's create an SSL certificate for the HTTPS proxy and add an SSL policy for it. Finally, we will create a target proxy and global forwarding rule by using the following commands:

```
gcloud compute ssl-certificates create <<<certificate name>>>
   --certificate <<<CRT_FILE_PATH>>>
   --private-key <<<KEY_FILE_PATH>>>
gcloud compute ssl-policies create cr_ssl_policy
--profile MODERN --min-tls-version 1.0
gcloud compute target-https-proxies create https-lb-proxy
 --url-map web-map --ssl-certificates <<<cert name>>>
gcloud compute forwarding-rules create <<<Rule name>>>
 --address <<<LB_IP_ADDRESS>>>
 --global
 --target-https-proxy <<<proxy name>>
 --ports 443
```

12. Now, our load balancing is configured. Let's guide traffic to it. First of all, let's find the IP address for our global forwarding rule:

```
gcloud compute forwarding-rules list
```

13. Finally, let's use the curl command and get our response:

```
curl https://<<<IPv4_ADDRESS>>>
```

Configuring Internal Load Balancing

Internal load balancing works with private load balancing IP which is exclusive to the VPC. Such load balancing is available for TCP/UDP based traffic. Perform following steps to setup internal load balancing:

1. Navigate to **Networking** | **Load balancing** and click on **Create load balancer**.

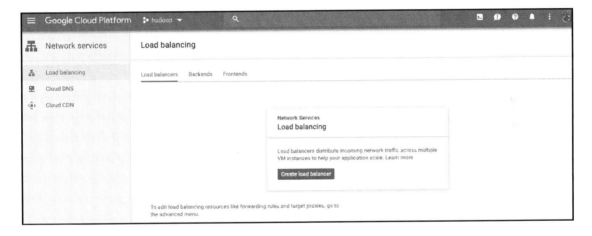

2. Select the type of load balancer (TCP/UDP) and click on **Start configuration**.

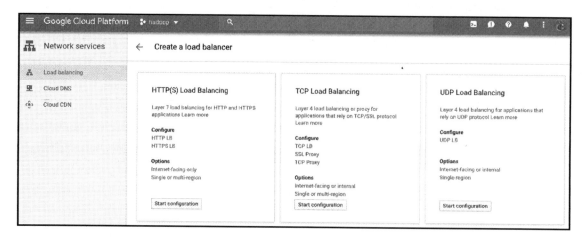

3. In the option of **Internet facing or Internal only** choose **Only between my VMs**.

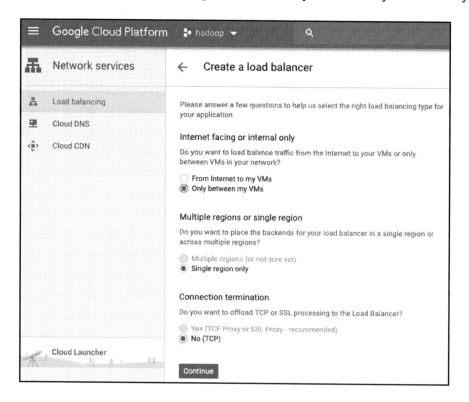

4. For configuring the backend, Choose your region (we will choose `us-central1`) and choose instance groups.
5. Finally, in the frontend configuration section, mention port as `8080` and keep rest of the values as default. Click on **Add frontend IP and Port**.
6. Click **Create** and your internal load balancing is setup.

Other load balancing

For non-HTTP(S) traffic, the load balancing policies vary a little but the objective remains essentially the same. Let's take a few examples:

- **SSL proxy load balancing**: With an SSL proxy, the SSL sessions are terminated at the beginning (at the global load-balancing layer).
- **TCP proxy**: Unlike an SSL proxy, this can handle HTTP(S) traffic, but is not the most recommended way. The advantage it does provide is the ability to use a single IP address for all of the routing, which may be required sometimes.
- **Internal load balancing**: This allows you to scale your services behind a private IP used for load balancing. This is internal, which means it is only applicable to networks used by GCP itself (for example, VPC). At the core, it uses TCP proxy and HTTP(S) load balancing.
- **Network load balancing**: This one is unique. It allows a load to be balanced based on the data of an incoming protocol IP (for example, network port, address, protocol type, and so on). Like HTTP(S) forwarding, this one also uses forwarding rules (limited to the network) and defines health checks for the pool. It is a pass-through load balancer, which means it does not proxy the connections.

Thus, Google Cloud Platform provides a load-balancing facility for all use cases. Load-balancing pricing is measured in units, where the first five rules cost $0.025 per hour and ingress data is $0.008 per GB. After five rules, each rule costs $0.010/hour. Thus, it is an economic way to keep your clusters efficient and balanced.

Summary

In this chapter, you learned why load balancing is important, along with the different types of load balancing and their uses. Finally, we took an in-depth look at HTTP(S) load balancing and how to establish it.

Networking in GCP
12

In previous chapters, we have seen various PaaS and IaaS offerings on Google Cloud Platform, such as the App Engine environment, Compute Engine VMs, and GKE (Kubernetes Engine). All of them involve independent or cluster-level networking. This is handled by **Virtual Private Cloud** (**VPC**) networks in GCP. Let's explore and understand the idea of VPCs in detail.

In this chapter, you will learn about the following:

- Virtual Private Cloud networks
- Subnets
- Firewall rules in GCP

Why GCP's networking model is unique

The way the GCP does networking is very different from what most networking professionals are used to, and other cloud providers such as AWS. This makes GCP networking confusing, especially since some of the important terms, such as VPC and subnet, have somewhat different meanings than in other contexts:

What's In A Name? The VPC Game

"What's in a name? That which we call a rose
By any other name would smell as sweet"

So said Shakespeare, but it's easy for a bard
For us engineers, that just makes things hard

VPC is a term that came from AWS
GCP uses it too, no more no less

But VPCs in AWS are in a region-bound
While VPCs in GCP are global all around

So if New York and London host two VMs in the same VPC
Though separated by the pond, internal IPs of each other they will see

Also a network used to mean an IP address tree
But in GCP, a VPC can be more than one hierarchy

So a VPC can have more than one disjoint IP address range
Great for logical separation, although still a bit strange

And in case you're wondering what a GCP subnet is
That's a great question and handy for a quiz

GCP subnets are regional and have a hierarchy
No disjoint IPs in a subnet - that would be anarchy

Every VPC is a distributed firewall
Routes and rules to control it all

Every project has a VPC that comes for free
The default subnet, with an inbuilt address tree

You can create more VPCs in a project if you'd like more
Auto or custom, the two types available in the store

VMs in the same VPC talk on IP addresses that are internal
Even if in different regions, their link is eternal

VMs in different VPCs talk on IP addresses that are external
Lower security and network costs can get infernal

If you've gone hybrid and need a secure link
Set up VPN and grab a soothing drink

To sense topology changes and routing that's dynamic
Add Cloud Router to VPN - said to be fantastic

There is a lot going on here, so let's go through and parse the implications of all of that:

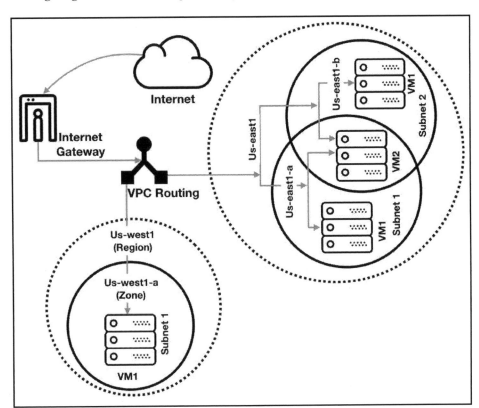

Each project in a GCP organization contains at least one default VPC. It can contain more than one network, depending on the resources requested. All VPCs of GCP are global resources, which means they are not bound to any particular zone or region. VPC resources have both internal and external IPs. The resources within the network communicate with each other using internal IPs, whereas external requests are served through external IP addresses. All of the traffic passes through a firewall and access to resources within the network is managed by IAM. Just like other networks, VPCs can also communicate with other VPC resources and VPNs.

In the backend as shown in the figure above, VPCs are distributed into partitions of smaller network also known as **Subnets**. Subnets are regional. One network can have one or more subnets in any region but a subnet will have all of the resources in the same region. In other words, we chose subnets and VPCs while defining regions for it. Once the regions are allocated to the subnets, IPs are instantly allocated to the resources created within them.

Every project has a quota, which limits the number of maximum VPCs to allocate. Apart from the quota, there are also limits. The specifics of and differences between them can be understood using the following table:

Item	Quota/limit	Amount	Meaning
VPC networks per project	Quota	5	Projects can have a maximum of five networks including default one
VMs per VPC network	Limit	7000	Maximum 7000 VMs per project
VM per subnet	Limit	NA	Any number of VMs as long as the total is less than 7000

The quota defines the number of VPC network instances that can be allotted to a project, and although the default value is 5, it can be increased. A limit is a fixed restriction of the number of resources, such as VMs, that can be housed in a VPC network. Limits are fixed and cannot be altered:

- **Auto mode VPC**: In an auto mode VPC, one subnet is created from each region. These subnets are assigned IPs within the `10.128.0.0/9` CIDR block and the process is automatic. Although GCP decides how many subnets to create, more subnets can be created manually.
- **Custom VPC**: VPC is created without creating subnets. Subnets are added manually afterwards. This provides more control over IP ranges and regions of subnets.

VPC networks and subnets

The term VPC is used in AWS to refer to the networking layer for EC2 Cloud Virtual Machines, and AWS VPC networks are regional. This implies that in AWS, if you have VMs in different regions, for example, one in the US and the other in the UK, they would have to be in different VPCs.

GCP VPCs Are Global

VPC is a term that came from AWS
GCP uses it too, no more no less

But VPCs in AWS are in a region-bound
While VPCs in GCP are global all around

In the Google Cloud world, on the other hand, resources on the same VPC can reside absolutely anywhere; two GCE VMs could be in different continents, while still residing in the same VPC. How is this possible? Well, clearly under the hood there is an internal routing mechanism that is hidden from the user and that makes this possible. This actually implies that Google VPC networks are a level up vis-a-vis their equivalents on other cloud platforms. We will have more to say on this just a bit later in the chapter when we discuss subnets:

Google networking term	Traditional networking equivalent
VPC network	Autonomous system (a collection of connected IP routing prefixes)
Subnet	VPC network on AWS, or an IP address range in the physical world (a hierarchy of IP addresses)

This table equates a GCP VPC to an **autonomous system** (**AS**) which is network of autonomous systems in the outside world. It is basically a union of IP address ranges with prefixed routing policies and are comprised of possibly different network operators. This implies that it is perfectly possible to have non-contiguous IP addresses inside the same VPC. For instance, the same VPC could have two subnets, one of which represents a `10.x.x.x` IP range, and the other represents a `192.x.x.x` range.

This idea can really take some getting used to, but it actually is quite a nice way to group resources and manage them. In a company with a physical networking setup, you could expect each department to have a subnet of its own, and in the same way, in the cloud you could group resources into subnets based on departments.

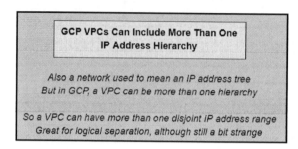

Clearly VPC subnets are akin to networks that we are used to; they represent a hierarchical IP address range, all resources in the same subnet must reside in the same region, and the address ranges of different subnets are not allowed to overlap. It is important to know that even within a subnet resources can still span zones, so you can explore options for HA inside a single subnet.

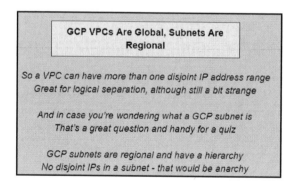

The default VPC

If you are from a networking background, all of this might make sense, but if you're not and just want to get up and running on the GCP, you'd quite possibly have a question: do I really need to know about VPCs, IP addresses and autonomous systems simply in order to use the GCP?

> **Default, Auto and Custom Networks**
>
> *Every project has a VPC that comes for free*
> *The default subnet, with an inbuilt address tree*
>
> *You can create more VPCs in a project if you'd like more*
> *Auto or custom, the two types available in the store*

The answer is a resounding **no**. By this point, you probably have enough GCP experience to realize that you don't start every new project by creating VPCs and configuring them. Clearly, that has been done for you by the platform. The mechanism for achieving this is the default VPC.

Every project comes with a default VPC and this default VPC is preconfigured with a bunch of essential plumbing:

- One subnet in each region (so that you can create VMs in any region and have them all exist on some subnet).
- A default internet gateway (this is the IP address to which packets get sent if no internal recipient can be found). It is possible to delete the default internet gateway to ensure network isolation.
- Default routes, which allow traffic to travel from one subnet to another.
- Firewall rules to allow network traffic to flow smoothly. These firewall rules are of two types:
    - The implied rules allow all egress and deny all ingress
    - An additional set of firewall rules to facilitate common protocols such as RDP, ICMP (ping), and SSH:

```
default-allow-internal, default-allow-ssh ,
  default-allow-rdp  and default-allow-icmp
```

Now, you can go ahead and create additional VPCs if you like, for instance if you would like to separate resources and make it hard for them to communicate with each other using internal IP addresses (more on that later). If you do decide to create additional VPCs, you can specify them to be either of type Auto, or of type custom.

Auto-mode networks are basically identical to the default VPC. A good way to think of this is to imagine a mold, or template, from which the default VPC is created. If you go ahead and create an auto-mode VPC, that too will be struck from this same template.

Custom-mode networks are very different though; they will come without much of the previous functionality. The idea is you only create a custom-model VPC if you want to take control of the nitty-gritty, in which case you probably don't want a set of pre-existing subnets, routes, or firewall rules.

Auto-mode networks can be converted to custom-mode ones, but the reverse is not possible. You can take charge, but once you do, you're in charge forever and can't return control to the platform.

Internal and external IP addresses

Resources that are in the same VPC can communicate using internal IP addresses, as well as using a project-internal DNS facility. This is true even if the resources are in different regions. For instance, consider two VMs, one in the US and the other in the UK; provided these are in the same VPC, they will be able to communicate using internal IP addresses despite their physical distance.

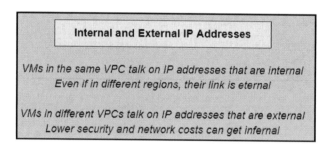

By contrast, if two resources are in different VPCs, even if they happen to be in the same region or even on the same underlying bare metal box (remember that GCP VMs are multi-tenanted), they will still have to communicate using external IP addresses, which implies that the network traffic between them will have to pass over the internet (or Google's global network in this case).

Internal IP addresses are assigned from the subnet range using the familiar DHCP protocol, and they are renewed every 24 hours. Each VM on a subnet is accessible using a network-scoped DNS. The **Fully Qualified Domain Name (FQDN)** for a VM is of the form:

```
[HOST_NAME].c.[PROJECT_ID].internal
```

External IP addresses, on the other hand, are ephemeral by default. If you'd like to fix an external IP address, you need to reserve it. Such reserved external IP addresses are said to be static and are chargeable if they are not in use. This is meant to deter folks from needlessly reserving IP addresses and then not using them.

Finally, you should be aware that a VM is not aware of its external IP address, that's a part of the metadata and is stored in a metadata server. So, if you run `ifconfig` on a VM, what you see is the internal IP address.

Communication on internal IP addresses has several advantages:

- **Cost**: Remember that network egress traffic incur charges. Communication over internal IP addresses costs as low as $0.01/GB.
- **Security**: Google's internal networks are relatively invulnerable to intrusion and security attacks. After all, Google has been under siege from hackers for over a decade now. However, once traffic leaves Google's internal networks and touches the internet, all bets are off.
- **Latency**: Google internal networks are blazingly fast. This is partially a legacy of Google's investments in YouTube, and in trying to get video served at acceptable latencies in all or most regions of the world. Internal traffic on the GCP is able to hitch a ride on these really fast internal links.

If you do have resources in different VPCs or even different projects that you'd like to hook up with internal links, two relatively advanced features you can consider are:

- **VPC peering**: This is a way to establish a pipe between a pair of VPCs. In case you are wondering how this differs from VPN, the encryption is done at network layer itself and is applied to private IPs within the same VPC.
- **Shared VPC**: This is a way to create a VPC in project A, and then have resources such as VMs that reside in a different project (projects B and C) which still reside on the same VPC. Project A is called the host project, and incurs the costs associated with the shared VPC.

VPN and cloud router

The term hybrid is usually used to describe a combination of an on-premises data center and a set of cloud-based resources. Hybrid architectures are becoming increasingly common for the simple reason that as big organizations move to the cloud, they need a hybrid setup during the migration period, and while they evaluate whether their cloud strategy is the right one.

```
┌─────────────────────────────────────────────────────┐
│  ┌─────────────────────────────────────────────┐     │
│  │             VPN and Cloud Router              │     │
│  └─────────────────────────────────────────────┘     │
│                                                       │
│      If you've gone hybrid and need a secure link     │
│        Set up VPN and grab a soothing drink           │
│                                                       │
│   Your local and cloud resources each other they can see │
│  On internal IPs - that's great and secure, even if not free │
│                                                       │
│      What if you'd like them to automatically know    │
│     When you add a rack or your VPC starts to grow?   │
│                                                       │
│    To sense topology changes and routing that's dynamic │
│     Add Cloud Router to VPN - said to be fantastic    │
└─────────────────────────────────────────────────────┘
```

The importance of hybrid infrastructures makes the VPN service a particularly important one for organizations that are moving to the cloud. It is trivial to set up a VPN connection between your on-premises setup and your organizations' cloud resources. This VPN connection will be secure, with a gateway at each end. The gateway at your on-premises end will be a physical one that you control, while the gateway at the GCP end is a virtual router, managed by the GCP.

There is a fair bit of advanced networking that goes on under the hood with VPN connections, notably the encryption of traffic at each end by the gateway device and the decryption at the other end. This requires the exchange of keys between those two devices, and happens using a specialized protocol called **Internet Key Exchange** (**IKE**). We will not dwell on the details of how this works, but you should be aware that VPN connections are secure. This also has the unfortunate side effect of making them relatively slow; if you have ever used a VPN connection to access your corporate network from home or while traveling, this is probably something you are familiar with. Here, the reason for slower speed will most likely be due to slower connections on the user's end. Apart from that, it is also important to remember that keeping a VPN up and running incurs charges which makes them costlier.

If your organization is considering a hybrid setup for the long term (rather than merely as a stopgap during migration or evaluation), you might want to consider some of the enterprise grade interconnection options that the GCP offers, notably Cloud Interconnect, which is a program where trusted third-party ISPs (such as AT&T, KDDI, SoftBank, and Tata) work with your organization and with Google to provide a high-quality interconnection without the overhead of VPN. Do check Google's list of supported service providers, the list is constantly growing.

Finally, VPN by itself is not going to provide dynamic routing capabilities. This means that if, for instance, a new rack of servers is added to your on-premises setup, your GCP VMs are not going to learn about it unless you turn down and turn back up your gateway device. To enable dynamic routing, you can make use of another GCP service called Cloud Router. This will make the VPN gateway device a BGP-enabled one, which provides dynamic route advertisement. This way, topology changes at either end will be picked up on the fly.

Working with VPCs

Working with GCP VPCs should be easy to adapt to if you have already gone through the previous chapters and are familiar with the GUI of web console:

1. Click on the menu button in the top left corner of web console, navigate to the **VPC network** tab, and go to the **VPC networks** section:

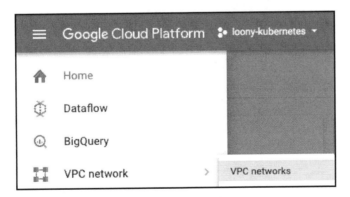

2. Click on **Create VPC Network**.

3. Fill in the specification fields and choose automatic in the **Subnets** field. Make sure that the name of the VPC only contains lowercase letters and no space characters in it:

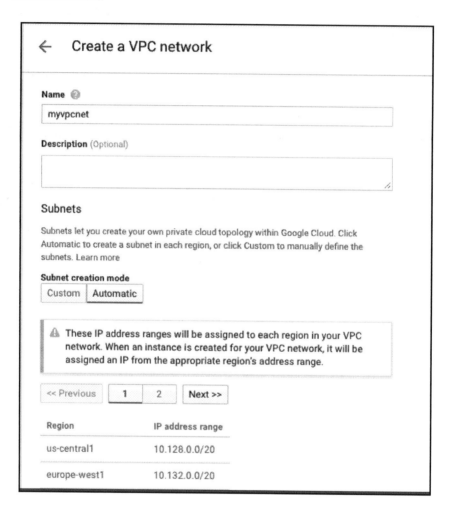

4. We can choose the firewall rules from a set of predefined ones, but we will create them later:

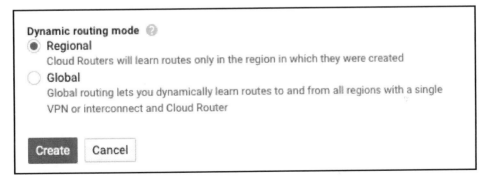

Firewall rules
Select any of the firewall rules below that you would like to apply to this VPC network.
Once the VPC network is created, you can manage all firewall rules on the Firewall rules page.

☐ Name	Type	Targets	Filters	Protocols / ports	Action	Priority
☐ myvpcnet-allow-icmp	Ingress	Apply to all	IP ranges: 0.0.0.0/0	icmp	Allow	65534
☐ myvpcnet-allow-internal	Ingress	Apply to all	IP ranges: 10.128.0.0/9	all	Allow	65534
☐ myvpcnet-allow-rdp	Ingress	Apply to all	IP ranges: 0.0.0.0/0	tcp:3389	Allow	65534
☑ myvpcnet-allow-ssh	Ingress	Apply to all	IP ranges: 0.0.0.0/0	tcp:22	Allow	65534
myvpcnet-deny-all-ingress	Ingress	Apply to all	IP ranges: 0.0.0.0/0	all	Deny	65535
myvpcnet-allow-all-egress	Egress	Apply to all	IP ranges: 0.0.0.0/0	all	Allow	65535

5. After choosing **Regional** or **Global** routing, click on **Create**. We will choose **Regional**:

Dynamic routing mode
- ● Regional
  Cloud Routers will learn routes only in the region in which they were created
- ○ Global
  Global routing lets you dynamically learn routes to and from all regions with a single VPN or interconnect and Cloud Router

[Create] [Cancel]

6. You can edit it later by switching to custom mode from auto mode.

7. Finally, you delete a VPC network by either going to the VPC Networks page and clicking on **DeleteVPC network** after selecting a network, or using the following command:

```
gcloud compute networks delete [NETWORK_NAME]
```

Working with custom subnets

As discussed earlier, it is possible to create a custom subnet in an already existing VPC. Follow these steps:

1. Navigate to the VPC networking page and choose one of the available networks.
2. Click on the **Add a subnet** option:

3. Fill in the details for name, region, IP range, and secondary IP range. Make sure you don't overlap IP ranges with any other existing subnet in your VPC.

4. After deciding to opt for logs and Private Google Access, click on the **Add** option.

5. Alternatively, you can use following command in the cloud shell:

```
gcloud compute networks subnets create <<<SUBNET_NAME>>>
--network <<<NETWORK>>>
--range <<<IP_RANGE>>>
[--secondary-range <<<RANGE_NAME>>>=<<<2ND_IP_RANGE>>>
```

6. To describe any subnet, use the following command:

```
gcloud compute networks subnets describe <<<SUBNET_NAME>>>
    --region <<<REGION>>>
```

7. Finally, to delete any subnet, use the following command:

```
gcloud compute networks subnets delete <<<SUBNET_NAME>>>
    --region <<<REGION>>>
```

Working with firewall rules

We have already discussed the idea that a VPC is effectively a distributed firewall; it enforces rules and monitors the flow of network traffic. These are the characteristics for the firewall rules:

- The rules defined for one VPC don't apply to others
- They only support IPv4 traffic, so addresses are also IPv4 only
- The only possible actions for firewall rules are allow and deny for ingress or egress
- Firewalls cannot allow traffic in one direction while denying it in the other
- The number of tracked connections vary with machine type

Any firewall rule component will contain direction of traffic, action, protocol, and a numerical value for priority. Priority can range from 0 (the most important) to 65535 (the least important).

Let's see how to create and manage custom firewall rules:

1. To create a firewall rule, you need to provide information such as action (allow/deny), network, protocol, and direction of the traffic (ingress/egress) to the following command. It is important to remember that if we choose to skip any of the following fields, GCP will stick to its default values:

```
gcloud compute firewall-rules create [NAME]
    [--network [NETWORK]; default="default"]
    [--allow   ([PROTOCOL][:PORT[-PORT]],[PROTOCOL[:PORT[-
    PORT]],...]] | all )
    [--action (deny | allow )]
    [--rules   ([PROTOCOL][:PORT[-PORT]],[PROTOCOL[:PORT[-
    PORT]],...]] | all )
    [--direction (ingress|egress|in|out); default="ingress"]
    [--priority [PRIORITY];default=1000]
    [--destination-ranges [CIDR-RANGE][,CIDR-RANGE...]]
    [--source-ranges [CIDR-RANGE][,CIDR-RANGE...]]
    [--source-tags [TAG][,TAG,...]]
    [--target-tags [TAG][,TAG,...]]
    [--source-service-accounts=[EMAIL]]
    [--target-service-accounts=[EMAIL]]
```

2. Any of the provided configurations can be updated with the following command:

```
gcloud compute firewall-rules create [NAME] <<<args>>>
```

3. The same rules can be reviewed by using the describe command:

```
gcloud compute firewall-rules describe <<<FIREWALL_RULE_NAME>>>
```

4. And finally, to delete the firewall rule, use this simple one-line command:

```
gcloud compute firewall-rules delete [FIREWALL_RULE_NAME]
```

Similarly, a firewall rule can also be created using web console. The steps for the same are as following:

1. Navigate to the **Firewall rules** page in the GCP console by searching it in the search bar:

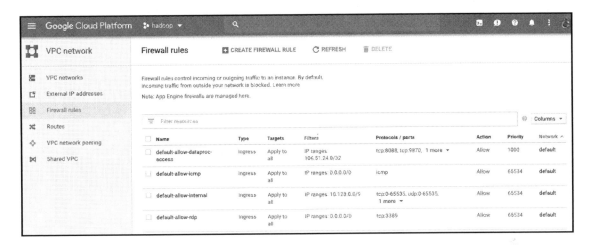

2. Click on **CREATE FIREWALL RULE.**
3. Enter a name for the firewall rule. The name needs to be unique within the project. We will name it `myrule`.
4. Specify a network for the firewall to be implemented along with the priority of the rule. We will keep it to **default**
5. Choose between **Ingress** and **Egress** as direction of your traffic. We will choose **Ingress**.

6. **Allow** or **Deny** the action on match. We will **Allow**.

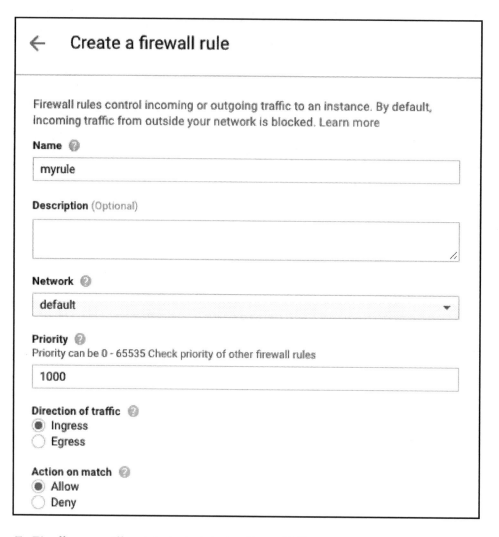

7. Finally, we will put 0.0.0.0/0 to allow all IP ranges.
8. Hit **Create** and your firewall rule is created.

Summary

We learned about the Virtual Private Cloud networks of GCP and their infrastructure, and how to create and manage our own VPC networks.

Finally, we took a look at how to manage custom subnets and firewall rules for our VPC networks.

13
Logging and Monitoring

In previous chapters, we have worked with many provisions and services of GCP, ranging from Compute Engine-hosted VMs to serverless, fully managed databases. When we are dealing with so many different components, keeping track of usage, errors, and activities becomes essential. This is where GCP's Stackdriver services are useful. Stackdriver is a cloud monitoring, metrics and analysis service by Google. Its main task is to provide performance and diagnostic data to GCP users. Stackdriver offers logging and monitoring services for GCP resources for free, up to a certain quota, and can monitor both GCP and AWS resources for premium account holders.

In this chapter, you will learn about the following:

- Logging in GCP
- Filtering in logs
- Exporting logs
- Stackdriver monitoring

Logging

In computing, logging refers to a record of events that have occurred over a certain time period. In GCP, logs are associated with projects; that is, each project will have separate logs. Logs can be used for debugging, tracking billing, analyzing performance, or just as proof of an event or task. Stackdriver allows users to view, filter, and export logs:

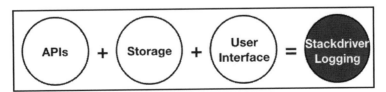

As shown in the diagram, the Stackdriver logging component is made up of three elements:

- Logging APIs, which are used to fetch record logs.
- Storage, that is, cloud storage buckets. The log export APIs have access to cloud storage buckets where logs can directly be streamed.
- A user interface to interact fluently with logs.

Logs are stored as objects of the type LogEntry. Log entries can be created by GCP or AWS services, and they use the `entries.write` method to write the logs. Mostly, the logs are automatically named, and the naming convention follows something simple like an identifier or a structured name consisting of author, identifier, and timestamp. Logs are kept for a certain time, even after deletion of the logged object itself, and this time period is called the retention period. To store the logs permanently, it is advisable to export them to cloud storage buckets before the retention period expires. In general, logs are recorded collectively for all of the resources, but while viewing and/or operating them, we can apply filters as per our needs. Logs are stored in plain text or JSON files. This is how filtering works:

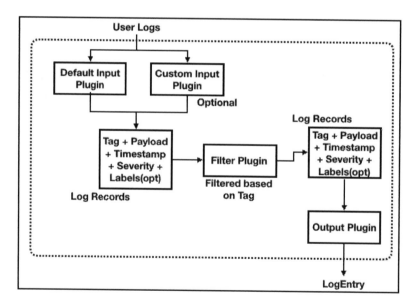

A user log is an accumulation of tag, payload, timestamp, severity, and labels. Here, payload refers to the data passed to APIs for performing operations (for example, the dataset of BigQuery), while severity distinguishes between config, information, warning, or errors. Tags are mandatory and labels are optional; both of them are used for filtering the logs. If the organization has multiple projects, it is advisable to keep relevant labels to avoid confusion.

GCP's Stackdriver pricing model includes two tiers.

- **Basic tier:** Usage is completely free but limited to GCP. Apart from that, this tier doesn't include Stackdriver monitoring agent.
- **Premium tier:** It charges $8 per month per resource and supports not only GCP but AWS as well. It also provides Stackdriver monitoring agent.

There are also internal uses of logs for GCP, such as auditing. Auditing is performed by audit logs, which are permanent logs recorded by GCP to monitor access and activities on resources and keep precise data for billing. Similar entities are admin activity logs, which are written to record administrative actions on resources, such as creation or deletion. As a byproduct of these cases, wider retention periods make it easier to keep the billing transparent. Logs are accessible to members of the project with appropriate roles. Roles are a convenient way to grant IAM permissions. Here is a list of roles, with descriptions:

Role	Description
Logs viewer	Gives read-only access to all logs, except data-access audit logs
Private logs viewer	Read-only access to all logs, including private logs
Logs writer	Gives access to service accounts to allow applications to write logs
Configuration writer	Gives access to create logs of logs (log metrics and export sinks)
Logging admin	The Big Boss, who has all permissions related to Stackdriver logging
Project viewer	The same as the logs viewer, but confined to a project
Project editor	Includes permissions to view, write, export, and delete logs for a project
Project owner	The same as the logging admin, but confined to a project

Working with logs

GCP web console is quite easy-to-handle way to work with logs and other resources. Following are the steps to setup logging on resources.

1. Navigate to the menu action button with three horizontal lines on the GCP web console.

2. Click on the button and navigate to **Logging** | **Logs**, and you will land on the logs viewing page:

3. To make sure you find the logs you desire, tweak the log type (activity or data access), log level (severity), and time window of the event.

4. You will find logs similar to these:

5. To create a log metric, you can click on **Create Metric** and name the metric of the logs that you filtered. This metric can be viewed in Stackdriver in a graphical format.

6. To export the logs to a sink (destination), you can navigate to the **Exports** tab under the **Logging** tab and click on the **Create Export** button:

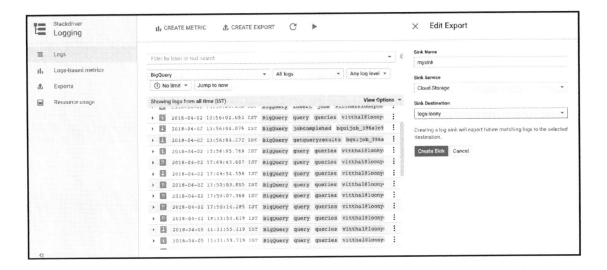

7. If you don't have a previously created sink, you should get a prompt to create one. Here, we will specify the destination as a cloud storage bucket named `logs-loony`.

8. By clicking on the **Play** button, it will start streaming the logs:

9. If you want to view the exported logs, you can navigate to the bucket and find them. For more information on cloud storage buckets, refer to `Chapter 5`, *Google Cloud Storage - Fishing in a Bucket*.

Thus, we saw how to setup logging and start logs streaming.

More Stackdriver – creating log-based metrics

Log-based metrics allow a logging agent to record certain number of logs of certain types of messages (such as error logs) over certain period of time. There are system-defined log-based metrics and user-defined log-based metrics. To create one, perform following steps:

1. Go to **Stackdriver logging | logs** and click on the **CREATE METRIC** button.

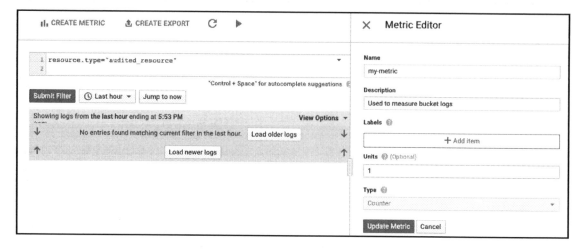

2. Name your metric. We will name them `my-metric` and describe its use. Provide labels as required. Here, we will give it as `resource.type="audited_resource"`.

3. Click on **Create** to create the metric.

4. You can edit or delete the metric once it is created by clicking on the three dots at the right end of the metric name.

5. Optionally, you can also create an alert for the metric from the same popup.

6. Clicking on it will guide you to Stackdriver UI. Here, you can mention the condition of the alert. We have asked for log entries above 4 for 5 minutes in past 1 hour.

7. Click on **Save Condition** to save the rule. Optionally, you can also define documentation for it by clicking on **+Add Documentation**.

8. Finally, save the policy.

Thus, this is how we create alerting policies for Stackdriver logs in GCP. Now, we will discuss the monitoring aspects of Stackdriver in GCP.

Monitoring

Monitoring mainly involves metrics, time series, and resources. Metrics help us get a better idea of how our deployments or applications are performing. Monitoring applies to resources, access, and activities. Here, we will understand it using a Compute Engine VM:

1. Create a Compute Engine VM (we will create one called `lamp-1` with the Debian OS) and SSH into it. For more information on how to create a Compute Engine VM instance, refer to `Chapter 3`, *Compute Choices – VMs and the Google Compute Engine*. Make sure you allow both HTTP and HTTPS traffic, to make network activity monitoring more efficient.

2. Install the Apache2 HTTP server with the following commands:

```
sudo apt-get update
sudo apt-get install apache2 php7.0
```

3. Go to the Stackdriver monitoring homepage using the following link and sign in using your GCP account. You will be given free 30-day-trial access. Navigate to it using the following link: `https://app.google.stackdriver.com/`.

4. Navigate to your project on the home page and go to **Resources | Instances**:

5. You will see the VM you created listed there. Click on it.

6. This will give the monitored stats of the VM. We are looking at CPU, network, and disk usage:

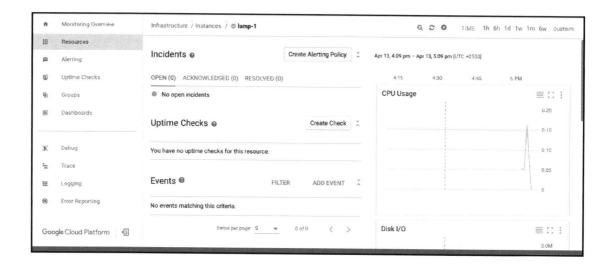

7. You can also apply filters based on your requirements and customize your metrics.

Summary

In this chapter, you learned how logging and monitoring facilities are provisioned in GCP via Stackdriver. You also learned about types of logs and roles affiliated to logs, and how to filter and explore logs.

Finally, you took a brief look at how to monitor resources using a Compute Engine VM example.

14
Infrastructure Automation

In this chapter, we turn our focus to infrastructure automation, a topic that is becoming quite hot these days and is also often referred to as **Infrastructure as a Code (IaaC)**. The idea is that provisioning resources can be done programmatically, using templates, commands, and even code. The implication of this is quite profound, particularly for companies that specialize in providing IT services and system integration. Such companies often have a large number of employees working on deploying infrastructure, servicing tickets, requisitioning hardware, and so on. The fundamental business model of such firms could change, and those that are not nimble might be at existential risk. In general, IAC can also be considered as the starting point of the DevOps movement. It acts as a foundation of Infrastructure automation which not only expedites the software development and delivery process but also makes it a lot more cost and quality efficient. Infrastructure as a Code is a big deal for large components of the workforce, so you should be sure to understand what it is all about.

You learn the following topics in this chapter:

- Managed Instance Groups
- Deployment manager

Managed Instance Groups

One cloud virtual machine instance is fine, but we've seen at the very start of the book that the reasons for switching to the cloud can be summed up in two words: autohealing and autoscaling. One cloud VM instance is not going to provide autohealing or autoscaling, so we need a higher-level abstraction, the **Managed Instance Group (MIG)**.

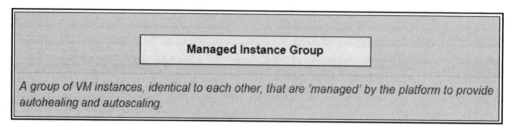

Understanding this one sentence is really important, so let's parse it carefully.

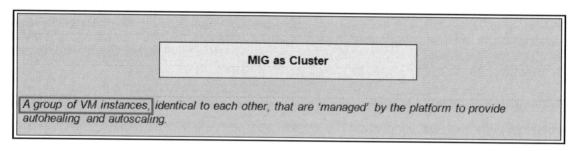

That fundamentally is what a Managed Instance Group is. Each element in MIG is GCE VM, just like any other GCE VM that you might have spun up. One VM instance is vulnerable; it can crash or be overwhelmed by a spike in client traffic, but a group of VM instances is effectively a cluster and much more robust.

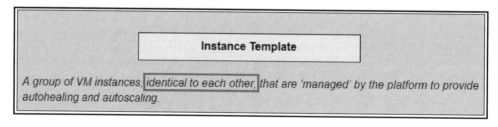

All the VM instances in an MIG are cast from the same mold; that mold is called an instance template. How does an instance template come into existence? In pretty much the same two ways that an individual VM comes into existence:

- You can create an instance template by specifying much the same properties that you would while creating an individual VM: the name, machine type, boot disk, and OS image
- You can import an instance template from an external image or Docker container

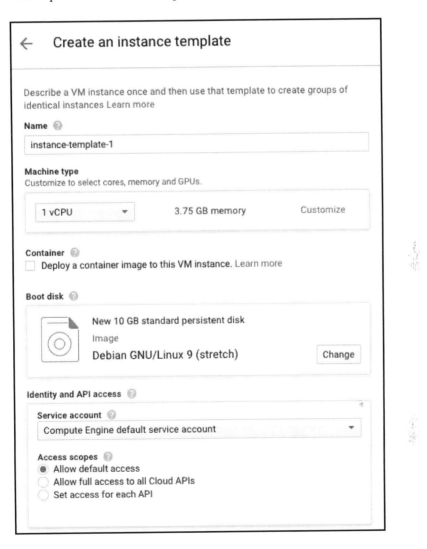

The platform takes responsibility for ensuring that each member of the MIG is running and ready to accept client requests. This is done by associating a health check with the MIG. The health check can be best thought of as a probe or polling program that will keep asking each member of the MIG whether it is healthy or not. This probe will need to be received and understood by the individual VM instances, which means that the protocol and port must be prespecified; the choices of protocol are HTTP(S), TCP, and SSL (TLS).

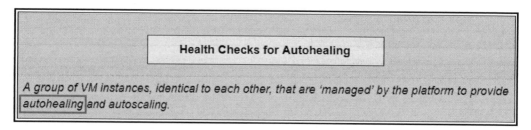

Health Checks for Autohealing

A group of VM instances, identical to each other, that are 'managed' by the platform to provide autohealing and autoscaling.

The health checker will ping each instance at a specified interval (named the check interval) and then wait. If no response is received within another specified interval (named the timeout), the health checker concludes that the VM instance is down. If a specific number of such probes all time out, the MIG will spin up a new instance to replace this sick one. That specified number of failures is called the unhealthy threshold. In the meantime, the service will ping the unhealthy instances as well, hoping that they have come back online. Once a new VM instance comes online, the checker will look for a number of consecutive successful pings (named the healthy threshold) before deciding that it is safe to send traffic to the instance.

Now, if you are paying close attention, you might note that the algorithm does not really sound like autohealing because the service does not actually restart the unhealthy instances, it merely continues polling them, hoping that some engineer has gone in and fixed them. So this, technically, is healing, but not quite autohealing.

If you thought this, well, you're wide awake, and absolutely right. The term autohealing refers specifically to an additional feature (currently in beta) in which the health check will recreate an instance once the health check fails. This automated restart really is autohealing although even the ordinary healing is quite important because it ensures that crashes of individual members of an MIG do not reduce the capacity of the MIG as a whole.

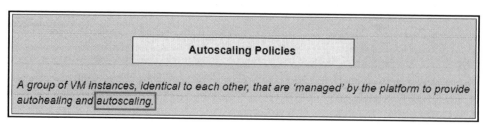

Autoscaling is another important additional feature of MIGs. You can specify a way for the MIG to measure how much load your VM instances are experiencing, and the number of elements in the MIG will go up or down in order keep that load close to a threshold you specify.

So, for instance, you might specify a CPU utilization threshold, say 60%. The service will then measure the average CPU utilization across the MIG, and if that number exceeds 60%, new VM instances will be spun up from the instance template we mentioned earlier. Later, say traffic dies down and the average CPU utilization falls to 55%, the MIG will also scale down by getting rid of some VM instances. This scale-down is graceful; connection draining will ensure that existing requests are serviced even as new ones are not accepted. Over time, those existing requests will be serviced, and once they are all done, the instance can shut down and exit the MIG.

Autoscaling is very fast, policies are checked, and updates to the state of the MIG are made every minute or so.

Another few important points worth keeping in mind: autoscaling policies can focus on CPU utilization, HTTP load balancing requests/second, or Stackdriver metrics. The last bit about Stackdriver is subtle: remember that Stackdriver allows us to create custom metrics, so we effectively can specify an autoscaling policy based on anything we want to measure (we do need to instrument our code and define the custom metric in Stackdriver though).

If you specify multiple policies, the MIG will go with the most liberal policy, that is, it will always to tend to provision the largest number of VM instances that might be needed by your app.

The advantage of autoscaling is obvious: you can scale up when traffic surges, but scale down (and save cost) when traffic falls. Autoscaling is a pretty important feature for any compute service, and indeed, GCE VMs are not alone in offering this functionality. Autoscaling comes with the territory in App Engine, you don't need to do anything to get it going. App Engine Flex is a bit slower to scale up and down than App Engine standard, but they both provide autoscaling. On the GKE, you can use an abstraction called a **Horizontal Pod Autoscaler (HPA)** to get similar functionality.

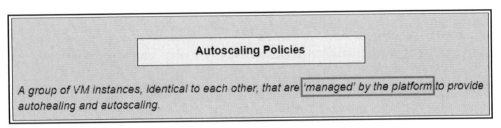

Hopefully, the manner in which the platform manages an instance group is clear, and there is a lot of behind-the-scenes processing going on to make sure that the actual and desired states of the MIG are in synch. One last bit, you should be aware that MIGs can be hooked up, pretty much automatically, to load balancers as backend server clusters. This use of MIGs with load balancers is a very important cloud use case.

Cloud deployment manager

Managed instance groups are a pretty fine way to automate virtual machines, but as we have already seen, VM instances are only a small part of the full suite of services a cloud platform has to offer. You might legitimately even question whether MIGs constitute IAC; after all, MIGs can be scripted using `gcloud` but not really using a programming language. To that extent, MIGs are a primitive form of infrastructure automation, but far from the real deal.

Let's say you needed to instantiate 1000 VM instances and each with a specific instance hostname and unique customized configuration. How would you go about this?

Here are some options:

- Get someone to sit and create them, one by one, using the web UI. This is not as inefficient as it sounds because the configurations are all different from each other, many organizations have teams that do exactly this.

- Organize the configurations, and put them in a database table. This table would have columns for each individual property, such as hostname, machine type, location, and zone. Then write a program that reads those from a database and invokes the Google Cloud API, either using the RESTful API directly, or using the gcloud command line.

- Create individual templates for each unique configuration, and create a managed instance group for each, using the exact number of instances of each type. Note that we would lose the ability to customize the hostname.

None of these options are particularly appealing. The middle option is the most robust from many points of view, but it has one important drawback: it involves writing a lot of code. Not just any code, but sensitive code that will automatically provision machines. If that code ran into an infinite loop and created a million VM instances rather than just a thousand, there would be real problems for everyone concerned.

Would it not be awesome if the platform provided some functionality that basically did the same thing, but spared us from writing code?

It turns out this exact same question has been asked several times in several different contexts, and the answer is almost always, yes, it would be awesome, and that would need a declarative syntax that is not quite code.

If you are wondering what some of these contexts are, here are three:

- **Structured Query Language (SQL)**, is a declarative language that allows users (even non-programmers) the ability to pull data from complicated RDBMS without bothering about their internals.

- The **Hypertext Markup Language (HTML)** is a declarative language that allows users (even non-programmers) the ability to create and render complicated web pages on browsers without bothering about their internals.

- **JavaScript Object Notation (JSON)** is a specification format that allows users (even non-programmers) the ability to query and pull data from document storage technologies such as Elasticsearch without bothering about its internals.

The idea is easy to extend to infrastructure deployments: create a template and specify what infrastructure you'd like to provision using that template and pass that template over to the platform, which will take care of the rest.

We can then bring to bear all the following advantages of working with code, without having to actually write code ourselves:

- **Reuse**: The same template can be used again and again without additional effort
- **Composability**: One template can include or reference another, and complex architectures can be put together this way
- **Source control**: The templates can be placed in source repositories (such as Git) and subject to all of the associated checks and balances

So, to create 1,000 VMs, the steps needed are as follows:

1. Create a configuration file, and let's call this `simple_config.yaml`:

```
resources:
- name: some-vm
  type: compute.v1.instance
  properties:
    zone: asia-south1-a
    machineType:
     https://www.googleapis.com/compute/v1/projects/myproject/
       zones/us-central1-f/machineTypes/f1-micro
    disks:
    - deviceName: boot
      type: PERSISTENT
      boot: true
      autoDelete: true
      initializeParams:
        sourceImage:
https://www.googleapis.com/compute/v1/projects/debian-cloud/glo
bal/images/family/debian-8
    networkInterfaces:
    - network:
https://www.googleapis.com/compute/v1/projects/myproject/global
/networks/default
      accessConfigs:
      - name: External NAT
        type: ONE_TO_ONE_NAT
```

2. Execute the `configuration` file using:

```
gcloud deployment-manager deployments create my-deployment --
config simple_config.yaml
```

If all goes well, at this point, if you navigate to your VM instances page, you will find a VM there, named `some-vm`, in the zone `asia-south1-a`. In addition, you will see a deployment created under the **Deployments** tab, you can then go ahead and delete it to roll back this deployment (that is, to get rid of the instance you just created).

Now all this sounds awesome and really simple, but you should be aware of a few caveats:

- As of this writing, Google Deployment Manager is not quite up there yet with other IAC tools such as Terraform or even CloudFormation on AWS. Deployments sometimes behave strangely and are painful to debug, relative to those other tools that are pretty robust now.
- YAML is a painful format to work with. The syntax needs to be pretty precise, indentations count (as in Python), and list elements need to be prefixed by a hyphen (–), else the configuration will be rejected as it is ill-formed. Azure uses JSON for similar specifications, and that is probably a far easier choice to work with.
- YAML, as it stands above, cannot be directly parameterized. To be able to specify parameters within the YAML, you'd need an associated programming language, which has to be either JINJA or Python. A useful analogy here is presented here to make this clear.

HTML:YAML :: Javascript:Jinja

HTML is declarative and does not feature loops or conditionals; if you need those features you ought to use Javascript and reference it from the HTML file.

YAML is declarative and does not feature loops or conditionals; if you need those features you ought to use Jinja and reference it from the YAML file.

Summary

Clearly, using deployment manager seems like quite a task given all of this. Here, though, is what you should be sure to remember about IAC:

- Managed Instance Groups are a powerful construct for autohealing and autoscaling groups of GCE VMs
- Infrastructure as a Code allows us to provision infrastructure using template files that can be reused, composed, and checked into source control
- Google's Cloud Deployment Manager offers an IAC framework using YAML configuration files, potentially parameterized using Jinja or Python
- Google's IaaC offering, Deployment Manager, is not quite on the same level of capabilities as the current segment leader (Terraform), but it is getting there

15
Security on the GCP

This chapter is rather different from virtually every other chapter in this book. The other chapters have mostly focused on the acquisition of skills such as how to provision resources (such as VMs or storage) or how to get results (such as BigQuery), while this chapter is mostly about knowledge such as how Google has gone about planning for security on the **Google Cloud Platform (GCP)**.

You will learn the following topics in this chapter:

- Some of the security features that the GCP provides
- Some tools that the GCP provides for your benefit, but that you still have to use
- Some best practices and design choices that are entirely yours to make

Google has a long history of run-ins with hackers and cybersecurity threats. As an organization, Google has not been shy of taking on governments the world over, and news reports have been rife for more than a decade about how governments in some parts of the world use cyberwarfare directed at specific companies and countries as an instrument of foreign and economic policy.

Okay, you may ask, why do we care? Well, we care because Google's long experience with, and success in, protecting itself against cyberattacks plays to our advantage as customers of the Google Cloud Platform. From years of warding off security threats, Google is well aware of the security implications of the cloud model. Thus, they provide a well-secured structure for their operational activities, data centers, customer data, organizational structure, hiring process, and user support.

Google has a global scale infrastructure to provide security for service deployments, data storage, interservice communication, private communication for customers, and admin operations. Google uses this global infrastructure to build commercial services, such as Gmail, Google search, Google Photos, and enterprise services, such as GCP and gsuite.

Security features at Google and on the GCP

Let's start by discussing what we get directly by virtue of using the GCP. This section is all about the platform; these are security protections that we very likely would not be able to engineer for ourselves. The big cloud providers, including Google, have a lot of time, money, and resources to pour into getting these little details right.

Let's go through some of the many layers of security provided by the GCP.

- **Data center physical security**: Only a small fraction of Google employees ever get to visit a GCP data center. Those data centers, the zones that we have been talking so much about, probably would seem out of a Bond film to those that did—security lasers, biometric detectors, alarms, cameras, and all of that cloak-and-dagger stuff.

- **Custom hardware and trusted booting**: A specific form of security attacks named privileged access attacks are on the rise. These involve malicious code running from the least likely spots that you'd expect, the OS image, hypervisor, or boot loader. There is only way to really protect against these, which is to design and build every single element in-house. Google has done that, including hardware, a firmware stack, curated OS images, and a hardened hypervisor. Google data centers are populated with thousands of servers connected to a local network. Google selects and validates building components from vendors and designs custom secure server boards and networking devices for server machines. Google has cryptographic signatures on all low-level components, such as BIOS, bootloader, kernel, and base OS, to validate the correct software stack is booting up. In addition, Google also designs custom hardware security chips installed on both server and peripherals to authenticate legitimate Google devices.

- **Data disposal**: The detritus of the persistent disks and other storage devices that we use are also cleaned thoroughly by Google. This data destruction process involves several steps: an authorized individual will wipe the disk clean using a logical wipe. Then, a different authorized individual will inspect the wiped disk. The results of the erasure are stored and logged too. Then, the erased driver is released into inventory for reuse. If the disk was damaged and could not be wiped clean, it is stored securely and not reused, and such devices are periodically destroyed. Each facility where data disposal takes place is audited once a week.

- **Data encryption**: We will have more to say on this, but in a nutshell, the default is for the GCP to always encrypt all customer data at rest as well as in motion. This encryption is automatic, and it requires no action on the user's part. Persistent disks, for instance, are already encrypted using AES-256, and the keys themselves are encrypted with master keys (which in turn are regularly rotated). All this key management and rotation is managed by Google. In addition to this default encryption, a couple of other encryption options exist as well, more on those in the following diagram:

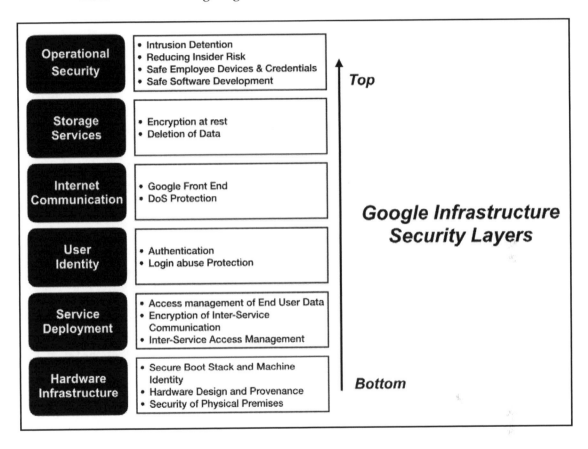

- **Secure service deployment**: Google's security documentation will often refer to secure service deployment, and it is important to understand that in this context, the term **service** has a specific meaning in the context of security: a service is the application binary that a developer writes and runs on infrastructure. For example, consider an App Engine sandbox running customer's application. Thousands of machines may run several copies of a single service, and they require a good orchestrator to manage and control the services on cluster. This secure service deployment is based on three attributes:

  - **Identity**: Each service running on Google infrastructure has an associated service account identity. A service has to submit cryptographic credentials provided to it to prove its identity while making or receiving **remote procedure calls** (RPC) to other services. Clients use these identities to make sure that they are connecting to an intended server and the server will use to restrict access to data and methods to specific clients.

  - **Integrity**: Google uses a cryptographic authentication and authorization technique at an application layer to provide strong access control at the abstraction level for interservice communication. Google has an ingress and egress filtering facility at various points in their network to avoid IP spoofing. With this approach, Google is able to maximize their network's performance and its availability.

  - **Isolation**: Google has an effective sandbox technique to isolate services running on the same machine. This includes Linux user separation, language and kernel-based sandboxes, and hardware virtualization. Google also secures operation of sensitive services such as cluster orchestration in GKE on exclusively dedicated machines (that is master nodes will be completely sandboxed from worker nodes in terms of physical resource allocation and security provisioning).

- **Secure interservice communication**: The term inter-service communication refers to GCP's resources and services talking to each other (for example, an App Engine application accessing BigQuery through APIs). For doing so, the owners of the services have individual whitelists of services which can access them. Using them, the owner of the service can also allow some IAM identities to connect with the services managed by them.

  Apart from that, Google engineers on the backend who would be responsible to manage the smooth and downtime-free running of the services are also provided special identities to access the services (to manage them, not to modify their user-input data).

  Google encrypts interservice communication by encapsulating application layer protocols (such as HTTP) in RPS mechanisms to isolate applications layer and to remove any kind of dependency of network security.

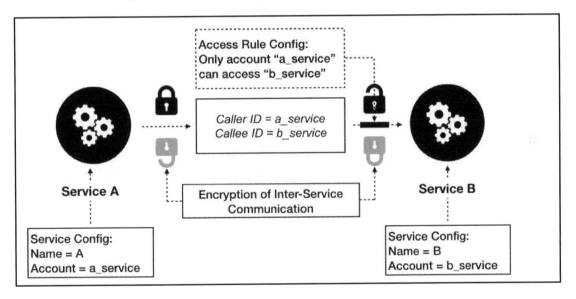

- **Using Google Front End**: Whenever we want to expose a service using GCP, the TLS certificate management, service registration, and DNS are managed by Google itself (instead of any third-party vendor). This facility is called **Google Front End (GFE)** service. For example, a simple file of Python code can be hosted as an application on App Engine that (application) will have its own IP, DNS name, and so on.

- **In-built DDoS protections**: Distributed Denial-of-Service attacks are very well studied, and precautions against such attacks are already built into many GCP services, notably in networking and load balancing. Load balancers can actually be thought of as hardened, bastion hosts that serve as lightning rods to attract attacks, and so are suitably hardened by Google to ensure that they can withstand those attacks. HTTP(S) and SSL proxy load balancers, in particular, can protect your backend instances from several threats, including SYN floods, port exhaustion, and IP fragment floods.
- **Insider risk and intrusion detection**: Google constantly monitors activities of all available devices in Google infrastructure for any suspicious activities. To secure employees' accounts, Google has replaced phishable OTP second factors with U2F, compatible security keys.

Google also monitors their customer devices that employees use to operate their infrastructure. Google also conducts a periodic check on the status of OS images with security patches on customer devices. Google has a special mechanism to grant access privileges named application-level access management control, which exposes internal applications to only specific users from correctly managed devices and expected network and geographic locations. Google has a very strict and secure way to manage its administrative access privileges. They have a rigorous monitoring process of employee activities and also a predefined limit for administrative accesses for employees.

Google-provided tools and options for security

As we've just seen, the platform already does a lot for us , but we still could end up leaving ourselves vulnerable to attack if we don't go about designing our cloud infrastructure carefully. To begin with, let's understand a few facilities provided by the platform for our benefit.

- **Data encryption options**: We have already discussed Google's default encryption; this encrypts pretty much everything and requires no user action. So, for instance, all persistent disks are encrypted with AES-256 keys that are automatically created, rotated, and themselves encrypted by Google.

- In addition to default encryption, there are a couple of other encryption options available to users. Both of these only make sense for those who really understand encryption, cryptography, and security. If you don't know how these work, it's best that you just stick with the default encryption.

  - **Customer-managed encryption keys (CMEK) using Cloud KMS**: This option involves a user taking control of the keys that are used, but still storing those keys securely on the GCP, using the key management service. The user is now responsible for managing the keys that are for creating, rotating and destroying them. The only GCP service that currently supports CMEK is BigQuery and is in beta stage for Cloud Storage. When might you use this option? Whenever you have sensitive data as well as the stipulation that that data be protected using your own key. Note that the keys are stored on the cloud, that is, they do leave your on-premise facility if you opt for CMEK.

  - **Customer-supplied encryption keys (CSEK)**: Here, the user specifies which keys are to be used, but those keys do not ever leave the user's premises. To be precise, the keys are sent to Google as a part of API service calls, but Google only uses these keys in memory and never persists them on the cloud. CSEK is supported by two important GCP services: data in cloud storage buckets as well as by persistent disks on GCE VMs. There is an important caveat here though: if you lose your key after having encrypted some GCP data with it, you are entirely out of luck. There will be no way for Google to recover that data. CSEK makes sense when you have sensitive data that needs to be encrypted using your own keys, and what's more, you have a stipulation that those keys cannot leave your on-premise facilities.

    - **Cloud security scanner**: Cloud security scanner is a GCP, provided security scanner for common vulnerabilities. It has long been available for App Engine applications, but is now also available in alpha for Compute Engine VMs. This handy utility will automatically scan and detect the following four common vulnerabilities:

      - **Cross-site scripting (XSS)**
      - Flash injection
      - Mixed content (HTTP in HTTPS)
      - The use of outdated/insecure libraries

- Like most security scanners, it automatically crawls an application, follows links, and tries out as many different types of user input and event handlers as possible.

Some security best practices

Here is a list of design choices that you could exercise to cope with security threats such as DDoS attacks:

- Use hardened bastion hosts such as load balancers (particularly HTTP(S) and SSL proxy load balancers).
- Make good use of the firewall rules in your VPC network. Ensure that incoming traffic from unknown sources, or on unknown ports, or protocols is not allowed through.
- Use managed services such as Dataflow and Cloud Functions wherever possible; these are serverless and so have smaller attack vectors.
- If your application lends itself to App Engine it has several security benefits over GCE or GKE, and it can also be used to autoscale up quickly, damping the impact of a DDOS attack.
- If you are using GCE VMs, consider the use of API rate limits to ensure that the number of requests to a given VM does not increase in an uncontrolled fashion.
- Use NAT gateways and avoid public IPs wherever possible to ensure network isolation.
- Use Google CDN as a way to offload incoming requests for static content. In the event of a storm of incoming user requests, the CDN servers will be on the edge of the network, and traffic into the core infrastructure will be reduced.

BeyondCorp – Identity-Aware Proxy

While every organisation wishes to have and maintain security of it's network infrastructure and data, maintaining zero-trust architecture (where all traffic is equally untrustworthy) with increasing scale is always a challenge. Google claims to have maintained it for 6 years and the result of such research and practices is BeyondCorp, an enterprise security model built on the idea of making individual users the units of security management instead of relying on network perimeter.

And now, BeyondCorp is available on GCP as a service. They call it **Identity-Aware-Proxy (IAP)**. Here, the IAM identities are used to create firewall and other security policies for the user. As a user, it implies following practices towards you:

- Service access can not be determined just by being a part of some network (unlike most of the University resource access management policies).
- Tokens to access services contain not only the user identity but also device information the user is connecting from (to avoid bots).
- All tokens of service access are end-to-end (GCP-to-User) encrypted.

All of this not only ensures greater amount of security but also eases the remote access to GCP resources which is an integral part of using a public cloud.

Summary

In this chapter, you learned that the GCP benefits from Google's long experience countering cyber-threats and security attacks targeted at other Google services, such as Google search, YouTube, and Gmail.

There are several built-in security features that already protect users of the GCP from several threats that might not even be recognized as existing in an on-premise world.

In addition to these in-built protections, all GCP users have various tools at their disposal to scan for security threats and to protect their data.

Finally, there are also some well-recognized best practices around cloud architecture design that ought to be kept in mind in order to reduce the likelihood of attacks and the impact of attacks that do indeed occur.

16
Pricing Considerations

Using a public cloud provider, such as the **Google Cloud Platform (GCP)**, has some important financial advantages—notably, that you can pay for what you use, and thus avoid large upfront financial commitments. However, public cloud services are not particularly cheap or easy to use. If you are not careful about how you use them, you can easily find yourself faced with a large, hard-to-understand bill. The risk of being nickel-and-dimed is real: like a traveler on an economy airline, you might find yourself paying for facilities that you have entirely taken for granted until now. This chapter is meant to help avoid sticker-shock and sudden unpleasant surprises.

We will cover the following topics in the chapter:

- The actual pricing models for different GCP services are interesting and very varied
- For any serious cloud architect, it makes sense to experiment with Google's very transparent pricing calculator and get a sense of the sensitivities of pricing to different usage parameters

All screenshots in this chapter are from Google's cloud pricing calculator, which is available at `https://cloud.google.com/products/calculator/`. The pricing and rates of these services keep changing, so you should be aware that these screenshots are all dated May 14, 2018. Please do your homework on the latest prices and policies when making real-world decisions. Also, in the comparisons provided in this chapter; we have considered lowest to quite high pricing extremes for the most part. It is trivial that your nature of application and requirement of resources will vary immensely so make sure to make your choices wisely.

Compute Engine

VM instances vary a great deal in price. Notice how the two following screenshots differ. The left-hand side screenshot shows a high-end configuration that includes TPUs (specialized processors for ML applications that are in high demand these days). These machines cost about $946/month, whereas the far simpler machine type in the right-hand side screenshot costs just $3.88/month:

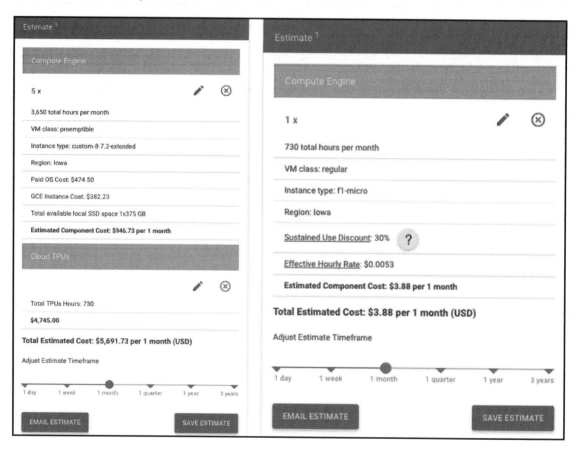

BigTable

BigTable is a high-end service that is blazingly fast and geared to very large data sizes (in the order of hundreds of TB or even PB). Therefore, it should come as no surprise that BigTable is expensive. Even at the small end, with a data size of 3 TB (that's three nodes, each with 1 TB), the cost is a considerable $1,597/month. If we scale up a bit to 20 nodes, our bill rises to more than $10,000/month. BigTable clusters definitely need to be taken down when not in use, you should brace yourself for unpleasant billing surprises:

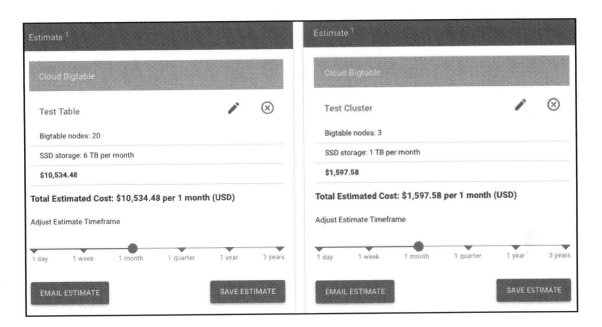

BigQuery

BigQuery is an incredibly attractive service to use, and the pricing is an important part of its appeal. Notice how the cost of a reasonably realistic, albeit light, use case is just 40 cents a month. Try the same level of usage on Teradata, and you'll understand why BigQuery is Google's most touted offering:

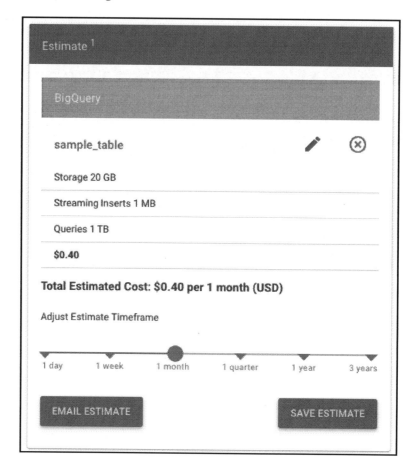

Datastore

Datastore is a document-oriented database with rather arcane pricing. The bill reflects several parameters: the size of data stored, the number of entity reads, writes, and deletes. Datastore is inexpensive, particularly when you take into account the free tier it offers:

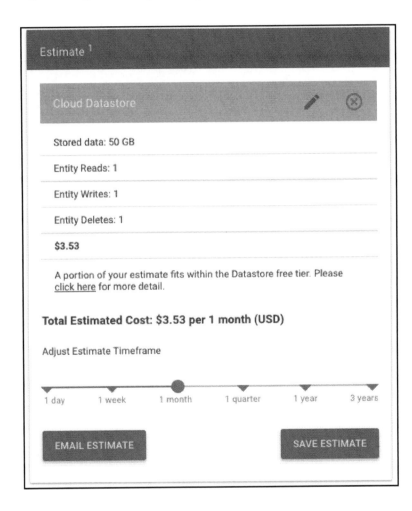

Cloud SQL

Cloud SQL can be thought of as a VM with MySQL (or PostgreSQL) installed on it, along with various associated services provided by the platform. So it ought to come as no surprise that the cost of a Cloud SQL instance can vary from $1,142/month to just $9/month. What's the big difference? It's all in the machine type we pick; the high bill refers to the custom machine type and the high-availability configuration (**High Availability (HA)**):

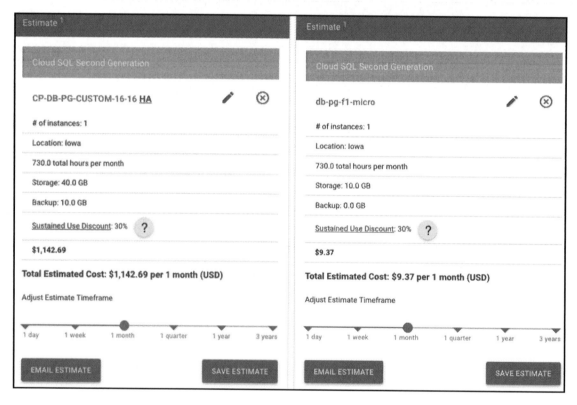

Google Kubernetes Engine

The Google Kubernetes service effectively runs a cluster of nodes (cloud VM instances) that host containers and the Kubernetes orchestration layer. Again, we can see how the type and number of VMs we pick dramatically alter how much we pay. The lesson is a recurring one: many GCP services are based on GCE VMs, and those VMs vary wildly in their costs. The left-hand side screenshot shows a five-node cluster running on `n1-standard-16` instances, and costing $1,941/month, whereas the right-hand side screenshot is a single-node cluster running on `f1-micro`, and it costs just $3.88/month.

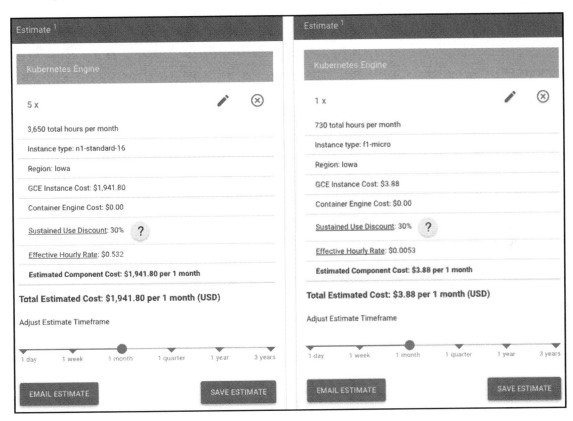

Pub/Sub

Pub/Sub pricing is relatively simple to model, and the sole determinant is the volume of message data. If your app rivals Twitter and generates 1 PB per month, the cost works out to almost $44,000. At the other extreme, a toy client/server app will set you back just 12 cents.

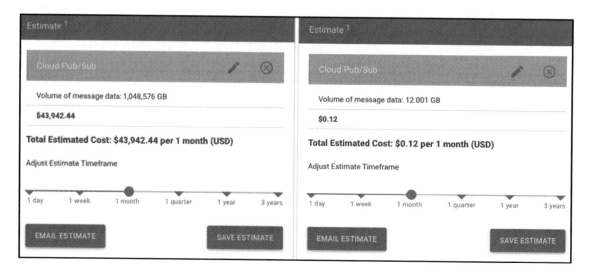

Cloud ML Engine

The Cloud ML Engine offers two distinct subservices: distributed training and distributed prediction. Training refers to the process of building a machine learning model from a corpus of data, whereas prediction refers to the use of that model to actually make forecasts.

Depending on how long your ML training jobs run and whether you use batch or online mode for prediction, the costs vary significantly. A fairly heavy-duty set of ML workloads will cost about $4,000 per month:

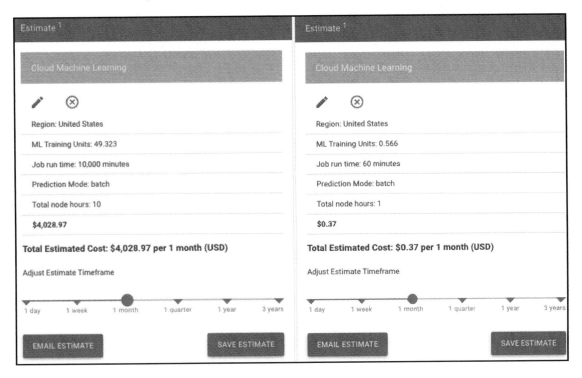

Stackdriver

The Stackdriver suite offers logging, monitoring, and other cloud ops services. As the volume of your log data and the number of monitored resources starts to rise, your Stackdriver bill goes up quickly too; notice how just 100 monitored resources and 100 custom metrics with 100 GB of logs rack up a bill of $800/month:

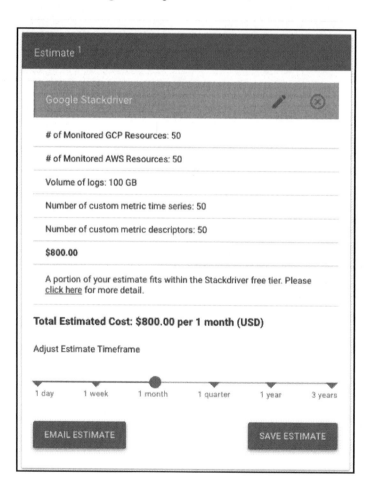

Video Intelligence API

Google, like AWS and Azure, has very powerful machine learning APIs that are available for a fee. These ML/AI APIs are pretrained, meaning that you don't need to bother writing any ML models of your own; you can just use the great models Google has already built. Use cases include the detection of explicit content, celebrities, and other specific features within video. Notice that scanning 10,000 minutes of video for a few different types of features costs about $2,250/month, as shown in the following screenshot:

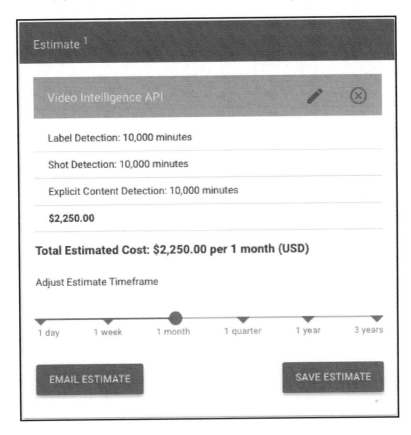

Key Management Service – KMS

You could choose to store your organization's keys on the Google Cloud using the Google KMS. The pricing of the KMS depends on the number of keys and the number of operations, and you can see that even for a large number of both. The bill works out to a relatively modest $600/month, as shown in the following screenshot:

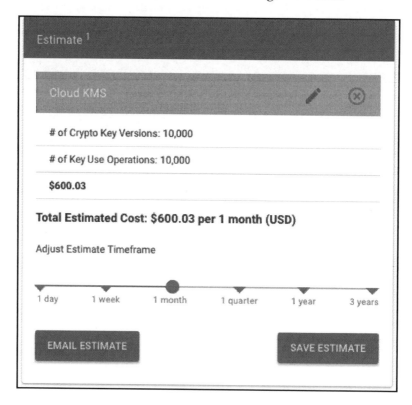

Vision API

The Vision API is yet another pretrained ML API, like the video intelligence API. Check out how many different kinds of operations are possible with this: OCR, face detection, explicit content detection, and so on. You might be tempted to build an entire startup around this one, and you would not be the only one. However, it won't come cheap; performing millions of such operations will cost almost $80,000/month. Starting out is easy enough though, and if you are performing operations in the thousands rather than millions, the price will be just about $15/month:

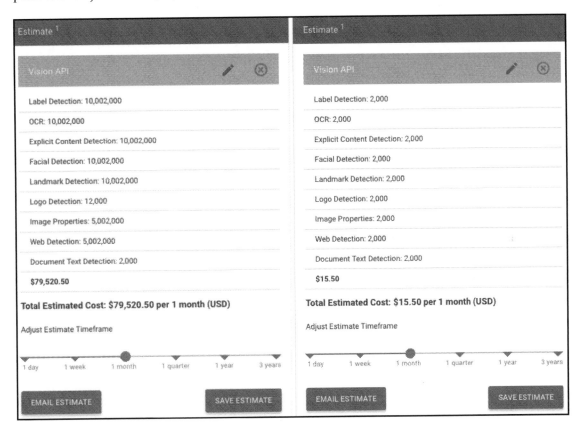

Summary

In this chapter, you learned that as we would expect, the prices of most GCP services vary widely, based on their usage, although the definition of usage varies widely by service. Some services, such as BigTable or Cloud Spanner, are inherently expensive and ought to be used with care. Several GCP services (for example, Cloud SQL and Kubernetes) are built atop GCE VMs, and the choices of VM type can dramatically change how much we pay.

17
Effective Use of the GCP

It is time to connect the dots! We started our journey with an introduction to public cloud platforms and why GCP is an important player in the game. We explored all of the GCP features and offerings and learned many of their use cases. We also learned the pricing differences between our choices of platforms/resources can bring. Now, let's sharpen all of this with some good practices and effective use cases to keep in mind to make sure we conclude our journey on a satisfactory note.

You will learn the following topics in this chapter:

- Designing cost-effective cloud apps can be harder than it seems; learn some of the tricks of the trade
- Designing for an effective scale: using Dataproc and Spark effectively can create a lot of impact even with existing code and existing skills
- Smart bets on new technologies, such as containers and Kubernetes, can transform your cloud architecture and your career

Eat the Kubernetes frog

There is a famous quote, attributed to Mark Twain, that goes like this:

> *Eat a live frog first thing in the morning and nothing worse will happen to you the rest of the day.*
>
> *-- Mark Twain*

This excellent quote has given rise to a flourishing industry of books and self-help coaches who urge you to eat various frogs in your life; we heartily agree with all of their advice (well, most of it). Don't shy away from upfront effort and unpleasantness; it will pay off in spades tomorrow. That's the general idea, and we heartily agree, particularly in the context of choosing a compute option on the cloud.

We saw, early in the book, how compute choices range from **Infrastructure as a Service (IaaS)** to **Platform as a Service (PaaS)**. Depending on where you are coming from, either the IaaS or the PaaS extremes are likely to seem most appealing to you. If you are coming from a small startup or an organization that does not have a lot of legacy infrastructure, the PaaS options will seem great—easy to get started having lots of friendly platform-specific APIs. If, on the other hand, you are from a large organization with a huge, on-premise data center, the easiest path will likely seem VM migration.

Now, of course, both the IaaS and the PaaS options are perfectly reasonable ones, and that's why, all cloud providers make sure that they have a full suite of such offerings. The Google suite of compute services is shown in the following diagram:

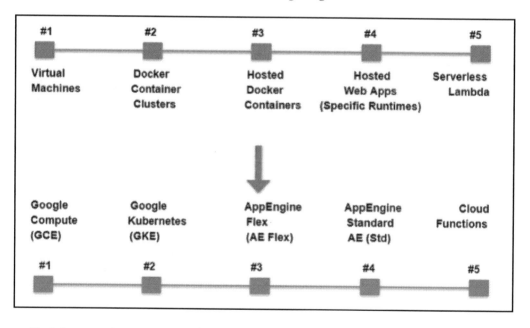

Now, all of these options are great, but we seriously recommend that you invest the time and effort containerizing your apps (that is, build Docker containers of them), and get them to run on Kubernetes.

This might seem like a big deal, a lot of work, and it is. But consider this, VM migration is no picnic either, particularly if you are doing it for hundreds or thousands of VMs. What's worse is that if you migrate your VMs from environment A (say your on-premise data center) to environment B (say the GCP) and then 6 months from now, you have a new CEO who used to work in an AWS shop and that new CEO asks you to move from environment B (GCP) to environment C (AWS), well, you're out of luck. All of the VM migration will have to be basically done again.

It might seem like we are being facetious here, but we are not. The world is, in our opinion, moving to a hybrid, multi-cloud world. The future, at least for the intermediate term, is a hybrid one. As large organizations can't afford to write down their existing DCs to zero and start from scratch on the cloud, migrations are going to be a reality of life for the next few years. The future is also likely multi-cloud because organizations have been bitten by vendor lock-in for products such as expensive relational databases, CRM software, and everything in between. In addition, Amazon in particular has been quite aggressive about getting into new lines of business; its acquisition of Whole Foods would give a whole set of current and prospective AWS customers pause. The most likely way the world will move is toward hybrid and multi-cloud infrastructure.

The PaaS options: App Engine on GCP or Elastic Beanstalk on AWS will certainly have their adherents, but do keep in mind that if you go down that route, you really are tied down to a specific cloud provider. That's the whole point of the P in PaaS, platform lock-in.

All of this explains why Kubernetes is just so hot right now. It has reached critical levels of acceptance, and leverages Docker, which is also stable and ubiquitously accepted. So, in a nutshell, eat that frog, containerize those apps, and move to Kubernetes.

Careful that you don't get nickel-and-dimed

> *"Look around the poker table; If you can't see the Sucker, you're It"*
> *-- Warren Buffett*

When you switch to the cloud, you might find yourself so thrilled at not having these huge fixed costs anymore, that you might forget a slightly sobering fact: the big cloud providers all report extremely healthy financial results from their cloud businesses. If being a cloud provider is so profitable, then consumers of a cloud provider's services need to be sure that they are not the patsies in the room.

This also gets back to the crucial difference between CAPEX and OPEX. **CAPEX**, or **capital expenditure**, refers to a large upfront spend of money used to get an asset (an asset is a resource—for example, a physical server—that will yield benefits over time, not just in the current period) OPEX, or operating expenses, refer to smaller, recurring spends of money for current period benefit:

> **CapEx vs. OpEx**
>
> *Buying a house is CapEx, renting a house is OpEx*
> *Buying a car is CapEx, hailing a cab or Uber is OpEx*
> *Running your own data center needs CapEx, using the cloud is OpEx*

The suckers in the cloud world are the careless users who don't carefully watch their bills, who don't pay attention to the pricing of products, and who don't optimize their usage to save costs. If you provision the biggest VM, your quota will allow you to, or if you forget to turn down your BigTable or Cloud Spanner instances, you will be directly responsible for the surging share prices of the big cloud providers.

Pay for what you allocate not what you use

This is an important mistake that even experienced technical folks make while switching from the on-premise world to the cloud. We are conditioned to think that the cloud world is all pay-what-you-use, and elastic, but that is not entirely true. There are numerous GCP services where you pay for resources that you allocate (even if you end up not using them). The three most important ones probably are as follows:

- Block storage (persistent disks and local SSDs)
- BigTable
- Cloud Spanner

BigTable and Cloud Spanner are resources where you provision nodes based on your data size, so at least in those cases you are unlikely to wildly overprovision. Block storage devices, the persistent disks, and local SSDs are quite likely to drop below your penny-pinching radar though. These disk abstractions can always be resized, so don't feel compelled to start by provisioning the biggest size you can find. Start small and add capacity as you need to.

Make friends with the gsuite admins

We discussed the Identity and Access Management bits of the GCP, and in that context, we observed that human identities are not actually defined in the GCP, rather they are seamlessly obtained from gsuite. Programmatic identities (service accounts) do in fact exist solely within the GCP though, as do roles.

Now, the reality of many organizations is that different teams manage the gsuite and GCP components. gsuite identities are often set up when a new employee joins the firm as a part of an onboarding process and might be organizationally linked to corporate IT, or even HR. GCP, on the other hand, is likely to be a core technology function that rolls up into the CTO.

This can have real practical implementations for how things get done. Say, for instance, that the GSuite team and the GCP teams don't get along well. Each time a new user joins or each time a user gets new responsibilities, that user might need to get added to the right gsuite groups (also known as Google groups). If the gsuite team is tardy getting this done, you as a cloud architect might find yourself taking little shortcuts like creating a service account that has whatever rights you want and then assigning those users the `ServiceAccountActor` role. This is a tempting shortcut, but one best avoided. You are almost certain to forget to revoke that `ServiceAccountActor` privilege once the Google group gets set up correctly and then years later that employee might go rogue and do bad things without any possibility of being traced because the `ServiceAccountActor` role makes those actions seem like a service account carried them out.

So, be a good corporate realist and make friends with the gsuite folks. You will need them a lot more than they will need you.

Try to find reasons to use network peering

Remember that VPCs in the GCP world are quite different from networks in the physical world or even on other cloud providers such as AWS. VPCs are more like **Autonomous Systems (AS)** because each VPC can include multiple disjoint IP address ranges.

Resources that are in the same VPC can communicate using internal IP addresses as well as using a project-internal DNS facility. This is true even if the resources are in different regions. For instance, consider two VMs, one in the US and the other in UK. Provided these are in the same VPC they will be able to communicate using internal IP addresses despite their physical distance.

By contrast if two resources are in different VPCs even if they happen to be in the same region or even on the same underlying bare metal box (remember that GCP VMs are multi-tenanted), they will still have to communicate using external IP addresses, which implies that the network traffic between them will have to pass over the internet.

Communication on internal IP addresses has several advantages:

- **Cost**: Remember that network egress traffic incurs charges, and communication over internal IP addresses avoids this.
- **Security**: Google's internal networks are relatively invulnerable to intrusion and security attacks. After all, Google has been under siege from hackers for over a decade now. However, once traffic leaves Google's internal networks and touches the internet, all bets are off.
- **Latency**: Google internal networks are blazingly fast; this is partially a legacy of Google's investments in YouTube and in trying to get video served at acceptable latencies in all or most regions of the world. Internal traffic on the GCP is able to hitch a ride on these really fast internal links.

This presents us with a trade-off: if we have lots of small, modular VPCs, organization of resources and firewall rules gets cleaner, but network traffic gets slower, costlier, and less secure.

A great way to square this circle is to make use of the feature named VPC peering. This allows a 1:1 link between VPCs so that resources on the peered VPCs can communicate using internal IP addresses. Unlike AWS, GCP is cheaper in this aspect since it only applies standard network charges. So, look for every possible opportunity to use VPC peering.

Understand how sustained use discounts work

Kubernetes notwithstanding, GCE VM instances are likely to remain an integral part of your organization's cloud strategy for the foreseeable future. Because you are certain to be using a lot of VM instances, you should invest the time to understand how exactly discounts on their usage work.

There are basically two major types of discounts currently available for VMs: sustained use and committed use discounts. Committed use discounts require you to make upfront commitments about how much you will use your VM instances, so if you really know, you will need some specific compute power; by all means, go ahead and make that commitment. Beware, always, of making such commitments. The cloud providers offer such discounts in the hope that users will overestimate their need and end up overpaying.

Sustained use discounts, on the other hand, are a lot more worthwhile. The basic idea here is: the GCP will combine all of your usage of VM instances of the same standard machine type, in the same project, and in the same zone, and apply a discount based on the total usage as if this were one, giant VM instance.

There is a lot of fine print in there that is worth understanding.

- The sustained use discount does not require any upfront commitment; it is automatically applied based on your actual usage.
- The discount applies for all VMs of the same standard type, in the same project, and in the same zone. This makes sense because VMs with these shared properties are in a sense fungible, they help GCP with capacity planning.
- Discount calculation for custom machine types is a bit different than for the standard machine types. So, there is a sustained use discount for custom machine types as well, but it is less likely to save you a ton of money.

Read the fine print on GCS pricing

Google Cloud Storage buckets are elastic, that is, you definitely pay for what you use, not what you allocate. That's great. However, there are a couple bits around their pricing that you should be certain to keep in mind:

- **Access charges on nearline and coldline buckets**: Recall that the hot bucket types (regional and multiregional) have relatively high storage charges, but no access charges. On the other hand, the cool and cold bucket types (nearline and coldline) do have access charges, and these can become quite substantial. Say you back up a laptop to a coldline bucket and want to retrieve all of that data because the laptop crashes, you might find yourself paying access charges not that different from the cost of an old laptop. So think through your use cases for the different bucket types very carefully. Again, I can't emphasise it enough to remember that use Nearline when access is once a month or once a few months; use coldline when access is once a year or even less frequent.

- **Class A and Class B operations**: GCS operations are categorized as Class A, Class B, and free. Class A and Class B operations are cheap on a per-operation basis but can become quite expensive if performed repeatedly. Take, for instance, something like Object Lifecycle management. This is the GCS feature that allows you to change the storage type of a bucket based on age, freshness, and so on. You might want to keep in mind that such operations are Class A operations, and they can end up costing you more than having the data item in a slightly suboptimal bucket type.

Use BigQuery unless you have a specific reason not to

There is an absolute candy store of data storage services available on the GCP. You probably have seen a taxonomy like the one in the following diagram, which tells you which service to use when. Now you certainly should take the time to go through this diagram and understand each part of it, but the bottom line can be summed up as: unless you really have a strong pressing reason, just use BigQuery:

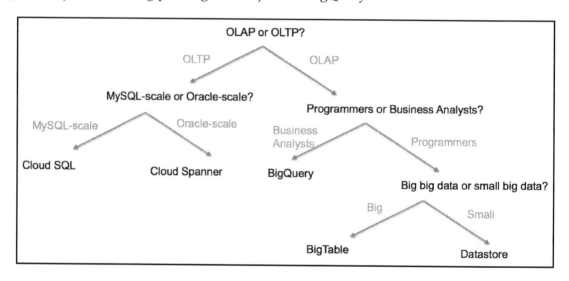

One asterisk about this preceding taxonomy is we intentionally list Datastore in the OLAP part of the tree because even though it does have a transactional mode, in the real world, if you need transactional support, you are far more likely to go with RDBMS than with a document-oriented NoSQL database such as Datastore.

What might some of those strong pressing reasons to not use BigQuery be? Well, you might need really ironclad transactional support in which case Cloud SQL or Cloud Spanner are your best options. Perhaps you need to support a large volume of writes and at a very high throughput, then BigTable is your best bet. However, in general, unless you have a strong explicit reason, just pick BigQuery.

Use pre-emptible instances in your Dataproc clusters

Hadoop (and Spark) jobs constitute perhaps the single-most important use case for organizations moving to the cloud. So, getting your Hadoop strategy right is really important, and here, Dataproc is a fairly obvious way to get started. One important bit of cost optimization that you ought to perform is using as many pre-emptible instances as possible.

Recall that pre-emptible instances are those that can be taken back by the platform at very short notice. So, if you are using a pre-emptible VM instance, you could have it snatched away at any point with just about 30 seconds to execute a shutdown script and clean up your state.

The flip side of this inconvenience is that pre-emptible VM instances are very cheap. On an apples-to-apples basis, you can expect a pre-emptible instance to cost about 60-80% less than a non-pre-emptible instance with the same specs. And here's the kicker: Hadoop has fault-tolerance built-in, and it is the perfect setting in which to exploit the affordability of pre-emptible instances.

Recall that Hadoop is the big daddy of distributed computing apps, it practically invented the idea of horizontal scaling in which large clusters of generic hardware are assembled and managed by some central orchestration software. This use of generic hardware implies that Hadoop always expects bad things to happen to nodes in clusters: it has elaborate mechanisms for sharding, replication, and making sure that node failures are managed gracefully.

In fact, within a Dataproc cluster, all of the pre-emptible VMs are collectively placed inside a Managed Instance Group, and the platform takes responsibility for clearing away the old pre-empted VMs so that they don't clog up your cluster.

There are some guidelines to keep in mind while allocating pre-emptible VMs to your Dataproc clusters. If your Hadoop jobs are skewed toward Map-only jobs and do not rely on HDFS a whole lot, you can probably push the envelope and use even 80-90% pre-emptible VMs without seeing performance degradation. On the other hand, if your Hadoop jobs tend to have a lot of shuffling, then using more than 50% preemptible VMs might be a bad idea: the pre-emption of a lot of VMs can significantly slow down your job, and the additional processing for fault-tolerance might end up even increasing the total cost.

Keep your Dataproc clusters stateless

Remember that Hadoop in its pure, non-cloud form maintains state in a distributed file system named HDFS. HDFS is on the same set of nodes where the Hadoop jobs actually run; for this reason, Hadoop is said to not separate compute and storage. The compute (Hadoop Jars) and storage (HDFS data) are on the same machines, and the Jars are actually shipped to where the data is.

This was a fine pattern for the old days, but in the cloud world, if you kept your data in HDFS, you would run up an enormous bill. Why? Because in the world of elastic Hadoop clusters, such as Dataproc on the GCP or Elastic MapReduce on AWS, HDFS is going to exist on the persistent disks of the cloud VMs in the cluster. If you keep data in HDFS, you will need those disks to always exist; therefore, the cluster will always be up. You will pay a lot, use only a little, and basically negate the whole point of moving to the cloud.

So, what you really ought to do is move your data from on-premise HDFS to cloud GCS. Do not move from on-premise HDFS to cloud HDFS. That way, you can spin up clusters whenever you like, point them to data on the GCS buckets, run your job, and kill the cluster. Such clusters are named stateless because they only reference state data from an external source (GCS buckets) rather than maintaining it internally in HDFS.

Dataproc As Managed Hadoop

Hadoop = YARN + HDFS + MapReduce
Dataproc = YARN + GCS + MapReduce

Dataproc clusters still have an internal HDFS area, but this is on the persistent disks of the Dataproc VMs, and will not exist beyond the life of the cluster

So - don't use HDFS, use GCS instead.

Understand the unified architecture for batch and stream

More and more big data applications rely on streaming data. There are many reasons for this: notably the increasing need for real-time insights where a system must output analytics as new data comes in on-the-fly. We will not spend a lot of time discussing the difference between batch and streaming data, but intuitively, batch data is at rest in a database or a file, whereas streaming data is, well, streaming from a source to a sink.

There is a specific architecture that Google mentions a lot, which combines batch and stream processing into a single pipeline, and it is worth our understanding this architecture, as follows:

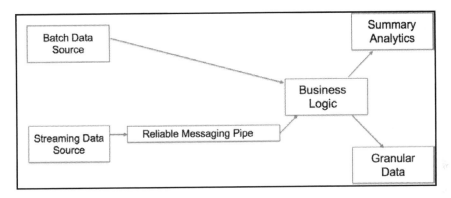

In the GCP word, the most common batch data source is GCS (that is, buckets) and the reliable messaging layer is Pub/Sub. Pub/Sub virtually always feeds into Dataflow, which is based on the Apache Beam APIs and combines batch and streaming logic into pipelines.

The classic source for summary analytics is BigQuery, and the best place to store granular, tick-by-tick processed data is BigTable (why BigTable? Because it supports fast writes and very large datasets, order of PB). So, penciling in all of those, we get the GCP version of the architecture.

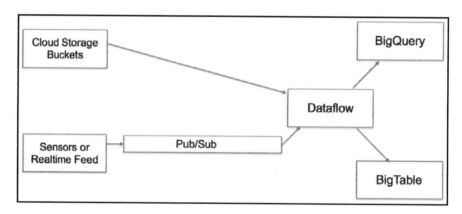

Now, this is an important architectural set piece, and you really should commit it to memory. However, this does not mean that you should actually adopt it, at least not as of the time of this writing, in early 2018. The weak link, right now, in this is Dataflow. In theory, Dataflow is an awesome technology. It unifies batch and streaming layers, de-dupes, and orders the streaming data coming in from Pub/Sub and can perform complex event-time and processing-time operations, such as windowing and watermarking. The downside? You have to write code to do this; there is no UI currently available. What's more? The code that can be in either Python or Java is not all that easy to write. In time, and probably very soon, Dataflow will be an attractive proposition, though, so we should not be quick to dismiss it.

Understand the main choices for ML applications

We have not spent a lot of time discussing machine learning on the GCP in this book, but at a very high level, you have two choices:

- TensorFlow and the Cloud ML Engine
- SparkML and Dataproc

Both options are good. The Cloud ML Engine has support for distributed training and prediction and is tightly coupled with TensorFlow, which is a great technology for deep learning. So, this option is probably a better one, on balance.

SparkML is a great option too, though. Spark is possibly the hottest big data technology today; therefore, there are a lot of existing Spark applications and a lot of talented Spark developers out there today. If your organization uses a lot of Spark right now, you might find the SparkML on Dataproc option to be a better one, at least until TensorFlow and the ML Engine catch on in popularity in your firm.

Understand the differences between snapshots and images

Persistent disks can be backed up using either images or snapshots; the two services seem similar but differ in some subtle ways, so let's be sure we understand the differences:

- Snapshots are best for data backups, they are cheaper, and incremental snapshots are possible too.
- Images are best for infrastructure re-use, such as exporting a VM image for use in a different project or as the basis for a Managed Instance Group.
- As we just mentioned previously, only images can be used as the basis for an instance template, which in turn is used to create Managed Instance Groups. Snapshots can't be used for this purpose.
- Images can be shared across projects and assigned versions and organized into families, marked with metadata, such as deprecated and obsolete.
- A fresh VM can be spun up using either a snapshot or an image, but with one difference: an image can directly be imported into a VM, whereas a snapshot will need to first instantiated into a persistent disk, and that persistent disk can then be used to spin up the VM.
- Snapshots are global, whereas persistent disks are zonal; so, if you'd like to move a persistent disk from one region to another, snapshots are the way to go.
- Neither images nor snapshots will work with local SSDs; they both only work with local or persistent disks.

Don't be Milton!

There's a line that goes, "*To a man with a hammer, everything looks like a nail*". That's a serious risk in the world of technology these days because of how fast new tools and technologies come and go. We all have a favorite hammer, a technology or a language that we mastered a decade or two ago, and that got us our first job or a big promotion. Well, that's great, but we have got to learn to move on. There are new hammers being devised every day, and in today's world of technology, the surest way to fall behind is to keep clinging to your old favorite hammer. Think of Milton, the stapler guy from the cult classic Office Space. Never mind if you have not seen the movie or even heard of it. The idea is simple to flourish; don't just accept new technologies grudgingly; run out, and embrace them.

Summary

In this chapter, you learned that containers and Kubernetes are a great compute option for the future. Dataproc can be a serious game-changer, particularly if you use it right. Pre-emptible VMs, images, snapshots, and buckets all have fine features to love and fine print to be aware of.

Other Books You May Enjoy

If you enjoyed this book, you may be interested in these other books by Packt:

Cloud Analytics with Google Cloud Platform
Sanket Thodge

ISBN: 978-1-78883-968-6

- Explore the basics of cloud analytics and the major cloud solutions
- Learn how organizations are using cloud analytics to improve the ROI
- Explore the design considerations while adopting cloud services
- Work with the ingestion and storage tools of GCP such as Cloud Pub/Sub
- Process your data with tools such as Cloud Dataproc, BigQuery, etc
- Over 70 GCP tools to build an analytics engine for cloud analytics
- Implement machine learning and other AI techniques on GCP

Google Cloud Platform Cookbook
Legorie Rajan PS

ISBN: 978-1-78829-199-6

- Host a Python application on Google Compute Engine
- Host an application using Google Cloud Functions
- Migrate a MySQL DB to Cloud Spanner
- Configure a network for a highly available application on GCP
- Learn simple image processing using Storage and Cloud Functions
- Automate security checks using Policy Scanner
- Understand tools for monitoring a production environment in GCP
- Learn to manage multiple projects using service accounts

Leave a review - let other readers know what you think

Please share your thoughts on this book with others by leaving a review on the site that you bought it from. If you purchased the book from Amazon, please leave us an honest review on this book's Amazon page. This is vital so that other potential readers can see and use your unbiased opinion to make purchasing decisions, we can understand what our customers think about our products, and our authors can see your feedback on the title that they have worked with Packt to create. It will only take a few minutes of your time, but is valuable to other potential customers, our authors, and Packt. Thank you!

Index

WordPress container
  creating 84, 85
  deploying 81, 82

Y

Yet Another Resource Negotiator 241

Z

zonal resources 17, 19

Made in the USA
Columbia, SC
15 May 2019